Here's What Writers and Critics Are Saying About the Publishing Marketplace Series

"A must for every Northwest writer or any writer interested in targeting the Northwest markets. Whether you're unpublished and want to hone your craft, just published and need to publicize your work, or an old hand looking for new markets, this book has it all for the Northwest writing scene."

Angela Butterworth, Advisor,
Seattle Chapter of Romance Writers of America,
bookseller and aspiring writer

"An indispensable guide for the nonfiction and fiction writer alike—much like money from home."

James B. Hall, established Oregon author,
editor, teacher, and poet

"These regional [Publishing Marketplace] directories are . . . sources of practical assistance to the professional or aspiring writer. The publishing sector listings and descriptions are very comprehensive. . . . these compilations are valuable reference items, and superb resources."

Publishers Reports, *April 1991*

"Two superb new guides from Writers Connection. These books are invaluable resources, not only for writers but for anyone in publishing."

Patricia Holt, Book Review Editor,
San Francisco Chronicle

". . . the growth of the small press movement has created new regional markets . . . From Writers Connection come two new directories that focus on local publishing opportunities. They [the books] are reasonably priced, easy to use, and provide information that is not readily available in other sources."

Booklist, *January 1991*

Northwest

PUBLISHING
MARKET
PLACE

Northwest

PUBLISHING MARKET PLACE

*A comprehensive directory
of markets, resources, and
opportunities for writers.*

Compiled by: Marjorie Gersh

Writers Connection

Cupertino, California

Northwest Publishing Marketplace

Published by: Steve Lester

Compiled by: Marjorie Gersh

Edited by: Jan Stiles, Meera Lester

Cover design by: Detta Penna

Publisher's Cataloging in Publication
(Prepared by Quality Books, Inc.)

Gersh, Marjorie, 1942-
　　Northwest publishing marketplace : a comprehensive directory of markets, resources, and opportunities for writers / Marjorie R. Gersh. --
　　p. cm.
　　Includes bibliographical references, glossary, and index.
　　ISBN 0-9622592-3-3

　　1. Publishers and publishing--Northwest, Pacific--Directories.
2. Authorship--Marketing. 3. Literary agents--Northwest, Pacific--Directories. I. Title.

PN161　　　　　　　　070.5209795
　　　　　　　　　　　　　QBI91-1044
　　　　　　　　　　　　　　　MARC

Books from Writers Connection Press:
　California and Hawaii Publishing Marketplace
　Southwest Publishing Marketplace
　Writing for the Ethnic Markets

To order copies, see page 183.

Writers Connection, 1601 Saratoga-Sunnyvale Road, Suite 180 Cupertino, CA 95014, (408) 973-0227, FAX (408) 973-1219

Printed and bound in the United States of America

Table of Contents

Acknowledgements

For their conscientious and diligent work verifying information, typesetting, and proofreading the manuscript, we thank Writers Connection staff members Cheryl Bowlin, Arlene Di Salvo, Mardeene Burr Mitchell, Dean Stark, Burton Sukhov, and Nancy B. Tamburello. We extend our thanks also to Sara Adler and Julie Oberbillig.

For sharing our belief that "writers helping writers strengthens our West Coast and Northwest writing and publishing community," and for supporting our work over the years, we extend a heartfelt thanks to all our Writers Connection members.

This book is dedicated to writers everywhere, but especially to those in the Northwest and on the West Coast for whom this definitive guide to publishing markets, information, and resources in these states has been produced.

Introduction

We know what writers need. Writers Connection has been in the business of providing information and services to writers, organizations, small presses, and self-publishers for nearly a decade. In *Northwest Publishing Marketplace*, the third in our *Marketplace* series, writers will find hundreds of new markets for their work.

Other books in this series include *California and Hawaii Publishing Marketplace*, covering the rapidly growing writing and publishing industry in California and Hawaii, and *Southwest Publishing Marketplace*, including listings for the six Southwestern states of Arizona, Colorado, Nevada, New Mexico, Texas, and Utah. Together, these books can help writers expand their horizons.

Markets

Independent publishing has been steadily increasing since the birth of the small press movement in the 1960s. The Northwest, with its varied markets and support of the arts, provides exciting opportunities for writers.

Because we designed and developed this book specifically for writers, we have provided as much of the critical information writers particularly want and need as we could gather. We've included the names of book and magazine submissions editors along with editorial guidelines, acceptance policies, preferred method of query, rights purchased, and tips from the respective editors or publishers. For newspapers, we've listed addresses and the names of general, book review, and travel editors.

Professional Organizations

For those interested in expanding their professional networks, we've included wherever possible the address, phone number, and contact for the headquarters of each organization and listed information on local chapters when applicable. Many organizations have local branches, and others provide services nationwide.

Writers' Conferences

Writers' conferences are prime sources of information, professional contacts, and motivation. In the conference section, you'll find listings that include locations, dates, fees, subjects, formats, number of faculty members, and special events. If you're serious about writing, plan to attend at least one conference this year.

Literary Agents

Of the agents specifically located in the Northwest, those who returned our surveys are included here. We have included not only names, addresses, and phone numbers, but substantial information on the kinds of literary properties the agencies are seeking, agency commission fees, and rights handled by the agency.

Merely writing to one agent does not guarantee acceptance, so expect the search to involve several contacts. Because a limited number of agents are based in the Northwest, you may need to expand your search to include additional resources, such as the *Literary Market Place* (LMP), available in most libraries, and references listed in the Books for Writers section of this book.

Books and Resources

For many years, Writers Connection's teachers, members, and seminar participants have offered insights and suggestions about the books they need to hone their skills. Writers Connection has responded with a bookstore of how-to-write books, style guides, reference books, market books, and business writing books. Since these books have proved so helpful to our writers, we thought you'd like to know about them, too. An annotated list of books is included in this directory, as well as other resources you, the writer, might need.

Updates

We realized from its inception that this book would require regular updating of information. Some market information will appear in the monthly 16-page *Writers Connection* newsletter. In addition, all *Marketplace* editions are updated regularly.

In compiling and verifying information for the book, we sent out thousands of questionnaires and spent weeks verifying information by phone. If any publishers, agents, organizations, or conferences are not listed, it is likely that their surveys were not returned, they requested deletion, or their information could not be verified.

We realize much of the information in this book will change with time: Organizations elect new officers each year; book publishers, magazines, and newspapers hire new editors; and conference directors find new locations, change formats, and offer new speakers.

When using this book, if you find information that is incomplete or has changed, please let us know. If you know of a book, magazine, or newspaper publisher that should be included, tell us—we'll send the appropriate survey forms. Let us know if you would like a free listing for your organization or conference.

If you wish to be notified of future editions of *Northwest Publishing Marketplace*, please send us your name and address. Finally, we appreciate feedback. Let us know if the book works well for you, or if it doesn't, and why.

Meera Lester, Editor
Co-founder Writers Connection

About Writers Connection

Writers Connection was founded in 1983 by Steve and Meera Lester to serve writers and publishing professionals in California. Writers Connection serves more than 2,000 members and provides a wide range of services, including seminars, a referral service to help writers connect with professional writers and editors who offer consultations or critique services, a bookstore offering a wide selection of titles on writing- and publishing-related topics, the annual Selling to Hollywood weekend conference, and a 16-page monthly newsletter.

With the establishment of the small press arm of the company, Writers Connection will be increasing its publishing activity. At present the company publishes the *Marketplace* series books and the *Writing for Hollywood* and *Selling to Hollywood* documentary videotapes. *Writing for the Ethnic Markets* is due out in late 1991.

Writers Connection membership offers discounts on seminars, conferences, and book and tape purchases, and facilitates access to a wide range of resource material.

The monthly *Writers Connection* newsletter features current information on markets, events, contests, and industry news as well as articles on various aspects of writing and publishing. Members receive the newsletter free, and subscriptions are available to nonmembers.

The company's seminar offerings target professional writers as well as hobbyists, average three to six hours in length, and cover subjects such as "Constructing the Novel," "Writing Mystery and Suspense," "Basic Grammar," "Travel Writing," "Writing from Points of Power and Passion," "Writing the Nonfiction Best Seller," and "Editing for Technical and Business Communicators."

If you would like to join Writers Connection or subscribe to the monthly newsletter, an order form appears on page 183. The form may also be used to request seminar information, a free sample newsletter, or additional information about Writers Connection and future editions of the *Marketplace* directories and other books from Writers Connection Press.

Book Publishers

We assume that you have a manuscript (or an idea for one) that you wish to have published. We have obtained and organized the following information to help you decide where to send your submission, what to include in and on the envelope, when to anticipate an initial response, and in general, what to expect in terms and payment if you are offered a publishing contract.

How to Use the Information in This Section

The first paragraph of each entry identifies the publishing company, lists its location, and describes its publishing history. Your initial contact should be directed to the submissions editor named in the entry.

Subjects of Interest

We divided this section into two fields: fiction and nonfiction (which includes poetry). We listed the publishers' areas of interest within each field and included titles of recent publications. What publishers don't want is as important as what they do want; don't waste your time trying to force through an exception.

Initial Contact

Follow the instructions. Send editors what they want. There are many resources in the Books for Writers section that will help you prepare an effective query letter or persuasive book proposal. Include any additional material requested. When sending a requested resumé, biography (bio), or curriculum vitae, include only those details of your life that are relevant to your authority and ability to write the book. Always include a self-addressed, stamped envelope (SASE) for the editor's response or return of your materials.

Acceptance Policies

Unagented manuscripts: Many larger publishing houses will look only at manuscripts submitted by an agent. Smaller presses are more often willing to consider unagented manuscripts submitted by the author directly. A few agents are located in the Northwest (see the section on Literary Agents), but for a wider choice you will need to use additional resources (see Books for Writers).

First novels: This category is included only if the publisher has indicated an interest in publishing an author's first novel.

Simultaneous submissions: If the publisher's information says "yes" to simultaneous submissions, you may submit your manuscript to several different publishers at the same time, but you should inform each publisher that the manuscript is being simultaneously submitted.

Disk submissions: Many publishers are willing to accept your *final* manuscript on a disk compatible with the publisher's computer system, but almost all of them prefer the initial contact be made in the form of hard copy (a printout on paper).

Response time to initial inquiry: Response time varies greatly. Be patient and avoid phoning unless you've been instructed to do so by the publisher. A week or two *after* the specified response time (listed in the publisher's entry), it is appropriate to send a written request for information concerning the status of your submission. As with submissions, include a SASE for the publisher's reply.

Average time until publication: This information (always dependent upon a number of factors) gives you an approximate idea of how long the process takes after the publisher has received the completed manuscript.

First run: The number of copies to be printed is usually based on the publisher's best estimate of the number of copies that can be sold in the initial one- to two-year period.

Subsidy or co-publishing: In general, this means that the author pays some portion of the production and promotion costs and potentially stands to earn more than a basic royalty if the book sells well. Many legitimate small publishing houses simply do not have the money to finance all costs, and for that reason they encourage author investment.

Co-publishing with responsible small presses can be a viable and advantageous option for authors with speciality books that target specific markets. Subsidy deals take many forms, so obtain all the facts, get the terms in writing, and seek legal advice before signing. Avoid so-called vanity publishers that do little more than collect your money.

Advance: When dealing with small or mid-size presses, the advances (if given at all) tend to be small. The money goes primarily into production and promotion. An advantage of working with small presses is that your book is not "just another on their big list." The lists tend to be smaller, and thus your book gets more attention.

Royalty: Some royalties are computed on the retail cover price, but most are computed on the publisher's net receipts. Net receipts are the monies the publisher actually receives for the book. Some publishers may deduct expenses from their net receipts before computing royalties. If your personal negotiations with a publisher have reached the contract stage, seriously consider paying an agent or a publishing attorney to review and evaluate the contract before you sign.

Marketing Channels

Most publishers market books through direct mail sales to individuals and libraries, rep sales to bookstores, and distributor sales (distributors stock, sell, and distribute books to bookstores and libraries). In addition, some publishers promote special sales through book clubs, professional and social organizations, and special interest groups. If your book has such special sales potential, be sure to mention that fact in your initial contact with the publisher.

Subsidiary Rights: If the publisher lists "all," that means he/she is buying and handling all subsidiary rights to ensure that the publishing house realizes as much profit from the book as possible. Often, however, subsidiary rights are negotiable. An experienced agent or publishing attorney can advise you if you're unsure whether or not to sell all these rights.

Additional Information

This is the publisher's opportunity to supply any supplemental information not covered in the preceding sections. Tips are specific recommendations from the publisher to the author and should be seriously considered.

Writers Guidelines: Whenever guidelines are offered, request them before you write or submit anything targeted for a particular publishing house. If no entry is listed, the publisher does not have printed guidelines available.

Catalog: We suggest that your first step toward any publisher be to send for the catalog of books already published. This will give you the "flavor" of that press and enable you to draft a more focused query or submission.

Abbreviations

n/i means no information was given to us by the publisher.

n/a means that this particular question did not apply to the publisher.

AGLOW PUBLICATIONS. (A ministry of Women's Aglow Fellowship International). PO Box 1548. Lynnwood, WA 98046-1557. (206) 775-7282. Fax: (206) 778-9615. Submissions Editor: Gloria Chisholm. Founded: 1969. Number of titles published: cumulative—151, 1992—10. Softback 100%.

Subjects of Interest. Nonfiction—Christian self-help, inspirational, teaching, and religious. Recent publications: *Lifetime Relationships; Eternal Living in an Everyday World; Love and Its Counterfeits; The Gift of Encouragement.* Do not want: anything not specifically geared to some area of Christian life.

Initial Contact. Query letter with synopsis/outline. Include sample chapters. SASE required.

Acceptance Policies. Unagented manuscripts: yes. Simultaneous submissions: no. Disk submissions: no. Response time to initial inquiry: 1 month. Average time until publication: 18 months. Average first press run: 10,000. **Advance:** yes. **Royalty:** 10% average; based on retail.

Marketing Channels. Distribution houses; direct mail; independent reps; in-house staff; special sales. Subsidiary rights: translation and foreign.

Additional Information. Tips: Familiarize yourself with some of our publications before submitting. Writer's guidelines and catalog: 9x12 SASE, 3 first class stamps.

AHSAHTA PRESS. Boise State University. 1910 University Dr. Boise, ID 83725. (208) 385-1999. Submissions Editor: Tom Trusky. Founded: 1974. Number of titles published: cumulative—41, 1992—3. Softback 100%.

Subjects of Interest. Nonfiction—poetry (relating to history, cultures, environment, or Western America). Recent publications: *Going Home Away Indian*. Do not want: conventional, "nice," academic or workshop poetry, cowboy poetry, or any poems not rooted in the American West.

Initial Contact. 15-poem sampler sent January-March only. (No cover letter, no vitae, no artwork.) SASE required.

Acceptance Policies. Unagented manuscripts: yes. Simultaneous submissions: yes. Disk submissions: any format. Response time to initial inquiry: 4-6 weeks. Average time until publication: 8-15 months. Average first press run: 500. **Advance:** not offered. **Royalty:** author's copies for first and second printings, 40% discount; 25% royalties commence with third printing.

Marketing Channels. Distribution houses; direct mail; independent reps. Subsidiary rights: none.

Additional Information. Tips: Know the quality we demand. Catalog: upon request.

ALASKA NATIVE LANGUAGE CENTER. University of Alaska. PO Box 900111. Fairbanks, AK 99775-0120. (907) 474-7874. Fax: (907) 474-5817. Submissions Editor: Tom Alton. Founded: 1967. Number of titles published: cumulative—212, 1992—4. Hardback .1%, softback 99.9%.

Subjects of Interest. Fiction—Alaska Native folklore; children's and young adult. Nonfiction—Alaska Native language texts, dictionaries, grammars, schoolbooks. Recent publications: *Ahtna Dictionary; K'etetaalkkaanee, Aleut Tales and Narratives*. Do not want: non-Alaska Native subjects or authors.

Initial Contact. Query letter only.

Acceptance Policies. Unagented manuscripts: no. Simultaneous submissions: n/a. Disk submissions: Macintosh. Response time to initial inquiry: immediate. Average time until publication: by arrangement. Average first press run: 300. **Advance:** not offered. **Royalty:** none; specialized situation.

Marketing Channels. Direct mail. Subsidiary rights: none.

Additional Information. We have a brochure available describing our work with Alaska Native languages. Catalog: write or phone.

Alaska Outdoor Books *see* **GREAT NORTHWEST PUBLISHING.**

Amadeus Press *see* **TIMBER PRESS, INC.**

AMERICAN GEOGRAPHIC PUBLISHING. PO Box 5630. Helena, MT 59601. (406) 443-2842. Fax: (406) 443-5480. Submissions Editor: Mark Thompson. Founded: 1970. Number of titles published: cumulative—75, 1992—20. Hardback 1%, softback 99%.

Subjects of Interest. Nonfiction—travel; illustrated geography; nature; photography; recreation; regional. Recent publications: *Southern Appalachia: Portrait of the Land and Its People* (half photo and half text).

Initial Contact. Book proposal.

Acceptance Policies. Unagented manuscripts: yes. Simultaneous submissions: yes. Disk submissions: IBM or Macintosh. Response time to initial inquiry: 2-4 weeks. Average time until publication: 6-9 months. Average first press run: 1500-10,000. **Advance:** yes. **Royalty:** yes.

Marketing Channels. Distribution houses; in-house staff; special sales. Subsidiary rights: first serialization; reprint; direct mail or direct sales; book club; translation and foreign; English language outside the United States and Canada.

Additional Information. Tips: Please look at our books in bookstores before submitting in order to learn a little about our publications. Catalog: copies sent as available.

Areopagitica Press *see* **TIMBER PRESS, INC.**

ARROWOOD BOOKS, INC. PO Box 2100. Corvallis, OR 97339. (503) 759-9539. Submissions Editor: Lex Runciman. Founded: 1985. Number of titles published: cumulative—8, 1992—2. Each book is published in both hardback and softback.

Subjects of Interest. Fiction—contemporary/modern set in Northwest or written by Northwest authors; short stories. Recent publications: *Deadly Virtues* (set in Willamette Valley). **Nonfiction**—drama; essays; poetry; history; biography; Northwest. Recent publications: *The Light Station on Tillamook Rock* (poetry). Do not want: how-to; children's literature.

Initial Contact. Query letter. Include sample chapters or poems, a short biography, and a list of recent publications. SASE required.

Acceptance Policies. Unagented manuscripts: yes. First novels: yes. Simultaneous submissions: yes, notify us. Disk submissions: no. Response time to initial inquiry: 3 months. Average time until publication: 1 year. Average first press run: 500-1000. **Advance:** $200 average. **Royalty:** 10-12% of retail.

Marketing Channels. Distribution houses; direct mail. Subsidiary rights: all.

Additional Information. Writer's guidelines: upon request. Catalog: upon request.

BARCLAY PRESS. (Subsidiary of Northwest Yearly Meeting of Friends Church). 600 E. Third St. Newberg, OR 97132. (503) 538-7345. Fax: (503) 538-7033. Submissions Editor: Dan McCracken. Founded: 1959. Number of titles published: cumulative—45, 1992—3. Hardback 33%, softback 67%.

Subjects of Interest. Nonfiction—religious; Christian living; contemporary and social issues. Recent publications: *Christians in the Crossfire.*

Initial Contact. Query letter with proposal. SASE required.

Acceptance Policies. Unagented manuscripts: yes. Simultaneous submissions: yes, inform us. Disk submissions: no. Response time to initial inquiry: 3 weeks. Average time until publication: 10 months. Average first press run: 1500. **Advance:** not offered. **Royalty:** yes.

Marketing Channels. Distribution houses; direct mail. Subsidiary rights: none.

Additional Information. Tips: Send a good proposal. Do not send entire manuscript. Catalog: SASE.

BEAR CREEK PUBLICATIONS. 2507 Minor Ave. E. Seattle, WA 98102. (206) 322-7604. Submissions Editor: Kathleen Shea. Founded: 1985. Number of titles published: cumulative—2, 1992—4. Softback 100%.

Subjects of Interest. Nonfiction—parenting; travel. Recent publications: *Take Your Baby and Go!* (guide for traveling with babies, toddlers). Do not want: children's books; religious materials; fiction; journals.

Initial Contact. Query letter with synopsis/outline. Include sample chapters. SASE required.

Acceptance Policies. Unagented manuscripts: yes. Simultaneous submissions: no. Disk submissions: Microsoft Word. Response time to initial inquiry: 60 days. Average time until publication: 6-12 months. Average first press run: 4000. **Advance:** negotiable. **Royalty:** negotiable.

Marketing Channels. Distribution houses; direct mail; special sales. Subsidiary rights: all.

Additional Informaticn. Interested in how-to books for parents of infants, toddlers, and young children. Catalog: SASE.

BEAR WALLOW PUBLISHING CO., THE. 57919 High Valley Rd. Union, OR 97883. (503) 562-5687. Submissions Editor: Jerry Gildemeister. Founded: 1976. Number of titles published: cumulative—6, 1992—1. Hardback 100%.

Subjects of Interest. Nonfiction—Western history; Americana; aviation; Native American; regional. Recent publications: *Around the Cat's Back, An American Vignette; A Letter Home; Where Rolls the Oregon.*

Initial Contact. Query letter only.

Acceptance Policies. Unagented manuscripts: yes. Simultaneous submissions: n/i. Disk submissions: no. Response time to initial inquiry: 1 week. Average time until publication: 1-2 years. Average first press run: 3000-10,000. Subsidy or co-publishing: consultant and production services to self-publisher. **Advance:** not offered. **Royalty:** yes.

Marketing Channels. Distribution houses; direct mail. Subsidiary rights: none.

Additional Information. Primarily in-house publishing; query prior to submission of material. Tips: We generally like materials that are Western history oriented, nonfiction, and one of a kind. Project must lend itself to fine illustration. Catalog: upon request.

BEAUTIFUL AMERICA PUBLISHING CO. (Imprints: Little America; Spirit of America). 9725 S. West Commerce Circle. PO Box 646. Wilsonville, OR 97070. (503) 682-0173. Fax: (503) 682-0175. Submissions Editor: Beverly A. Paul. Founded: 1986. Number of titles published: cumulative—24, 1992—8. Hardback 50%, softback 50%.

Subjects of Interest. Fiction—holiday stories; children's and young adult. Nonfiction—architecture; history; home and garden; Native American; nature; scenic; regional; travel; children's. Recent publications: *East Coast Victorians; Highway 101; Public and Private Gardens of the Northwest; Christmas Collie; Incredible Adventures of Donovan Willoughby.* Do not want: poetry; fiction (romantic novels, etc.).

Initial Contact. Query letter only.

Acceptance Policies. Unagented manuscripts: yes. Simultaneous submissions: no. Disk submissions: yes. Response time to initial inquiry: 1 month. Average time until publication: 1 year. Average first press run: 7500-10,000. Subsidy or co-publishing: yes. **Advance:** yes. **Royalty:** yes.

Marketing Channels. Distribution houses; direct mail; independent reps; in-house staff; special sales. Subsidiary rights: all.

Additional Information. Catalog: upon request.

BEYNCH PRESS PUBLISHING CO. 1928 SE Ladd Ave. Portland, OR 97214. Not accepting submissions.

BOX DOG PRESS. (Subsidiary of Box Dog Enterprises). PO Box 9609. Seattle, WA 98109. Submissions Editor: Craig Joyce. Founded: 1982. Number of titles published: cumulative—15, 1992—7. Softback 100%.

Subjects of Interest. Fiction—avant-garde; erotica; horror; humor; science fiction. Recent publications: *Milk of the Poison Mojo*. Nonfiction—film; gay/lesbian; humor; men's issues; philosophy; poetry; photography; real estate; sexual issues; sports (baseball); writing/ publishing. Recent publications: *Hands of Linda Blair; Dandy* (poetry-lyrics). Do not want: how-to; gardening.

Initial Contact. Query letter with synopsis/outline. Include sample chapters, bio, education, and other interests. SASE required.

Acceptance Policies. Unagented manuscripts: yes. First novels: yes. Simultaneous submissions: yes. Disk submissions: no. Response time to initial inquiry: 2-4 weeks. Average time until publication: varies. Average first press run: 500. **Advance:** not offered. **Royalty:** yes.

Marketing Channels. Distribution houses; direct mail (mostly). Subsidiary rights: all.

Additional Information. Know our writers. Tips: Be original, be good. Writer's guidelines: upon request. Catalog: SASE, or send 2 first class stamps.

BRIGHT RING PUBLISHING. PO Box 5768. Bellingham, WA 98226. (206) 734-1601. Submissions Editor: Mary Ann Kohl. Founded: 1985. Number of titles published: cumulative—3, 1992—1. Softback 100%.

Subjects of Interest. Nonfiction—resource/activity books for children and adults; education; parenting. Recent publications: *Good Earth Art* (environmental art for kids); *Mudworks: Creative Clay, Dough, and Modeling Experiences; Scribble Cookies: Independent Art Experiences for Children*. Do not want: picture books or story books; any fiction.

Initial Contact. Any form of contact is okay. Include age of intended market. SASE required.

Acceptance Policies. Unagented manuscripts: yes. Simultaneous submissions: yes. Disk submissions: PC (save as text). Response time to initial inquiry: 2-6 weeks. Average time until publication: 1 year. Average first press run: 10,000. **Advance:** $500. **Royalty:** 5% average; based on wholesale and retail.

Marketing Channels. Distribution houses; cooperative distribution; direct mail; special sales. Subsidiary rights: all.

Additional Information. We're very small but successful. Tips: Works must encourage creativity of an open-ended nature in children. Writer's guidelines: SASE. Catalog: write or call.

CAXTON PRINTERS, LTD., THE. 312 Main St. Caldwell, ID 83605. (208) 459-7421. Fax: (208) 459-7450. Submissions Editor: Kathy Gaudry. Founded: 1895, began publishing in 1925. Number of titles published: cumulative—unknown, 1992—8. Hardback 25%, softback 75%.

Subjects of Interest. Nonfiction—Western Americana with emphasis on history, travel, adventure, and lifestyle. Recent publications: *Camera Eye on Idaho: Pioneer Photography 1863-1913; In Search of Western Oregon* (travel). Do not want: fiction; poetry.

Initial Contact. Query letter with synopsis/outline. Include sample chapters, a brief resumé with author qualifications. SASE required.

Acceptance Policies. Unagented manuscripts: yes. Simultaneous submissions: yes, inform us. Disk submissions: no. Response time to initial inquiry: 2-3 months. Average time until publication: 8-12 months. Average first press run: 4000. **Advance:** $500-$2000 average, when we offer one. **Royalty:** 10%; based on retail sales.

Marketing Channels. Distribution houses; direct mail; independent reps; in-house staff. Subsidiary rights: all.

Additional Information. Book editing, design, and production are all done in house—one of only a few American publishers to do so. Tips: Read the guidelines and catalog before submitting, then make sure your manuscript fits with what we publish. Writer's guidelines: SASE. Catalog: upon request.

CENTER FOR EAST ASIAN STUDIES. (Subsidiary of Western Washington University). Western Washington University. Bellingham, WA 98225-9056. (206) 676-3401. Submissions Editor: Professor Henry G. Schwarz. Founded: 1971. Number of titles published: cumulative—19, 1992—3. Hardback 50%, softback 50%.

Subjects of Interest. Nonfiction—scholarly subjects on East Asia (China, Japan, Korea, Mongolia). Recent publications: *The Minorities of Northern China; Buddhist Art of East Asia; The Korean Peasant at the Crossroads.*

Initial Contact. Book proposal. Include sample chapters. SASE required.

Acceptance Policies. Unagented manuscripts: yes. Simultaneous submissions: no. Disk submissions: no. Response time to initial inquiry: 2 weeks. Average time until publication: 1 year. Average first press run: varies greatly. **Advance:** not offered. **Royalty:** usually a negotiated number of free copies and a number of additional copies at specified discount.

Marketing Channels. Distribution houses; direct mail; special sales. Subsidiary rights: none.

Additional Information. Writer's guidelines: upon request. Catalog: upon request.

CIRCA PRESS. PO Box 482. Lake Oswego, OR 97034. (503) 636-7241. Submissions Editor: address inquiries to Editor. Founded: 1985. Number of titles published: cumulative—6, 1992—3. Hardback 50%, softback 50%.

Subjects of Interest. Nonfiction—business/economics; contemporary/social issues; government/politics; philosophy; psychology; sociology; new ideas (inquire). Recent publications: *The Human Position* (philosophy/free will); *Chamru* (world government); *Politics: An American Perspective.* Do not want: how-to; self-help; religion; new age; cooking; gardening.

Initial Contact. Query letter clearly describing manuscript. SASE required.

Acceptance Policies. Unagented manuscripts: yes. Simultaneous submissions: yes, inform us. Disk submissions: yes (we will notify author as to format). Response time to initial inquiry: 3-4 weeks. Average time until publication: 6-12 months. Average first press run: 2000-3000. **Advance:** not offered. **Royalty:** 10%; based on cover price.

Marketing Channels. Distribution houses; cooperative distribution. Subsidiary rights: all.

Additional Information. Writing must be well researched, free of jargon, and suitable for a general, well-educated adult reader. Tips: Query first with a letter of any length which clearly describes the manuscript. Writer's guidelines: sent if we like query letter. Catalog: SASE (first class postage for one ounce).

CIVETTA PRESS. PO Box 1043. Portland, OR 97207. (503) 228-6649. Submissions Editor: Thomas Bjorklund. Founded: 1989. Number of titles published: cumulative—2, 1992—5. Softback 100%.

Subjects of Interest. Nonfiction—how-to; writing; travel; self-help; professional directories; general. Recent publications: two books on how to write and get published. Do not want: children's; novels; poetry.

Initial Contact. Query letter only. SASE required.

Acceptance Policies. Unagented manuscripts: yes. Simultaneous submissions: yes. Disk submissions: no. Response time to initial inquiry: within 2 weeks. Average time until publication: 6 months. Average first press run: 5000. **Advance:** not offered. **Royalty:** 6% average.

Marketing Channels. Distribution houses; cooperative distribution; direct mail; in-house staff; special sales. Subsidiary rights: first serialization; second serialization; book club rights; translation and foreign.

Additional Information. We publish books that demonstrate an author's strong writing abilities. We don't like to rewrite a whole book, no matter how interesting the topic. Tips: Write an interesting, detailed query letter. Also, be detailed about your credentials for writing this book. Writer's guidelines: request from editor. Catalog: request from marketing department.

CLARK CO., THE ARTHUR H. PO Box 14707. Spokane, WA 99214. (509) 928-9540. Submissions Editor: Robert A. Clark. Founded: 1902. Number of titles published: cumulative—450, 1992—8. Hardback 100%.

Subjects of Interest. Nonfiction—Western Americana in areas of biography, history, and reference.

Initial Contact. Query letter with synopsis/outline. SASE required.

Acceptance Policies. Unagented manuscripts: yes. Simultaneous submissions: no. Disk submissions: no. Response time to initial inquiry: 10 days. Average time until publication: 9 months. Average first press run: 750-1500. Subsidy or co-publishing: higher royalty percentage. **Advance:** none offered. **Royalty:** 10% average; based on net sales.

Marketing Channels. In-house staff; display advertising. Subsidiary rights: dramatization, motion picture, and broadcast; paperback.

Additional Information. We specialize in nonfiction Western history. Catalog: 6x9 SASE.

Classics of the Fur Trade *see* **MOUNTAIN PRESS PUBLISHING CO.**

CLEANING CONSULTANT SERVICES, INC. 1512 Western Ave. PO Box 1273. Seattle, WA 98111. (206) 682-9748. Fax: (206) 622-6876. Submissions Editor: William R. Griffin. Founded: 1976. Number of titles published: cumulative—20, 1992—3. Hardback 10%, softback 90%.

Subjects of Interest. Nonfiction—technical cleaning procedures; cleaning and maintenance-related small business start-up manuals; business economics and opportunity; education; crafts and hobbies; consumer services; text and reference; education. Recent publications: *Food Service Health Sanitation and Safety; How to Sell and Price Contract Cleaning; Comprehensive Rug and Carpet Cleaning*. Do not want: fiction.

Initial Contact. Query letter with synopsis/outline or a book proposal with sample chapters or entire manuscript. Include marketing information, potential audience, and how to reach market. Phone calls are accepted. SASE required.

Acceptance Policies. Unagented manuscripts: yes. Simultaneous submissions: no. Disk submissions: no. Response time to initial inquiry: 1-4 weeks. Average time until publication: 3-12 months. Average first press run: 1000-2500. Subsidy or co-publishing: would consider. **Advance:** $50-$1000 average. **Royalty:** 5-10% average; based on income.

Marketing Channels. Distribution houses; cooperative distribution; direct mail; independent reps; in-house staff; special sales. Subsidiary rights: all.

Additional Information. We are interested in the following subjects only: references, directories, and how-to on cleaning and maintenance, health, self-employment, and entrepreneurship. Tips: Send only what we ask for. Writer's guidelines: write or call. Catalog: write or call.

CONSCIOUS LIVING PRESS. (Subsidiary of Conscious Living Foundation).
PO Box 9. Drain, OR 97435. Fax: (503) 836-2930. Submissions Editor: Dr. Tim Lowenstein. Founded: 1978. Number of titles published: cumulative—3, 1992—n/i. Softback 100%.

Subjects of Interest. Nonfiction—health; self-help; family issues; music; new age; psychology; human resources.

Initial Contact. Query letter only. SASE required.

Acceptance Policies. Unagented manuscripts: yes. Simultaneous submissions: no. Disk submissions: IBM WordPerfect. Response time to initial inquiry: 2-3 weeks. Average time until publication: 6 months. Average first press run: 3000. Subsidy or co-publishing: yes. **Advance:** not offered. **Royalty:** yes.

Marketing Channels. Distribution houses; cooperative distribution; direct mail; independent reps. Subsidiary rights: none.

Continuing Education Press *see* **PORTLAND STATE UNIVERSITY.**

COUNCIL FOR INDIAN EDUCATION. 517 Rimrock Rd. Billings, MT
59102. (406) 252-7454. Submissions Editor: Hap Gilliland. Founded: 1970. Number of titles published: cumulative—120, 1992—6. Hardback and softback editions for most books.

Subjects of Interest. Fiction—Native American life, past and present, suitable for use in schools. Recent publications: *Sun Dance for Andy Horn* (modern Sioux Indian novel). Nonfiction—Native American history, crafts, activities, and teacher-training materials; poetry; games and puzzles. Do not want: materials unrelated to Indian life or culture; pornography.

Initial Contact. Query letter with synopsis/outline or sample chapters or entire manuscript. SASE required.

Acceptance Policies. Unagented manuscripts: yes. First novels: yes. Simultaneous submissions: yes. Disk submissions: no. Response time to initial inquiry: 2-6 months. Average time until publication: 10 months. Average first press run: 1000. Subsidy or co-publishing: rarely, but we will work on a shared cost basis for books too large for us to finance. **Advance:** not offered. **Royalty:** 10%; based on wholesale.

Marketing Channels. Direct mail. Subsidiary rights: none.

Additional Information. Writer's guidelines: #10 SASE. Catalog: #10 SASE.

CROSS CULTURAL PRESS. 1166 S. 42nd St. Springfield, OR 97478.
(503) 746-7401. Submissions Editor: Kenneth Fenter. Founded: 1984. Number of titles published: cumulative—6, 1992—2. Softback 100%.

Subjects of Interest. Nonfiction—Japanese or Asian/American encounters. Recent publications: *Tokyo Observer; Asian Observer; Gaijin! Gaijin!*

Initial Contact. Query letter with synopsis/outline. Include 2 sample chapters and an author bio. SASE required.

Acceptance Policies. Unagented manuscripts: yes. Simultaneous submissions: yes. Disk submissions: MS DOS. Response time to initial inquiry: 2-3 weeks. Average time until publication: 6-8 months. Average first press run: 2000. Subsidy or co-publishing: percentage with author repayment plus royalty. **Advance:** not offered. **Royalty:** 10% average; based on actual sale price.

Marketing Channels. Cooperative distribution; direct mail. Subsidiary rights: none.

Additional Information. Catalog: (brochure) upon request.

CULINARY ARTS, LTD. PO Box 2157. Lake Oswego, OR 97035. (503) 639-4549. Submissions Editor: Cheryl Long. Founded: 1979. Number of titles published: cumulative—8, 1992—12. Softback 100%.

Subjects of Interest. Nonfiction—cookbooks; food hobbies; Scandinavian subjects. Recent publications: *Classic Liqueurs: The Art of Making and Cooking with Liqueurs; Gourmet Mustards: How to Make and Cook with Them; Light Fantastic: Health Conscious Entertaining; Happy Birthday: A Guide to Special Parties for Children; Yes You Can Microwave!*

Initial Contact. Query letter with synopsis/outline. Include expertise in subject. SASE required.

Acceptance Policies. Unagented manuscripts: yes. Simultaneous submissions: no. Disk submissions: only after acceptance. Response time to initial inquiry: 1 month. Average time until publication: 1 year. Average first press run: 2500. **Advance:** not offered. **Royalty:** yes.

Marketing Channels. Distribution houses; cooperative distribution; direct mail; independent reps; special sales. Subsidiary rights: all.

Additional Information. Tips: Look for specialty areas, i.e. herbs, food hobbies, etc., something unique but popular. Catalog: upon request.

DENALI PRESS, THE. PO Box 021535. Juneau, AK 99802-1535. (907) 586-6014. Fax: (907) 463-6780. Submissions Editor: Alan Edward Schorr. Founded: 1986. Number of titles published: cumulative—15, 1992—6. Hardback 10%, softback 90%.

Subjects of Interest. Nonfiction—ethnic groups (Hispanic, Native American); refugees; anthropology; cultural diversity; Alaskana; reference; scholarly. Recent publications: *Refugee and Immigrant Resource Directory; Hispanic Resource Directory*. Do not want: fiction; new age.

Initial Contact. Query letter with synopsis/outline and one sample chapter. Include author bio.

Acceptance Policies. Unagented manuscripts: yes. Simultaneous submissions: yes. Disk submissions: not initially, but manuscript must be available as computer file. Response time to initial inquiry: 4 weeks. Average time until publication: 9-15 months. Average first press run: 2500. **Advance:** not offered. **Royalty:** 10% average; based on net receipts.

Marketing Channels. Cooperative distribution; direct mail; in-house staff. Subsidiary rights: all.

Additional Information. Tips: Send letter, outline, and perhaps one sample chapter. Manuscript must be available as computer file. Catalog: upon request.

DIMI PRESS. PO Box 3363. Salem, OR 97302. (503) 364-7698. Fax: (503) 364-9727. Submissions Editor: Dick Lutz. Founded: 1981. Number of titles published: cumulative—3, 1992—n/i. Softback 100%.

Subjects of Interest. Nonfiction—relaxation techniques (self-help books and tapes); self-help; Tarahumara Indians; directory of senior services in Marion and Polk Counties, Oregon; general interest. Recent publications: *Feel Better! Live Longer! Relax* (review of relaxation techniques); *The Running Indians* (account of interesting Indian tribe). Do not want: cookbooks; children's books; religion; personal accounts.

Initial Contact. Query letter with book proposal. Include proposed market. SASE required.

Acceptance Policies. Unagented manuscripts: yes. Simultaneous submissions: yes. Disk submissions: Macintosh preferred; IBM accepted. Response time to initial inquiry: 4 weeks. Average time until publication: varies. Average first press run: 2000. Subsidy or co-publishing: cost plus, on specific tasks needed. **Advance:** variable. **Royalty:** 10% average; based on retail price.

Marketing Channels. Distribution houses; direct mail. Subsidiary rights: all.

Additional Information. At present, we want only practical self-help or nonfiction targeted to a specific market. We also provide self-publishing information and services. Tips: Query letter should be objective, practical, and targeted to a specific market. Writer's guidelines: write, call, or fax. Catalog: write, call, or fax.

Dioscorides Press *see* **TIMBER PRESS, INC.**

DORAL PUBLISHING. (Imprint: The Pure Bred Series). PO Box 596. Wilsonville, OR 97070. (503) 694-5707. Submissions Editors: Dr. Alvin Grossman (dog breed books); Lynn Grey (general pet books); Robin Roberts (other dog books). Founded: 1986. Number of titles published: cumulative—9, 1992—4. Hardback 70%, softback 30%.

Subjects of Interest. Nonfiction—books about purebred dogs and cats. Recent publications: *The Basenji, Out of Africa to You; Meet the Pug for Years of Happiness.* Do not want: fiction.

Initial Contact. Query letter with synopsis/outline. Include author's credentials and previous publications. SASE required.

Acceptance Policies. Unagented manuscripts: yes. Simultaneous submissions: no. Disk submissions: Macwrite II. Response time to initial inquiry: within 3 weeks. Average time until publication: 6 months. Average first press run: 3000. **Advance:** not offered. **Royalty:** 10% average on the first 5000.

Marketing Channels. Distribution houses; direct mail; independent reps. Subsidiary rights: all.

Additional Information. We cater to the needs of the dog show breeder/exhibitor and, to a lesser extent, the cat fancier. Tips: A good bibliography and index are mandatory. Catalog: upon request.

EDMONDS ARTS COMMISSION BOOKS. 700 Main St. Edmonds, WA 98020. (206) 775-2525, ext. 269. Fax: (206) 778-5322. Submissions Editor: Literary Arts Committee Chair. Founded: 1987. Number of titles published: cumulative—2, 1992—undecided. Softback 100%.

Subjects of Interest. Fiction—short stories; folklore. Recent publications: *Sasquatch Sightings, Imagined and True* (anthology). Nonfiction—folklore; general interest; historical; literary. Recent publications: *A Centennial Sampler of Edmonds Writing* (anthology). Do not want: unsolicited material.

Initial Contact. Only in response to calls for entries, which are mailed to local writers and found in releases to the local media. Be sure to acquire a copy of "Request for Proposal" first. SASE required.

Acceptance Policies. Unagented manuscripts: yes. Simultaneous submissions: no. Disk submissions: no. Response time to initial inquiry: 1 month. Average time until publication: 6 months. Average first press run: 2500. **Advance:** not offered. **Royalty:** free copies of book.

Marketing Channels. Distribution houses; in-house staff; special sales. Subsidiary rights: reprint; direct mail or direct sales.

Additional Information. Writer's guidelines: included in "Request for Proposal."

EPICENTER PRESS, INC. (Imprint: Umbrella Guides). 18821 64th Ave. NE. Seattle, WA 98155. (206) 485-6822. Fax: (206) 485-9772. Submissions Editor: Kent Sturgis. Founded: 1988. Number of titles published: cumulative—7, 1992—3. Hardback and softback (about 40% in both).

Subjects of Interest. Nonfiction—art books, photography, biography, history, travel, and children's books focused on Alaska or the Pacific Northwest. Recent publications: *Carmack of the Klondike* (biography of the man whose discovery triggered the Klondike gold rush).

Initial Contact. Query letter with synopsis/outline and book proposal. Include sample chapters. SASE required.

Acceptance Policies. Unagented manuscripts: yes. Simultaneous submissions: yes. Disk submissions: no. Response time to initial inquiry: 6 weeks. Average time until publication: 18 months. Average first press run: 7000. **Advance:** not offered. **Royalty:** 10% average; based on retail price.

Marketing Channels. Distribution houses; cooperative distribution; direct mail; in-house staff; special sales. Subsidiary rights: all.

Additional Information. We love to deal with authors who have useful ideas for marketing and promoting their titles and are willing to help. Catalog: upon request.

Evergreen Pacific Publishing *see* **ROMAR BOOKS, LTD.**

FALCON PRESS PUBLISHING CO. PO Box 1718. Helena, MT 59624. Fax: (406) 442-2995. Submissions Editor: Christopher Cauble. Founded: 1978. Number of titles published: cumulative—100+\-, 1992—25. Hardback 50%, softback 50%.

Subjects of Interest. Nonfiction—outdoors; recreation and hiking; fishing; scenic driving for entire United States; large-format, scenery giftbooks. Recent publications: hiker's guides to New Mexico, Utah, and California. *America on My Mind* (large-format, photo giftbook). Do not want: manuscripts or inquiries on anything except the above-mentioned topics.

Initial Contact. Query letter. Include sample chapters and market data.

Acceptance Policies. Unagented manuscripts: yes. Simultaneous submissions: no. Disk submissions: yes. Response time to initial inquiry: 4-6 weeks. Average time until publication: 1 year. Average first press run: 5000. **Advance:** varies. **Royalty:** 10% average.

Marketing Channels. Distribution houses. Subsidiary rights: all.

Additional Information. Tips: We are looking for people to write recreation guides in the areas of hiking, fishing, scenic drives, rockhounding, etc., within our already set format. These people must be experienced writers and be experienced in the area about which they are writing. Catalog: upon request.

FAST FORWARD PUBLISHING. PO Box 45153. Seattle, WA 98145-0153.
(206) 527-3112. Fax: (206) 523-4829. Submissions Editor: Wayne Parker.
Founded: 1989. Number of titles published: cumulative—1, 1992—4. Softback
100%.

Subjects of Interest. Nonfiction—computer and business "how-to" books. Recent
publications: *The Computer Buyer's Handbook.* Do not want: poetry; fiction.

Initial Contact. Query letter with synopsis/outline or book proposal. Include sample chapters
and the qualifications and experience of the author. SASE not required.

Acceptance Policies. Unagented manuscripts: yes. Simultaneous submissions: yes; other
publishers must be notified on acceptance. Disk submissions: IBM compatible; ASCII.
Response time to initial inquiry: 30 days. Average time until publication: 6-12 months.
Average first press run: 3000-5000 depending on advance orders. **Advance:** none offered.
Royalty: amount negotiable; based on trade practices.

Marketing Channels. Distribution houses; direct mail. Subsidiary rights: all.

Additional Information. We are looking to expand rapidly in the computer and consumer
book markets. We need good titles! Tips: Demonstrate the sales potential of your title, how it
is unique, why it is important, what is exciting and appealing about it to a broad readership.
Writer's guidelines: as part of inquiry process. Catalog: write, call, or fax.

FERNGLEN PRESS, THE. 473 Sixth St. Lake Oswego, OR 97034. Only in-
house publishing at present, with an emphasis on travel and Hawaii.

FLYING PENCIL PUBLICATIONS. PO Box 19062. Portland, OR 97219.
(503) 245-2314. Submissions Editor: Madelynne Diness. Founded: 1983. Number
of titles published: cumulative—6, 1992—2. Softback 100%.

Subjects of Interest. Fiction—will consider only if plot is heavily influenced by
protagonist's involvement in fishing/Western outdoors activity. **Nonfiction**—fishing; Western
travel guides; natural history; outdoor recreation. Recent publications: *Fishing with Small Fry
(How to Hook Your Kids on Fishing); Yellowstone Fishing Guide.* Do not want: hunting-
related manuscripts.

Initial Contact. Query letter with synopsis/outline. Include sample chapters and information
about the directed market. SASE required.

Acceptance Policies. Unagented manuscripts: yes. Simultaneous submissions: yes. Disk
submissions: no. Response time to initial inquiry: 1 month. Average time until publication: 9
months. Average first press run: 5000. **Advance:** $1200 average. **Royalty:** 8-15% average;
based on retail.

Marketing Channels. Distribution houses. Subsidiary rights: all.

GLACIER HOUSE PUBLICATIONS. PO Box 201901. Anchorage, AK
99520. (907) 272-3286. Fax: (907) 274-9614. Submissions Editor: Dave Thorp.
Founded: 1987. Number of titles published: cumulative—6, 1992—18. Hardback
20%, softback 80%.

Subjects of Interest. Fiction—adventure; short stories. **Nonfiction**—adventure; Alaska;
natural history; fishing; travel; directories; dictionaries. Recent publications: *Skiing Alaska's
Back Forty; Rockhound Guide to Alaska; Bed and Breakfast in Alaska; Alaska Salmon Atlas;
Dictionary of Alaska Place Names.*

Initial Contact. Query letter with synopsis/outline. Include sample chapters.

Acceptance Policies. Unagented manuscripts: yes. First novels: yes. Simultaneous submissions: no. Disk submissions: Macintosh. Response time to initial inquiry: 1 week. Average time until publication: varies. Average first press run: 2000-20,000. **Advance:** not offered. **Royalty:** negotiable.

Marketing Channels. Distribution houses; cooperative distribution; direct mail; independent reps; in-house staff; special sales. Subsidiary rights: all.

Additional Information. We were founded by two writers. Tips: Be brief. Writer's guidelines: call. Catalog: call.

GLEN ABBEY BOOKS, INC. (Imprint: Lakeside Recovery Press). 735 N. Northlake Way, Ste. 1090. Seattle, WA 98103. (206) 548-9360. Fax: (206) 632-0353. Submissions Editor: Bill Pittman. Founded: 1986. Number of titles published: cumulative—14, 1992—8. Softback 100%.

Subjects of Interest. Nonfiction—books for people in 12-step recovery programs that relate to areas of contemporary and social issues, family issues, and health and fitness; self-help; sociology; new age; history/biography. Recent publications: *Dealing with Depression in 12 Step Recovery; Stepping Stones to Recovery: For Women*. Do not want: any material that does not deal with the recovery process; fiction.

Initial Contact. Query letter with synopsis/outline. Include sample chapters or entire manuscript. SASE required.

Acceptance Policies. Unagented manuscripts: yes. Simultaneous submissions: no. Disk submissions: PC; prefer Microsoft Word 5.0. Response time to initial inquiry: 3 months. Average time until publication: 1 year. Average first press run: 5000-10,000. **Advance:** not offered. **Royalty:** negotiable.

Marketing Channels. Distribution houses; direct mail. Subsidiary rights: all.

Additional Information. We are very specialized; our publications fit within an extremely narrow category. Tips: Read the materials we have already published: for example, any of our titles, Melody Beattie's books, or anything from Hazelden or Compcare publishers. Writer's guidelines: upon request. Catalog: upon request.

GRAPEVINE PUBLICATIONS, INC. PO Box 2449. Corvallis, OR 97339-2449. (503) 754-0583. Submissions Editor: Daniel R. Coffin. Founded: 1983. Number of titles published: cumulative—32, 1992—18. Softback 100%.

Subjects of Interest. Nonfiction—self-instruction in math, science, technology; curriculum materials; computers. Recent publications: *An Easy Course in Using WordPerfect 5.1.*

Initial Contact. Book proposal. Include sample chapters, a detailed outline, and market survey. SASE required.

Acceptance Policies. Unagented manuscripts: yes. Simultaneous submissions: yes. Disk submissions: Macintosh (preferred); or DOS 5 1/4 or 3 1/2. Response time to initial inquiry: 4 weeks. Average time until publication: 6-8 months. Average first press run: 5000. **Advance:** not offered. **Royalty:** yes.

Marketing Channels. Direct mail; in-house staff; special sales. Subsidiary rights: none.

Additional Information. We are looking for writers who can teach or teachers who can write. Writer's guidelines: 8 1/2 x 11 SASE, $.98. Catalog: 5 1/2 x 8 1/2 SASE, $.52.

GRAPHIC ARTS CENTER PUBLISHING CO. PO Box 10306. Portland, OR 97210. (503) 226-2402. Fax: (503) 223-1410. Submissions Editor: Douglas A. Pfeiffer. Founded: 1968. Number of titles published: cumulative—150, 1992—15. Hardback 90%, softback 10%.

Subjects of Interest. Fiction—children's illustrated titles. Recent publications: *The Dream Stealer; Prancer*. Nonfiction—state, regional, and country photo-essays. Recent publications: *Sweden; Arizona; The Best of Alaska*. Do not want: unsolicited adult fiction; biography; historical manuscripts.

Initial Contact. Query letter with synopsis/outline. Include previously published titles and a clearly identified target audience. SASE required.

Acceptance Policies. Unagented manuscripts: no. Simultaneous submissions: yes. Disk submissions: no. Response time to initial inquiry: 1 week; may take 6 months for acceptance. Average time until publication: 2 years. Average first press run: 10,000. **Advance:** not offered. **Royalty:** no.

Marketing Channels. Distribution houses; independent reps; in-house staff; special sales. Subsidiary rights: all.

Additional Information. We specialize in color reproduction of photographs and illustrations. Tips: Identify the target audience clearly. Writer's guidelines: upon request. Catalog: upon request.

GREAT NORTHWEST PUBLISHING AND DISTRIBUTING CO., INC. (Imprint: Alaska Outdoor Books). PO Box 103902. Anchorage, AK 99510. (907) 373-0122. Fax: (907) 376-0826. Submissions Editor: Marvin Clark. Founded: 1979. Number of titles published: cumulative—25, 1992—5. Hardback 80%, softback 20%.

Subjects of Interest. Nonfiction—Alaska; hunting; life in the Alaskan outdoors. Recent publications: *Empire on Ice; One Man's Homestead*. Do not want: anything unrelated to Alaska or the Alaskan outdoors.

Initial Contact. Query letter with synopsis/outline.

Acceptance Policies. Unagented manuscripts: yes. Simultaneous submissions: yes. Disk submissions: only after acceptance. Response time to initial inquiry: 1 month. Average time until publication: 1-2 years. Average first press run: n/i. Subsidy or co-publishing: occasionally; terms vary. **Advance:** not offered. **Royalty:** 10% average; based on net.

Marketing Channels. Distribution houses; direct mail. Subsidiary rights: n/i.

Halcyon House *see* **NATIONAL BOOK CO.**

HANCOCK HOUSE PUBLISHERS. 1431 Harrison Ave. Blaine, WA 98230. (206) 354-6953. Fax: (604) 538-2262. Submissions Editor: Diane Brown. Founded: 1968. Number of titles published: cumulative—300, 1992—25. Hardback 20%, softback 80%.

Subjects of Interest. Nonfiction—aviculture; conservation; Indian; animals; anthropology; folklore; nature; regional; Northern biography. Recent publications: *To Heal the Earth; Ah Mo*. Do not want: fiction.

Initial Contact. Query letter with synopsis/outline. Include length of manuscript and whether visuals are available. SASE required.

Acceptance Policies. Unagented manuscripts: yes. Simultaneous submissions: yes. Disk submissions: no. Response time to initial inquiry: 2 weeks. Average time until publication: 6-12 months. Average first press run: 5000. **Advance:** yes. **Royalty:** yes.

Marketing Channels. Direct mail; independent reps; in-house staff. Subsidiary rights: all.

Additional Information. Writer's guidelines: upon request. Catalog: 9x12 SASE.

HAPI PRESS, THE. 512 SW Maplecrest Dr. Portland, OR 97219. (503) 246-9632. Submissions Editor: Joe E. Pierce. Founded: 1970. Number of titles published: cumulative—35, 1992—3. Hardback 5%, softback 95%.

Subjects of Interest. **Fiction**—off beat. Recent publications: *Thorns, Thistles and Chrome* (futuristic science fiction). **Nonfiction**—social sciences; personal accounts about Oregon history. Recent publications: *Obied Dickson's War on Sin in Salem* (early church history in Oregon); *Language Acquisition or Learning* (English as a second language). Do not want: run-of-the-mill fiction.

Initial Contact. Query letter with 2 sample chapters. Include author's qualifications for this particular book. SASE required.

Acceptance Policies. Unagented manuscripts: n/i. Simultaneous submissions: yes. Disk submissions: WordPerfect 4.3 or 5.1. Response time to initial inquiry: 3 months. Average time until publication: 1 year. Average first press run: 350. Subsidy or co-publishing: partial subsidies are accepted on books that we do not think will sell. **Advance:** not offered. **Royalty:** 15% average; based on retail price.

Marketing Channels. In-house staff. Subsidiary rights: all.

Additional Information. We are very small and our list must necessarily be very limited. Tips: Give us some hints as to your probable markets. Writer's guidelines: We are very flexible. Catalog: upon request.

HARPERCOLLINS CHILDREN'S BOOKS, PACIFIC NORTHWEST. (Subsidiary of HarperCollins Publishers, New York). 8948 SW Barbur Blvd., Ste. 154. Portland, OR 97219. Submissions Editor: Linda Zuckerman. Number of titles published: 1992-12. Hardback 100%.

Subjects of Interest. **Fiction**—for children, preschool through young adult. Recent publications: *On the Third Ward* (child with tuberculosis in post-war Germany). **Nonfiction**—for children, pre-school through young adult. Recent publications: *Big Cats* (by Seymour Simon, well-known science writer); *Eight Hands Round* (picture book about quilts).

Initial Contact. Query letter with synopsis/outline. Send 1 or 2 chapters for nonfiction and the entire manuscript for fiction. Include information on previous books published, publisher, and date of publication.

Acceptance Policies. Unagented manuscripts: yes. First novels: yes. Simultaneous submissions: yes, inform us. Disk submissions: no. Response time to initial inquiry: 3 months. Average time until publication: 18-24 months. Average first press run: n/i. **Advance:** yes. **Royalty:** yes; based on retail price.

Marketing Channels. In-house staff; special sales. Subsidiary rights: all.

Additional Information. We are a small editorial office that is part of HarperCollins Children's Books, New York. Writer's guidelines: SASE. Catalog: SASE, $1.56 postage to HarperCollins, 10 E. 53rd St., New York, NY 10022-5299.

HARVEST HOUSE PUBLISHERS. 1075 Arrowsmith. Eugene, OR. 97402. (503) 343-0123. Fax: (503) 342-6410. Submissions Editors: Mary Conner, Editorial Secretary; LaRai Weikert, Manuscript Coordinator. Founded: 1974. Number of titles published: cumulative—50, 1992—5. Hardback 15%, softback 85%.

Subjects of Interest. **Fiction**—pioneer romance; fireside romance; children's picture books. Recent publications: *Love's Enduring Hope* (pioneer romance); *The Archon Conspiracy* (adventure, Christian science fiction); *Bedtime Hugs for Little Ones*. **Nonfiction**—Christian living. Recent publications: *Global Peace and the Rise of Antichrist* (prophecy). Do not want: poetry.

Initial Contact. Query letter with synopsis/outline. Include sample chapters, previously published works, and author bio. SASE required.

Acceptance Policies. Unagented manuscripts: yes. Simultaneous submissions: yes. Disk submissions: no. Response time to initial inquiry: 2-8 weeks. Average time until publication: 1 year. Average first press run: 10,000. **Advance:** variable. **Royalty:** variable.

Marketing Channels. Distribution houses; direct mail; independent reps; in-house staff. Subsidiary rights: all.

Additional Information. We are an Evangelical Christian publishing company. Tips: Ask for guidelines first. Always include a synopsis with query. Be brief and to the point in the cover letter. Writer's guidelines: SASE. Catalog: SASE.

HEMINGWAY WESTERN STUDIES SERIES. Boise State University.

1910 University Dr. Boise, ID 83725. (208) 385-1999. Submissions Editor: Tom Trusky. Founded: 1985. Number of titles published: cumulative—7, 1992—1. Hardback 20%, softback 80%.

Subjects of Interest. **Nonfiction**—relating to intermountain West in areas of popular scholarship (anthropology, contemporary and social issues, and ethnic). Recent publications: *Preserving the Game* (essays on gambling, mining, and hunting in the West). Do not want: local history.

Initial Contact. Query letter with synopsis/outline.

Acceptance Policies. Unagented manuscripts: yes. Simultaneous submissions: yes. Disk submissions: all formats. Response time to initial inquiry: 2-3 months. Average time until publication: 1 year. Average first press run: 2000. **Advance:** not offered. **Royalty:** 12% average; based on wholesale.

Marketing Channels. Distribution houses; direct mail; independent reps. Subsidiary rights: none.

Additional Information. Not interested in jargon-laden academic works or Utah's Bermuda Triangle (i.e., footnote heaven or regional voodoo). Tips: We want reliable, authoritative, lively nonfiction studies relating to Rocky Mountain art, history, environment, politics, religions, sociology, anthropology (any "ology"). Writer's guidelines: upon request. Catalog: upon request.

HIGH PLAINS PRESS. PO Box 123. Glendo, WY 82213. (307) 735-4370.

Submissions Editor: Nancy Curtis. Founded: 1985. Number of titles published: cumulative—11, 1992—2. Hardback 20%, softback 80%.

Subjects of Interest. **Nonfiction**—Western historical; women in the American West; autobiography; humor; rural; travel; poetry (occasionally). Recent publications: *Wyoming's Last Frontier; No Roof But Sky* (poetry).

Initial Contact. Query letter with synopsis/outline. SASE required.

Acceptance Policies. Unagented manuscripts: yes. Simultaneous submissions: yes, inform us. Disk submissions: not initially. Response time to initial inquiry: 4 weeks. Average time until publication: 18 months. Average first press run: 1500. **Advance:** yes. **Royalty:** 10% average; based on discounted cover price.

Marketing Channels. Distribution houses; direct mail; in-house staff; special sales. Subsidiary rights: first serialization; reprint; book club.

Additional Information. Although we are small, we've worked to gain a good reputation in the Rockies. Tips: Your direct relationship to the West is a priority. Catalog: SASE.

HOME EDUCATION PRESS. PO Box 1083. Tonasket, WA 98855.
(509) 486-1351. Submissions Editor: Helen Hegener. Founded: 1983. Number of titles published: cumulative—12, 1992—3. Softback 100%.

Subjects of Interest. Nonfiction—home education; alternative education. Recent publications: *The Homeschool Handbook; Alternatives in Education, I Learn Better by Teaching Myself.* Do not want: anything not relating to alternative education or home schooling.

Initial Contact. Query letter with synopsis/outline. SASE required.

Acceptance Policies. Unagented manuscripts: yes. Simultaneous submissions: yes, inform us. Disk submissions: yes. Response time to initial inquiry: 4-6 weeks. Average time until publication: 6-9 months. Average first press run: 1500. **Advance:** not offered. **Royalty:** percentage negotiable.

Marketing Channels. Distribution houses; cooperative distribution; direct mail; special sales. Subsidiary rights: all.

Additional Information. Only interested in home schooling and alternative education nonfiction. Writer's guidelines: SASE. Catalog: SASE.

HOMESTEAD PUBLISHING. PO Box 193. Moose, WY 83102. Submissions
Editor: Carl Schreier. Founded: 1981. Number of titles published: cumulative—18, 1992—5. Hardback 30%, softback 70%.

Subjects of Interest. Nonfiction—illustrated books on natural history; biography; children/young adult (natural history, nature); anthropology; animals; art; history; photography; travel; reference. Recent publications: *Yellowstone Selected Photographs 1870-1960* (coffee-table book). Do not want: textbooks.

Initial Contact. Query letter with synopsis/outline. Include sample chapters or complete manuscript. Also include sample artwork where appropriate. SASE required.

Acceptance Policies. Unagented manuscripts: yes. Simultaneous submissions: yes. Disk submissions: ask us. Response time to initial inquiry: 2 weeks. Average time until publication: 1 year. Average first press run: 10,000-15,000. **Advance:** $1000 average. **Royalty:** 8-12% average; based on net.

Marketing Channels. Distribution houses; direct mail. Subsidiary rights: all.

Additional Information. Our audience is sophisticated, with an interest in nature, conservation, and art. Tips: Manuscripts should be professional and literate and be of the highest quality. Catalog: #10 SASE, 2 first class stamps.

INTERTEXT. 2633 E. 17th Ave. Anchorage, AK 99508-3207. Submissions
Editor: Sharon Ann Jaeger. Founded: 1982. Number of titles published: cumulative—4, 1992—6. Hardback 25%, softback 75%.

Subjects of Interest. Fiction—contemporary/modern; literary; surrealism. Nonfiction—poetry; literary translations; literary criticism; fine arts; Alaska. Recent publications: *The Mirror Dances; River Haiku; 17 Toutle; Lake County Diamond; The Pope in Space.* (All titles listed are poetry.) Do not want: politics; religion; ephemera; amateur verse; memoirs; kitsch.

Initial Contact. Query letter. Include 3-4 sample poems, story, or sample chapter. SASE required.

Acceptance Policies. Unagented manuscripts: yes. Simultaneous submissions: yes; queries only. Disk submissions: no. Response time to initial inquiry: 3-6 months. Average time until publication: 1-2 years. Average first press run: 500-1000. **Advance:** not offered. **Royalty:** 10% average; based on net after all costs have been paid.

Marketing Channels. Direct mail. Subsidiary rights: reprint; direct mail or direct sales; translation and foreign; English language publication outside the United States and Canada.

Additional Information. Not for beginners! We are extremely selective. Press is not funded by grants. We are not looking for any unsolicited work until 1994, as we have several projects in progress. Writer's guidelines: SASE. Catalog: SASE.

JACKSON MOUNTAIN PRESS. PO Box 2652. Benton, WA 98056. (206) 255-6635. Fax: (206) 255-6663. Submissions Editor: Carole Goodsett. Founded: 1974. Number of titles published: cumulative—20, 1992—2. Softback 100%.

Subjects of Interest. Nonfiction—popular science; local interest cookbooks; Pacific Northwest geology; field guides. Recent publications: *Gems and Minerals of Washington.*

Initial Contact. Query letter with synopsis/outline. SASE required.

Acceptance Policies. Unagented manuscripts: yes. Simultaneous submissions: no. Disk submissions: no. Response time to initial inquiry: 1 week. Average time until publication: 6 months. Average first press run: 3000. **Advance:** not offered. **Royalty:** 40% average; based on wholesale.

Marketing Channels. Distribution houses; cooperative distribution; direct mail; special sales. Subsidiary rights: reprint rights.

Additional Information. Catalog: upon request.

Lakeside Recovery Press *see* **GLEN ABBEY BOOKS, INC.**

Little America *see* **BEAUTIFUL AMERICA PUBLISHING CO.**

LOCKHART PRESS, THE. PO Box 1207. Port Townsend, WA 98368. (206) 385-6413. Fax: (206) 385-6412. Submissions Editor: Russell A. Lockhart, Ph.D. Founded: 1986. Number of titles published: cumulative—3, 1992—6. Handmade books; trade paperbacks beginning in 1991.

Subjects of Interest. Nonfiction—poetry; Jungian psychology; dream-related works.

Initial Contact. Query letter with synopsis/outline. Include entire manuscript and biographical information. SASE required.

Acceptance Policies. Unagented manuscripts: yes. Simultaneous submissions: yes. Disk submissions: yes. Response time to initial inquiry: 3 months. Average time until publication: 6 months. Average first press run: 100 (handmade); 2500 (trade). **Advance:** $500 average. **Royalty:** 15% average; based on net.

Marketing Channels. Direct mail. Subsidiary rights: all.

Additional Information. We will continue to do both a handmade series and a new trade series. Poetry and nonfiction should be related to dreams. Writer's guidelines: upon request. Catalog: upon request.

MAVERICK PUBLICATIONS, INC. PO Box 5007B. Bend, OR 97708. (503) 382-6978. Fax: (503) 382-4831. Submissions Editor: Gary Asher. Founded: 1968. Number of titles published: cumulative—80, 1992—10. Hardback 5%, softback 95%.

Subjects of Interest. Fiction—historical or Native American located in the Northwest. Nonfiction—Northwest focus in the areas of history, natural history, recreation, cookbooks, and reference. Recent publications: *Antelope: The Saga of a Western Town; Naughty Ladies of the Old Northwest; Introduction to Beachcombing; Introduction to Seashells; Introduction to Nautical Relics.*

Initial Contact. Book proposal with entire manuscript.

Acceptance Policies. Unagented manuscripts: yes. Simultaneous submissions: yes. Disk submissions: IBM. Response time to initial inquiry: 3 weeks. Average time until publication: 1 year. Average first press run: 2000. Subsidy or co-publishing: co-publishing. **Advance:** not offered. **Royalty:** 10% average; based on publisher's selling price.

Marketing Channels. Distribution houses. Subsidiary rights: all.

Additional Information. We have our own in-plant printing capabilities and offer our services to self-publishers. Tips: Have enough faith in your book to consider self-publishing or co-publishing.

MCGRAW MOUNTAIN, INC. (Imprint: Peanut Butter Publishing). 200 2nd Ave. W. Seattle, WA 98119-4105. (206) 281-5965. Fax: (206) 286-4433. Submissions Editor: Elliott Wolf. Founded: 1972. Number of titles published: cumulative—400, 1992—20. Hardback 10%, softback 90%.

Subjects of Interest. Nonfiction—cookbooks; family histories; regional.

Initial Contact. Book proposal with sample chapters.

Acceptance Policies. Unagented manuscripts: yes. Simultaneous submissions: yes. Disk submissions: yes. Response time to initial inquiry: 6 weeks. Average time until publication: 4 months to 2 years. Average first press run: 5000-10,000. Subsidy or co-publishing: yes. **Advance:** n/i. **Royalty:** n/i.

Marketing Channels. Cooperative distribution; direct mail; independent reps; special sales. Subsidiary rights: all.

Additional Information. Catalog: call 1-800-451-7771.

METAMORPHOUS PRESS. PO Box 10616. Portland, OR 97210. (503) 228-4972. Fax: (503) 223-9117. Submissions Editor: Nancy Wyatt-Kelsey. Founded: 1982. Number of titles published: cumulative—24, 1992—5. Hardback 20%, softback 80%.

Subjects of Interest. Nonfiction—behavioral science (new, well-thought-out ideas); personal growth; philosophy; self-help; neurolinguistics; health; psychology; sociology; education. Recent publications: *Sales: The Mind's Side; Classroom Magic; Righting the Educational Conveyor Belt; Re-Creating Your Self; Self Rescue; Seventh Dragon; Get the Results You Want; Magic of NLP Demystified.*

Initial Contact. Query letter with outline and table of contents. Include writing sample and projected market. SASE required.

Acceptance Policies. Unagented manuscripts: yes. Simultaneous submissions: yes. Disk submissions: send written inquiry first. Response time to initial inquiry: 30-45 days. Average time until publication: 8-12 months. Average first press run: 2000-5000. **Advance:** not offered. **Royalty:** 10% average; net after expenses.

Marketing Channels. Distribution houses; cooperative distribution; direct mail; in-house staff. Subsidiary rights: all.

Additional Information. We are interested in books that help people further their own search and gain control of their lives in areas of health/fitness, business, education, therapy, communication, and personal growth. Writer's guidelines: call or write. Catalog: call or write.

MOTHER OF ASHES PRESS. PO Box 66. Harrison, ID 83833-0066.
(208) 689-3738. Submissions Editor: Joe M. Singer. Founded: 1980. Number of titles published: cumulative—4, 1992—1. Hardback 25%, softback 75%.

Subjects of Interest. **Fiction**—literary. Recent publications: *The Blink of an Eye*. **Nonfiction**—possibly graphic arts for the small press; poetry. Recent publications: *El Salvador—A House Divided* (a story in comic book form); *Rural News* (poetry). Do not want: unsolicited book-length manuscripts.

Initial Contact. Manuscripts (non-book length) should be submitted to either of the press's magazines, *The Village Idiot* and *The Printer's Devil*. SASE required.

Acceptance Policies. Unagented manuscripts: yes. First novels: yes. Simultaneous submissions: no. Disk submissions: no. Response time to initial inquiry: n/a. Average time until publication: n/a. Average first press run: n/i. **Advance:** not offered. **Royalty:** 15% of press run.

Marketing Channels. Distribution houses; direct mail. Subsidiary rights: none.

Additional Information. What few books we issue are outgrowths of our two periodicals, *The Village Idiot*, a general interest journal, and *The Printer's Devil*, graphic arts for the small press. Writer's guidelines: #10 SASE. Catalog: #10 SASE.

MOUNTAINEERS BOOKS, THE. 306 2nd Ave. W. Seattle, WA 98119.
(206) 285-2665. Fax: (206) 285-8992. Submissions Editor: Margaret Foster-Finan. Founded: 1961. Number of titles published: cumulative—200+, 1992—24. Hardback 15%, softback 85%.

Subjects of Interest. **Nonfiction**—guidebooks and how-to's for the outdoors (hiking, bicycling, cross-country skiing, climbing, mountaineering, backpacking, trekking, paddle-sports); some adventure narratives; conservation and mountaineering history. Recent publications: *Hiking the Southwest's Canyon Country; South America's National Parks; Mountain Bike Adventure Washington's Cascades and Olympics; Miles from Nowhere.* Do not want: guides involving motorized transportation; hunting; public transport adventure narratives.

Initial Contact. Query letter or book proposal. Contact may include the entire manuscript, but it is not required. Include market information, competing titles, and the author's credentials. SASE required.

Acceptance Policies. Unagented manuscripts: yes. Simultaneous submissions: yes, but advise status. Disk submissions: no. Response time to initial inquiry: 2-8 weeks. Average time until publication: 1-2 years. Average first press run: 3000-5000. **Advance:** negotiable. **Royalty:** negotiable; based on net of projected sales.

Marketing Channels. Major wholesalers and retailers, both book and outdoor trade; independent reps (commissioned); in-house staff (customer service). Subsidiary rights: generally all.

Additional Information. We also have a biennial adventure narrative award. Request information. We are willing to work with first-time writers and are interested in guides for all over the world. The overwhelming majority of our books are where-to guides. Tips: We prefer writers with genuine knowledge about their subjects. Our guides cannot be superficial. We cannot include commercial information in our books. Writer's guidelines: write or call. Catalog: write or call.

MOUNTAIN MEADOW PRESS.
PO Box 1170. Wragell, AK 99929. (907) 874-2565. Submissions Editor: Borg Hendrickson. Founded: 1987. Number of titles published: cumulative—5, 1992—3. Softback 100%.

Subjects of Interest. Fiction—wilderness related; Western historical; Native American. Recent publications: *Knight's Rule: A Tale of Modern Wilderness.* Nonfiction—Western historical. Recent publications: *Clearwater Country, The Traveler's Historical and Recreational Guide.* Do not want: We are not looking for manuscripts, but we will read and comment on incidental submissions and may, in rare cases, accept a manuscript.

Initial Contact. Entire manuscript. Include author background and depth of research done for the manuscript. SASE required.

Acceptance Policies. Unagented manuscripts: yes. First novels: yes. Simultaneous submissions: yes. Disk submissions: no. Response time to initial inquiry: 1 month. Average time until publication: 1 year. Average first press run: 2000-4000. Subsidy or co-publishing: negotiable. **Advance:** not offered. **Royalty:** negotiable.

Marketing Channels. Distribution houses; special sales. Subsidiary rights: none.

Additional Information. We are not actively seeking manuscripts. Tips: Excellence alone impresses us. Catalog: #10 SASE.

MOUNTAIN PRESS PUBLISHING CO.
(Imprints: Roadside Geology Series; Roadside History Series; Classics of the Fur Trade). PO Box 2399. Missoula, MT 59806. (406) 728-1900. Fax: (406) 728-1635. Submissions Editors: David Alt or Donald Hyndman (geology); Daniel Greer (history); David Flaccus (general). Founded: 1947. Number of titles published: cumulative—223, 1992—14. Hardback 25%, softback 75%.

Subjects of Interest. Nonfiction—geology; regional history; natural history; regional plant, mammal, and bird guides. Recent publications: *Agents of Chaos: Earthquakes, Volcanoes, and Other Natural Disasters; The Range; Northwest Weeds; Roadside Geology of Utah; Roadside History of Oregon.* Do not want: poetry; fiction.

Initial Contact. Query letter with synopsis/outline or book proposal.

Acceptance Policies. Unagented manuscripts: yes. Simultaneous submissions: yes. Disk submissions: yes. Response time to initial inquiry: 4 weeks. Average time until publication: 14-24 months. Average first press run: 5000. **Advance:** not offered. **Royalty:** 12% average; based on publisher's net.

Marketing Channels. Direct mail; independent reps. Subsidiary rights: all.

Additional Information. Mountain Press is a nonfiction publisher, specializing in geology, natural history, and regional history titles. Tips: Write for our catalog to get an idea of the wide scope of our press. Study it and make sure your work fits. Catalog: upon request.

MR. COGITO PRESS.
Pacific University. Humanities Department. Forest Grove, OR 97116. (503) 226-4135. Submissions Editors: Robert Davies, John Gogol. Founded: 1978. Number of titles published: cumulative—11, 1992—12. Softback 100%.

Subjects of Interest. Nonfiction—poetry; poetry translations; art. Recent publications: *Canoeing in the Rain* (poems regarding an adopted Indian child); *To Recognize This Dying* (on Central America). Do not want: any unsolicited books or inquiries regarding same. All submissions (4-5) should go to the magazine *Mr. Cogito.*

Initial Contact. Submission first to magazine. SASE required.

Acceptance Policies. Unagented manuscripts: n/a. Simultaneous submissions: n/a. Disk submissions: no. Response time to initial inquiry: up to 2 months. Average time until publication: up to 6 months. Average first press run: 250-500. Subsidy or co-publishing: possible negotiation in future. **Advance:** not offered. **Royalty:** 10% of copies.

Marketing Channels. Distribution houses; direct mail; special sales. Subsidiary rights: none.

Additional Information. We accept line graphics and poetry only. We like moving poems (political and social context welcome). Tips: Send 4-5 poems to *Mr. Cogito* magazine with SASE. Writer's guidelines: SASE. Catalog: upon request.

MULTNOMAH PRESS. (Subsidiary of Multnomah School of the Bible).

10209 SE Division St. Portland, OR 97266. (503) 257-0526. Fax: (503) 255-7690. Submissions Editor: Editorial Department. Founded: 1969. Number of titles published: cumulative—800, 1992—40. Hardback 25%, softback 75%.

Subjects of Interest. Fiction—children (4-7, 8-12) and teen Bible and value-related series. Recent publications: *Teach Me About* Series (Bible, salvation, prayer, Holy Spirit); *You'll Never Guess What Happened* Series (deals with the consequences of lying, stealing, bullying, and being obnoxious). **Nonfiction**—Christian values in family/marriage, social issues, feelings, recovery, theology, and devotion. Recent publications: *Stress Fractures: Biblical Splints for Everyday Pressures; Total Life Management; Mastering Worship; If God Is in Control, Why Is My World Falling Apart?* Do not want: poetry; calendars; music; cartoons.

Initial Contact. Query letter with synopsis/outline and 1-2 sample chapters. Also include author's credentials, book's objective, and target audience. SASE required.

Acceptance Policies. Unagented manuscripts: yes. Simultaneous submissions: yes. Disk submissions: no. Response time to initial inquiry: 45 days. Average time until publication: 1 year. Average first press run: 10,000. **Advance:** negotiable, when needed. **Royalty:** 14% average; based on wholesale price.

Marketing Channels. Distribution houses; direct mail; independent reps; in-house staff; special sales. Subsidiary rights: reprint; video; sound and recording; direct mail or direct sales; book club; translation and foreign; computer and other magnetic and electronic media; commercial; English language publication outside the United States and Canada.

Additional Information. Writer's guidelines: #10 SASE, 1 first class stamp. Catalog: 9x12 SASE, 5 first class stamps.

NATIONAL BOOK CO. (Division of Educational Research Associates.

Imprints: Halcyon House). PO Box 8795. Portland, OR 97207-8795. (503) 228-6345. Submissions Editor: Carl W. Salser. Founded: 1965. Number of titles published: cumulative—n/i, 1992—20. Hardback 10%, softback 90%.

Subjects of Interest. Nonfiction—educational materials in areas of art, business, economics, social sciences, technical, language arts, textbooks, politics, science. Recent publications: *Tall Tales* (audio cassettes for children 4-12); *Black Americans in Congress; House of Cards: The Unmaking of America's Educational System; Personal Shorthand* (Cardinal Series Book 1, College Edition). Do not want: fiction.

Initial Contact. Query letter with synopsis/outline. Include sample chapters or complete manuscript. SASE required.

Acceptance Policies. Unagented manuscripts: yes. Simultaneous submissions: no. Disk submissions: no. Response time to initial inquiry: 2 months. Average time until publication: 9 months. Average first press run: n/i. **Advance:** none offered. **Royalty:** 5-15% average; based on retail or wholesale.

Marketing Channels. Direct mail. Subsidiary rights: all.
Additional Information. Catalog: 9x12 SASE, 2 first class stamps.

NEW MOON PUBLISHING. 215 SW 2nd St., Ste. 201. PO Box 1027. Corvallis, OR 97339. (503) 757-0027. Fax: (503) 757-0028. Submissions Editor: Tom Alexander. Founded: 1980. Number of titles published: cumulative—3, 1992—2. Softback 100%.

Subjects of Interest. Nonfiction—marijuana cultivation and politics; general high-tech gardening. Recent publications: *Best of Sinsemilla Tips; Best of the Growing Edge.* (Both are anthologies of magazines we publish.) Do not want: anything other than gardening titles.

Initial Contact. Query letter with synposis/outline. Include sample chapters. SASE required.

Acceptance Policies. Unagented manuscripts: yes. Simultaneous submissions: no. Disk submissions: yes. Response time to initial inquiry: 1-2 months. Average time until publication: 6-9 months. Average first press run: 10,000. **Advance:** not offered. **Royalty:** 8% average; based on gross sales.

Marketing Channels. Distribution houses; cooperative distribution; direct mail; independent reps; in-house staff. Subsidiary rights: all.

Additional Information. Writer's guidelines: SASE.

NORTHWEST PARENT PUBLISHING. PO Box 22578. Seattle, WA 98122. (206) 322-2594. Fax: (206) 328-6172. Submissions Editor: Ann Bergman. Founded: 1979. Number of titles published: cumulative—3, 1992—2. Softback 100%.

Subjects of Interest. Fiction—children's. Nonfiction—parenting guide books and activity books for families.

Initial Contact. Query letter only. SASE required.

Acceptance Policies. Unagented manuscripts: yes. Simultaneous submissions: no. Disk submissions: yes. Response time to initial inquiry: 8 weeks. Average time until publication: 18-24 months. Average first press run: 5000. **Advance:** yes. **Royalty:** 7% average; based on retail.

Marketing Channels. Distribution houses; direct mail; independent reps; in-house staff; special sales. Subsidiary rights: first serialization; reprint rights.

Oasis Press, The *see* **PSI RESEARCH.**

OREGON HISTORICAL SOCIETY PRESS. Oregon Historical Society. 1230 SW Park. Portland, OR 97205. (503) 222-1741. Fax: (503) 221-2035. Submissions Editor: Bruce Hamilton. Founded: 1973. Number of titles published: cumulative—120, 1992—not known. Hardback 50%, softback 50%.

Subjects of Interest. Nonfiction—Americana; regional (adult and juvenile); nature; history; politics; photography; women's. Recent publications: *The City Builders; Silicon Forest; Electrifying Eden*; Ronald MacDonald Eager Beaver Series: *Treasure Mountain; Chief Sarah.*

Initial Contact. Query letter only or synopsis/outline and sample chapters or complete manuscript. SASE required.

Acceptance Policies. Unagented manuscripts: yes. Simultaneous submissions: yes. Disk submissions: ask first. Response time to initial inquiry: 1 week. Average time until publication: 18 months. Average first press run: 1500. Subsidy or co-publishing: 70% nonauthor. **Advance:** not offered. **Royalty:** yes; based on wholesale price. Often makes direct purchase.

Marketing Channels. Distribution houses; cooperative distribution; direct mail; in-house staff; special sales. Subsidiary rights: all.

Additional Information. Writer's guidelines: #10 SASE. Catalog: upon request.

OREGON STATE UNIVERSITY PRESS. 101 Waldo Hall. Corvallis, OR 97331-6407. (503) 737-3166. Submissions Editor: Jo Alexander. Founded: 1961. Number of titles published: cumulative—150+\-, 1992—6. Hardback 50%, softback 50%.

Subjects of Interest. Nonfiction—history (environmental or regional); biography (regional); Pacific Northwest studies; natural resource management; contemporary and social issues; scholarly. Recent publications: *Following the Nez Perce Trail, A Historical Travel Guide; Birds of Malheur National Wildlife Refuge.* Do not want: poetry; fiction; any subjects not listed above.

Initial Contact. Query letter with synopsis/outline or book proposal. Include sample chapters. SASE required.

Acceptance Policies. Unagented manuscripts: yes. Simultaneous submissions: no. Disk submissions: no. Response time to initial inquiry: 2-4 weeks. Average time until publication: 1 year. Average first press run: 1000 paper; 300 hard. Subsidy or co-publishing: subventions sometimes necessary; not from author personally. **Advance:** not offered. **Royalty:** 10-15% average; based on net receipts.

Marketing Channels. Distribution houses; direct mail; independent reps. Subsidiary rights: those appropriate to regional and scholarly books.

Additional Information. Catalog: upon request.

PACIFIC PRESS. PO Box 7000. Boise, ID 83707. (208) 465-2500. Fax: (208) 465-2531. Submissions Editor: Marvin Moore. Founded: 1874. Number of titles published: cumulative—30, 1992—30. Hardback 10%, softback 90%.

Subjects of Interest. Fiction—Christian lives based on true stories only. Recent publications: *Best for Me, Story of Becki Trueblood, Miss Idaho 1990* (how she handled conflict of values and loss of Miss America crown as a Christian). **Nonfiction**—doctrinal Seventh-Day Adventist lifestyle. Do not want: anything not related to religion.

Initial Contact. Query letter or query letter with synopsis or book proposal. Include sample chapters and author's writing experience. SASE required.

Acceptance Policies. Unagented manuscripts: yes. Simultaneous submissions: inform us. Disk submissions: yes, with hard copy. Response time to initial inquiry: 2 months. Average time until publication: 6 months. Average first press run: 5000. Subsidy or co-publishing: occasionally; terms negotiable. **Advance:** $500 average. **Royalty:** 8% average; based on retail.

Marketing Channels. Distribution houses; in-house sales. Subsidiary rights: all.

Additional Information. We are a Seventh-Day Adventist publisher. Tips: Send us a proposal. Writer's guidelines: upon request. Catalog: upon request.

PARADISE PUBLICATIONS. 8110 SW Wareham. Portland, OR 97223. (503) 246-1555. Submissions Editor: Christie Stilson. Founded: 1983. Number of titles published: cumulative—10, 1992—14. Softback 100%.

Subjects of Interest. Nonfiction—travel guidebooks. Recent publications: comprehensive and personalized guides to each of the Hawaiian Islands. Do not want: anything other than travel.

Initial Contact. Query letter. Include author's background. Sample chapters okay. SASE required.

Acceptance Policies. Unagented manuscripts: yes. Simultaneous submissions: yes. Disk submissions: yes. Response time to initial inquiry: 2 months. Average time until publication: 6 months. Average first press run: 8000. **Advance:** not offered. **Royalty:** yes.

Marketing Channels. Distribution houses; direct mail. Subsidiary rights: all.

Additional Information. We are a small press dealing with specialized travel subjects written by authors who have lived and traveled extensively. The books are updated every two years. Catalog: SASE.

Peanut Butter Publishing *see* **MCGRAW MOUNTAIN, INC.**

PICTORIAL HISTORIES PUBLISHING CO. 713 S. 3rd St. Missoula, MT 59801. (406) 549-8488. Submissions Editor: Stan Cohen. Founded: 1976. Number of titles published: cumulative—135, 1992—10. Hardback 5%, softback 95%.

Subjects of Interest. Nonfiction—WW II military history; Civil War. Do not want: fiction.

Initial Contact. Query letter only.

Acceptance Policies. Unagented manuscripts: yes. Simultaneous submissions: yes. Disk submissions: no. Response time to initial inquiry: several weeks. Average time until publication: 1 year. Average first press run: 3000. **Advance:** not offered. **Royalty:** 10% average; based on gross sales.

Marketing Channels. Distribution houses; direct mail; special sales. Subsidiary rights: all.

Additional Information. We are very selective about subjects; have too many in the hopper already. Tips: Make your query specific. Catalog: call or write.

POETS. PAINTERS. COMPOSERS. 10254 35th Ave. SW. Seattle, WA 98146. (206) 937-8155. Submissions Editors: Joseph F. Keppler, Carl Diltz, Jim Andrews (Canada). Founded: 1984. Number of titles published: cumulative—12, 1992—4. Softback 100%.

Subjects of Interest. Nonfiction—poetry; essays; philosophy; spiritual/metaphysical; scholarly works; book reviews; art; computers; technology; writing/publishing. Recent publications: distinctive small editions of poems; special journals with emphasis on interface between technology and literature. Do not want: long novels.

Initial Contact. Entire manuscript. Include author bio and a statement of aesthetics, if possible. SASE required.

Acceptance Policies. Unagented manuscripts: yes. Simultaneous submissions: no. Disk submissions: Macintosh. Response time to initial inquiry: immediately. Average time until publication: 8 months. Average first press run: 300. **Advance:** not offered. **Royalty:** no.

Marketing Channels. Cooperative distribution; direct mail; special sales. Subsidiary rights: none.

Additional Information. We specialize in poetry, art, and criticism in small, fine editions. Catalog: SASE.

PORTLAND STATE UNIVERSITY. (Subsidiary of Oregon State System of Higher Education. Imprint: Continuing Education Press). PO Box 1394. Portland, OR 97207. (503) 725-4891. Fax: (503) 725-4882. Submissions Editor: Tony Midson. Number of titles published: cumulative—26, 1992—1. Hardback 10%, softback 90%.

Subjects of Interest. Nonfiction—educational (non-textbook); informational manuals in areas of agriculture, anthropology, business, child care/development, social sciences, government and politics, science and technology, and senior adults', women's, and men's issues. Recent publications: *Getting Funded: A Complete Guide to Proposal Writing; Write Now, A Complete Self Teaching Program for Better Handwriting.* Do not want: poetry; autobiographies.

Initial Contact. Query letter or query letter with synopsis/outline. Include author's credentials.

Acceptance Policies. Unagented manuscripts: yes. Simultaneous submissions: yes, other contracts declared. Disk submissions: not until requested. Response time to initial inquiry: 2 months. Average time until publication: 1 year. Average first press run: 3000. **Advance:** not offered. **Royalty:** yes.

Marketing Channels. Distribution houses; direct mail; in-house staff. Subsidiary rights: none.

Additional Information. We are interested in books of nonfiction, educational interest. Author must have appropriate credentials on subject. Catalog: upon request.

PSI RESEARCH. (Imprint: The Oasis Press). 300 N. Valley Dr. Grants Pass, OR 97526. (503) 479-9464. Fax: (503) 476-1479. Submissions Editor: Rosanno Alejonadro. Founded: 1975. Number of titles published: cumulative—80, 1992—7. Hardback and softback for almost all editions.

Subjects of Interest. Nonfiction—how-to, reference, self-help, and textbooks in areas of business (finance, public relations, franchising, export/import), computers, economics, education, finance, marketing. Recent publications: *Franchise Bible; How to Write Your Own Business Contracts.* Do not want: fiction; poetry.

Initial Contact. Query letter with synopsis/outline. Include bio, background information, and sample chapter, if available. SASE required.

Acceptance Policies. Unagented manuscripts: yes. Simultaneous submissions: yes. Disk submissions: ASCII. Response time to initial inquiry: 1-3 weeks. Average time until publication: 6 months. Average first press run: 1500. **Advance:** none offered. **Royalty:** based on net sales.

Marketing Channels. Distribution houses; cooperative distribution; direct mail; independent reps; in-house staff, special sales. Subsidiary rights: all.

Additional Information. Catalog: call or write.

Pure Bred Series, The *see* **DORAL PUBLISHING.**

QUESTAR PUBLISHERS, INC. PO Box 1720. Sisters, OR 97759. (503) 549-1144. Fax: (503) 549-2044. Submissions Editor: Thomas Womack. Founded: 1987. Number of titles published: cumulative—35, 1992—8-10. Hardback 25%, softback 75%.

Subjects of Interest. Fiction—biblical Christian (adult and children); children's Bible storybooks. Recent publications: *The Beginner's Bible; Wisdom Hunter; What Would Jesus Do?* Nonfiction—Christian living; practical theology; marriage and family. Recent publications: *Incompatibility: Grounds for a Great Marriage.* Do not want: poetry.

Initial Contact. Query letter with synopsis/outline or book proposal. Include sample chapters and biographical sketch. SASE required.

Acceptance Policies. Unagented manuscripts: yes. First novels: yes. Simultaneous submissions: yes. Disk submissions: no. Response time to initial inquiry: 1-2 months. Average time until publication: 1-2 years. Average first press run: 5000-10,000. **Advance:** not offered. **Royalty:** starts at 12.5%.

Marketing Channels. Distribution houses; in-house staff; special sales. Subsidiary rights: all.

Additional Information. All our materials must have a Christian orientation. Catalog: SASE, $.52 postage.

Roadside Geology Series, Roadside History Series *see* **MOUNTAIN PRESS PUBLISHING CO.**

ROMAR BOOKS, LTD. (Imprints: Romar Books; Evergreen Pacific Publishing). 18002 15th Ave. NE, Ste. B. Seattle, WA 98155. (206) 368-8157. Fax: (206) 368-7968. Submissions Editors: Karen Duncan, Larry Reynolds. Founded: 1987. Number of titles published: cumulative—35, 1992—6. Hardback 10%, softback 90%.

Subjects of Interest. Fiction—children's; mysteries (detective). Recent publications: *Smiles* (mystery); *Mama Llama's Pajamas* (ages 7-9). **Nonfiction**—cookbooks; special topics; marine-related sports and recreation. Recent publications: *The Art of Sandcastling; Black Granite Reflections* (for Vietnam veterans); *Peasant to Palace* (Russian cookbook). Do not want: mass-market fiction; romance.

Initial Contact. Query letter with synopsis/outline. Include sample chapters and author's résumé, including any specific qualifications that lend writer credibility on topic. SASE required.

Acceptance Policies. Unagented manuscripts: yes. First novels: yes. Simultaneous submissions: yes. Disk submissions: no. Response time to initial inquiry: 8-10 weeks. Average time until publication: 1 year. Average first press run: 1500. **Advance:** not offered. **Royalty:** 10% average; based on publisher's net.

Marketing Channels. Distribution houses; in-house staff; special sales. Subsidiary rights: all, or as negotiated.

Additional Information. Catalog: none presently available.

SANDPIPER PRESS. PO Box 286. Brookings, OR 97415. (503) 469-5588. Submissions Editor: Marilyn Reed Riddle. Founded: 1979. Number of titles published: cumulative—7, 1992—1. Softback 100%.

Subjects of Interest. Fiction—Each book is on a single subject and is printed in large print, 18 points. Recent publications: Tolstoy's *Where Love Is, There is God Also; Otherwhere, One Step Beyond* (Rod Serling-style stories); *Unicorns for Everyone.* **Nonfiction**—Each book is on a single subject (i.e., humor, Native American, philosophy) and published in large print. Recent publications: *Large Print Innovative Cookbook; Physically Challenged Can-Do* (anthology); *Poems from the Oregon Sea Coast; Walk with Me.* Do not want: novels.

Initial Contact. Query letter only. SASE required.

Acceptance Policies. Unagented manuscripts: yes. Simultaneous submissions: yes. Disk submissions: no. Response time to initial inquiry: 1-2 months. Average time until publication: 1-2 years. Average first press run: 2000. **Advance:** not offered. **Royalty:** no.

Marketing Channels. In-house staff. Subsidiary rights: all.

Additional Information. Each book is on a different subject. All are in 18-point large print. Our next anthology is by Native Americans, *Visions and Prophecies* (nonfiction). Tips: Query first with SASE. Writer's guidelines: SASE. Catalog: SASE.

SASQUATCH BOOKS. 1931 Second Ave. Seattle, WA 98101. (206) 441-5555. Fax: (206) 441-5555. Submissions Editor: Anne Depue. Founded: 1978. Number of titles published: 1992—9. Hardback 10%, softback 90%.

Subjects of Interest. Nonfiction—Pacific Northwest in the areas of art/architecture, folklore, nature, history, politics, photography, sports, recreation, and travel. Recent publications: *The Border in Bloom: A Northwest Garden through the Seasons.*

Initial Contact. Query letter with synopsis/outline and sample chapters. SASE required.

Acceptance Policies. Unagented manuscripts: yes. Simultaneous submissions: yes. Disk submissions: ask us. Response time to initial inquiry: 6-8 weeks. Average time until publication: 6 months average. Average first press run: 5000. **Advance:** yes. **Royalty:** 7% average (paperback); based on retail.

Marketing Channels. Independent sales reps; in-house staff. Subsidiary rights: all.

Additional Information. Although the subjects of our books focus on the Pacific Northwest, we distribute appropriate books on a national level. Tips: Book must have a Pacific Northwest angle. Writer's guidelines: SASE. Catalog: upon request.

SIGNPOST PRESS, INC., THE. 1007 Queen St. Bellingham, WA 98226. (206) 734-9781. Submissions Editor: Knute Skinner. Founded: 1975. Number of titles published: cumulative—14, 1992—2. Hardback 10%, softback 90%.

Subjects of Interest. Nonfiction—poetry. Recent publications: *Dream of Long Headdresses; Daughter; Western Movie.* Do not want: anything other than poetry.

Initial Contact. Query letter only. Do not submit query between June 10 and September 10. SASE required.

Acceptance Policies. Unagented manuscripts: yes. Simultaneous submissions: inform us. Disk submissions: no. Response time to initial inquiry: 2-3 weeks. Average time until publication: 3-12 months. Average first press run: 500. Subsidy or co-publishing: occasionally; author purchases copies. **Advance:** none offered. **Royalty:** based on 10% of books printed.

Marketing Channels. Direct mail. Subsidiary rights: none.

Additional Information. Catalog: upon request.

Spirit of America *see* **BEAUTIFUL AMERICA PUBLISHING CO.**

STORY LINE PRESS. Three Oaks Farm. 27006 Gap Rd. Brownsville, OR 97327. (503) 466-5352. Fax: (503) 466-3200. Submissions Editor: Robert McDowell. Founded: 1985. Number of titles published: cumulative—36, 1992—17. Hardback 50%, softback 50%.

Subjects of Interest. Fiction—mystery; short stories; novels. Recent publications: *Close Softly the Doors* (mystery). **Nonfiction**—literary memoirs; critical essays; poetry (first books of poetry are only accepted as entrants to the Nicholas Roerich Poetry Prize). Recent publications: *New Italian Poets; English and Italian Poets; Army Brat* (memoirs).

Initial Contact. Query letter with synopsis/outline. Include sample chapters and publishing history. SASE required.

Acceptance Policies. Unagented manuscripts: yes. First novels: yes. Simultaneous submissions: no. Disk submissions: Macintosh, 3 1/2 disks; Microsoft Word. Response time to initial inquiry: 3 months. Average time until publication: 1-2 years. Average first press run: 3000. **Advance:** negotiable. **Royalty:** negotiable; based on advance.

Marketing Channels. Distribution houses; cooperative distribution; direct mail. Subsidiary rights: first serialization; reprint; dramatization, motion picture, and broadcast; sound reproduction and recording; direct mail or direct sales; book club; translation and foreign; English language publication outside the United States and Canada.

Additional Information. We are looking for any subject matter written with high literary quality. Tips: telephone first. Catalog: upon request.

TIMBER PRESS, INC. (Imprints: Dioscorides Press, botany; Amadeus Press, music; Areopagitica Press, history.) 9999 SW Wilshire. Portland, OR 97225. (503) 292-0745. Fax: (503) 292-6607. Submissions Editor: Richard Abel. Founded: 1976. Number of titles published: cumulative—100+\-, 1992—40. Hardback 80%, softback 20%.

Subjects of Interest. Nonfiction—Northwest; forestry; serious music; history; horticulture (ornamental and business); botany; natural history; translations. Recent publications: *Northwest Coast: A Natural History; Bulbs* (2 vols.); *Enrico Caruso: My Father and My Family*. Do not want: picture books.

Initial Contact. Query letter or synopsis/outline and 3-4 sample chapters. SASE required.

Acceptance Policies. Unagented manuscripts: yes. Simultaneous submissions: yes. Disk submissions: yes, ask first. Response time to initial inquiry: 2 months. Average time until publication: 1 year. Average first press run: 3000. **Advance:** varies. **Royalty:** 10-15% average.

Marketing Channels. Distribution houses; mail order; professional and trade outlets. Subsidiary rights: all.

Additional Information. Catalog: 9x12 SASE, 3 first class stamps.

TWIN PEAKS PRESS. PO Box 129. Vancouver, WA 98666. (206) 694-2462. Submissions Editor: Helen Hecker. Founded: 1984. Number of titles published: cumulative—6, 1992—12. Softback 100%.

Subjects of Interest. Nonfiction—cooking, food, and nutrition; how-to; self-help; reference; business; economics; health; hobbies; sports; travel, camping, and recreation; senior adults; film, television, and video; psychology; self-help; careers; relationships. Do not want: fiction; poetry.

Initial Contact. Query letter with outline only. Do not send unsolicited manuscripts. SASE required.

Acceptance Policies. Unagented manuscripts: yes. Simultaneous submissions: yes. Disk submissions: n/i. Response time to initial inquiry: 1 month. Average time until publication: 6 months. Average first press run: 5000. **Advance:** not offered. **Royalty:** varies.

Marketing Channels. Distribution houses; direct mail; in-house staff; special sales. Subsidiary rights: n/i.

Additional Information. We respond only when interested in query; otherwise, no response. Catalog: none.

Umbrella Guides *see* **EPICENTER PRESS, INC.**

UNIVERSITY OF ALASKA PRESS. First Floor, Gruening Bldg., UAF.
Fairbanks, AK 99775-1580. (907) 474-6389. Fax: (907) 474-7225. Submissions
Editor: Debbie Van Stone. Founded: 1967. Number of titles published:
cumulative—36, 1992—6. Hardback 50%, softback 50%.

Subjects of Interest. Nonfiction—scholarly nonfiction relating to Alaska, the circumpolar
north, and North Pacific rim. Recent publications: *Chills and Fever: Health and Disease in the
Early History of Alaska.* Do not want: fiction; poetry.

Initial Contact. Query letter with synopsis/outline.

Acceptance Policies. Unagented manuscripts: yes. Simultaneous submissions: no. Disk
submissions: Macintosh. Response time to initial inquiry: 2 months. Average time until
publication: 6-8 months. Average first press run: 1500. **Advance:** not offered. **Royalty:** 7-
10% average; based on type of work.

Marketing Channels. Distribution houses; direct mail; independent reps; in-house staff.
Subsidiary rights: none.

Additional Information. We are a small, regional, scholarly publisher. Writer's guidelines:
upon request. Catalog: upon request.

UNIVERSITY OF IDAHO PRESS. 16 Brink Hall. Moscow, ID 83843.
(208) 885-6245. Fax: (208) 885-6911. Submissions Editor: James J. Heaney.
Founded: 1972. Number of titles published: cumulative—80, 1992—9. Hardback
20%, softback 80%.

Subjects of Interest. Fiction—related to academic creative writing programs. Recent
publications: *Unearned Pleasures and Other Stories.* Nonfiction—Western Americana;
history; Native American studies; literature; environmental and resource policy studies;
religion; archaeology; anthropology; agriculture; women's issues. Recent publications:
Offering Smoke. Do not want: historical fiction; fictionalized history.

Initial Contact. Query letter with synopsis/outline or book proposal. Include sample chapters
and resumé, if possible.

Acceptance Policies. Unagented manuscripts: yes. First novels: maybe. Simultaneous
submissions: no. Disk submissions: IBM; WordPerfect. Response time to initial inquiry: 3
weeks. Average time until publication: 1 year. Average first press run: 1000. **Advance:** not
offered. **Royalty:** 10% average; based on net.

Marketing Channels. Distribution houses; direct mail; independent reps; in-house staff.
Subsidiary rights: all.

Additional Information. Writer's guidelines: upon request. Catalog: upon request.

WASHINGTON STATE UNIVERSITY PRESS. Cooper Publications Bldg.
Pullman, WA 99164-5910. (509) 335-3518. Fax: (509) 335-8568. Submissions
Editor: Glen Lindeman. Founded: 1927. Number of titles published: cumulative—40
(current), 1992—8. Hardback 30%, softback 70%.

Subjects of Interest. Nonfiction—regional history; ethnic studies (Afro-American, Asian,
Native American). Recent publications: *North Bank Road: The Spokane, Portland, and Seattle
Railway; In the Shadow of the Mountain: The Spirit of the CCC; Peoples of Washington:
Perspectives on Cultural Diversity.* Do not want: fiction; children's books.

Initial Contact. Query letter with synopsis/outline. Include sample chapters and resumé.

Acceptance Policies. Unagented manuscripts: yes. Simultaneous submissions: yes, if given the first right of refusal. Disk submissions: Microsoft Word preferred. Response time to initial inquiry: 2-4 weeks. Average time until publication: 12-18 months. Average first press run: 2000. **Advance:** not offered. **Royalty:** 10% average; based on net profit on second and subsequent printings.

Marketing Channels. Direct mail; independent reps; in-house staff. Subsidiary rights: reprint; dramatization, motion picture, and broadcast; direct mail or direct sales; book club; translation and foreign; computer and other magnetic and electronic media.

Additional Information. Catalog: upon request.

YE GALLEON PRESS. PO Box 287. Fairfield, WA 99012. (509) 283-2422. Submissions Editor: Glen C. Adams. Founded: 1937. Number of titles published: cumulative 500+, 1992—20. Hardback 75%, softback 25%.

Subjects of Interest. Fiction—only if subsidized. **Nonfiction**—Pacific Northwest history; rare Western United States history (reprints); Native American. Recent publications: *Joseph Seltice, Saga of Coeur d'Alene Indians* (an account of Chief Joseph); *Jesse Applegate, A Day with the Cow Column* (reprint). Do not want: far-out religious material. (I sell to seminaries and do not wish to offend this market.)

Initial Contact. Query letter with entire manuscript. SASE required.

Acceptance Policies. Unagented manuscripts: yes. Simultaneous submissions: no. Disk submissions: no. Response time to initial inquiry: 1 month. Average time until publication: 9 months. Average first press run: 1000. Subsidy or co-publishing: yes. **Advance:** not offered. **Royalty:** 5-10% average.

Marketing Channels. Distribution houses; direct mail; independent reps; in-house staff. Subsidiary rights: none.

Additional Information. We print Pacific Northwest history and rare Western United States history, Northwest Coast material, and a little rare Pacific material. Tips: We do mostly reprint work and help authors to self-publish. I have reprinted some exceedingly rare California gold rush titles. All fiction is sponsored (paid for). Titles accepted on a royalty basis would need to be of high quality, with good sales potential. Catalog: upon request.

Magazines and Newsletters

A single issue of a periodical (magazine or newsletter) is constructed from many different manuscripts, including articles, interviews, fiction, columns, reviews, poetry, etc. Some of this material is produced in-house by the publisher's staff, and some is purchased from freelance writers. We collected and organized the following information to help you find and approach publishers of periodicals in the Northwest most likely to accept your inquiry and your submission.

How to Use the Information in This Section

The first paragraph of each entry identifies the publication and gives its location, submissions editor(s), and focus or type. Also included is information on the frequency of publication, circulation, and the number of manuscripts bought each year if the publication buys freelance material. Whether payment is made in cash or copies is also indicated.

Editorial Needs

This section identifies the publication's interests. However, when indicating nonfiction index topics for their publications, some editors selected more subjects than were named in their initial list of interests. In some cases, additional topics may indicate future interests; in others, they identify subcategories within the periodical's basic focus, such as celebrity profiles for a regional publication or ethnic issues for a family magazine. Check the subject index to see which publications are listed for your specific interest or expertise.

Editorial needs are listed for fiction and/or nonfiction. For periodicals that accept fiction, we have listed the subject area or genre followed by the forms or types, such as short stories, excerpts, etc. Information on length and/or payment (if made in cash) follows in parentheses when that information varies for each form. When payment and/or word length are the same for all forms, a general statement at the end of the fiction section contains that information.

For nonfiction, we have indicated general subject interests followed by the forms accepted. Information in parentheses may include specific subjects for each form, preferred length, and payment (when made in cash). Whenever information is the same for all forms, we have included it in a comprehensive sentence at the end of the section.

Initial contact

This information indicates how the editor wants to be contacted. You increase your chances for selling to a particular editor if you follow the suggestions listed here. Whether stated or not, always include a SASE.

Acceptance Policies

Byline offered: While most publications include an author's byline, some do not—an important issue for most writers and thus listed first.

Publishing rights: This information specifies the particular use of your manuscript the periodical is paying for. Most magazine editors purchase first North American serial rights—the right to publish your material first in their periodical for distribution in United States and Canada. For information concerning other rights purchased, we suggest that you consult one of the many legal handbooks for writers or see the Books for Writers section of this book.

Payment made: Some smaller publications offer contributor's copies and publish your byline as payment. We have listed the exact number of copies offered whenever possible. When payment is offered in cash rather than copies, the timing is listed—most commonly on acceptance or on publication. For payments made in cash, the listing includes information on kill fees and expenses.

Kill fee: Some publications pay the writer a portion of the regular payment for articles that are assigned but later cancelled (or killed). Kill fees generally do not apply to unassigned articles.

Writer's expenses: Keep in mind that expenses are generally paid only when preapproved by the editor, so always clarify policies ahead of time. Editors rarely authorize payment of expenses incurred by authors unknown (and unproven) to them. Assignments are generally reserved for writers with proven ability and reliability.

Simultaneous submissions: If the publisher says "yes," you may submit your manuscript to several different publications at the same time, but you must inform each publisher that the manuscript is being simultaneously submitted.

Response time to initial inquiry: Be patient and avoid phoning the editor unless you have an agreement with that individual to do so. Two to three weeks *after* the specified response time, it is appropriate to send a written request for information concerning the status of your submission. As with any correspondence to a publisher or agent, remember to include your SASE.

Average time until publication: Always dependent upon a number of factors, this information provides an approximate idea of how long the publishing process takes after the editor has received and accepted the completed manuscript.

Computer printouts: Most publishers will now accept computer printouts, but many accept dot matrix only if it is of near-letter quality. While the majority want your material submitted in the form of manuscript pages, many will now accept your finished submission on a disk compatible with their computer systems.

Photography Submissions

We've included the publication's preference for film type and format (black-and-white or color prints or transparencies) and size. Requests for additional information (listed under "Photographs should include") may cover model releases, captions, and identification of subjects. Payment for photographs may be made separately or in conjunction with the article submitted. Photographic rights may also be handled in the same manner.

Additional Information

This section of the entry reflects additional comments by the editor aimed specifically at the writer. Tips are suggestions that can help ensure your success in placing an article with a particular periodical. The best first step toward approaching any publication is to obtain its writer's guidelines and a sample copy.

Abbreviations

n/i means no information was given to us by the periodical.

n/a means that this particular question did not apply to the periodical.

ALASKA BUSINESS MONTHLY. PO Box 241288. Anchorage, AK 99524. (907) 276-4373. Fax: (907) 279-2900. Submissions Editor: Judith Fuerst Griffin. Type: regional business magazine. Frequency of publication: monthly. Circulation: 10,000+. Number of manuscripts accepted per year: 36. Payment offered.

Editorial Needs. Nonfiction—issues; people; companies. **Forms:** features (800-3000 words; payment negotiable); interview/profile (business people; 800-1500 words; payment negotiable).

Initial Contact. Query letter or article proposal with subject outline. SASE required.

Acceptance Policies. Byline given: yes. Publishing rights: first North American serial rights; second serial rights; one-time rights; work-for-hire. Payment made: upon publication. Kill fee: negotiable. Expenses: no. Response time to initial inquiry: 2-4 weeks. Average time until publication: 2-4 months. Submit seasonal material 3 months in advance. Simultaneous submissions: depends on circumstances. Disk submissions: several formats with conversions.

Photography Submissions. Format and film: prints; contact sheets; negatives; transparencies. Photographs should include: query first. **Payment:** negotiable. Photographic rights: one-time rights.

Additional Information. We are written for an Alaskan business audience and those who want to do business in the state. Ninety-eight percent of our material is written by Alaskans. Tips: Be brief and send writing samples. Writer's guidelines: none. Sample copy: SASE.

ALASKA FISHERMAN'S JOURNAL. 1115 NW 46th St. Seattle, WA 98107. (206) 789-6506. Fax: (206) 789-9193. Submissions Editors: John Van Amerongen (articles); Chris Horton (general articles, news). Type: for the fishing industry. Frequency of publication: monthly. Circulation: n/i. Number of manuscripts accepted per year: 25-50.

Editorial Needs. Fiction—sea aventures. **Forms:** book excerpts.

Nonfiction—fishing related. **Forms:** book reviews; features; interview/profiles; poetry; news.

Initial Contact. Article proposal with subject outline or entire article. Include phone number. SASE required.

Acceptance Policies. Byline given: yes. Publishing rights: n/i. Payment made: upon publication. Kill fee: no. Expenses: no. Response time to initial inquiry: n/i. Average time until publication: 1 month. Submit seasonal material 4 months in advance. Simultaneous submissions: no. Disk submissions: WordPerfect.

Photography Submissions. Format and film: black-and-white or color contact sheets. Photographs should include: identification of subjects. **Payment:** $15-$100 (cover). Photographic rights: n/i.

Additional Information. Tips: Make sure your story has someting to do with the fishing industry. Keep it clean and tight. Call us.

ALASKA GEOGRAPHIC. PO Box 93370. Anchorage, AK 99509-3370. (907) 258-2515. Submissions Editor: Penny Rennick. Type: geography and natural history of Alaska, Northwest Canada, Pacific and polar rims. Frequency of publication: quarterly. Circulation: 10,000. Number of manuscripts accepted per year: all writing is staff written or on assignment only. Payment offered.

Editorial Needs. Nonfiction—each issue covers 1 specific area. **Forms:** features; photo features.

Initial Contact. Query as to what subject or areas are currently being worked on. SASE required.

Acceptance Policies. Byline given: yes. Publishing rights: n/a. Payment made: upon publication. Kill fee: no. Expenses: depends. Response time to initial inquiry: 2 months. Average time until publication: 6 months. Simultaneous submissions: no. Disk submissions: inquire.

Photography Submissions. We welcome freelance photo submissions or queries about our photo needs. Format and film: color transparencies. Photographs should include: captions; identification of subjects. **Payment:** based on space rates. Photographic rights: first rights.

Additional Information. Our issues are 100-page, full-color publications, and we don't send samples. Single copies are for sale in bookstores or through our office. Price is $17.95.

ALASKA QUARTERLY REVIEW. College of Arts and Sciences. University of Alaska Anchorage. Anchorage, AK 99508. (907) 786-4775. Submissions Editors: Ronald Spatz (executive and fiction editor); Thomas Sexton (poetry). Type: literary. Frequency of publication: 2 double issues per year. Circulation: 1000. Number of manuscripts accepted per year: 45. Payment in copies.

Editorial Needs. Fiction—avant-garde/experimental; contemporary/modern; Native American. **Forms:** book excerpts (30-40 pages); novellas; plays.

Nonfiction—reviews; criticism; philosophy. **Forms:** essays (30 pages maximum); poetry.

Initial Contact. Entire article. Include short bio with cover letter. SASE required.

Acceptance Policies. Byline given: yes. Publishing rights: first North American serial rights. Payment made: in copies. Response time to initial inquiry: 4-12 weeks. Average time until publication: 6 months maximum. Simultaneous submissions: inform us in cover letter. Disk submissions: no.

Additional Information. Quality is our main concern. We seek it both in the traditional and experimental forms submitted to us. Writer's guidelines: upon request. Sample copy: $4.

ALASKA WOMEN, A JOURNAL OF YESTERDAY, TODAY, AND TOMORROW. HCR 64 Box 453. Seward, AK 99664. (907) 288-3168.
Submissions Editors: Honnie Kaye Pressley (art); Diane Gill (book reviews); Janet Taylor (performing arts); Editor (all others). Type: Alaskan women. Frequency of publication: quarterly. Circulation: n/i. Number of manuscripts accepted per year: n/i. Payment made in subscription.

Editorial Needs. Fiction—anything about Alaskan women.

Nonfiction—Alaskan women. **Forms:** book reviews; cartoons; columns; entertainment reviews; fillers; interview/profile; photo feature; poetry.

Initial Contact. Query letter and entire article. Include short bio. SASE required.

Acceptance Policies. Byline given: yes. Publishing rights: we purchase no rights. Payment made: in subscription. Response time to initial inquiry: 2 weeks. Average time until publication: 3-4 months. Simultaneous submissions: no. Disk submissions: no.

Photography Submissions. Format and film: black-and-white prints. Photographs should include: captions; identification of subjects; short bio on photographer.

Additional Information. The article must be about a living Alaskan woman who has accomplished something in her life. Articles must include photographs. We are also interested in articles about Alaskan museums and historical sites. Tips: We are looking for articles with a "homey" style. Be sure to read our guidelines. Writer's guidelines: upon request. Sample copy: only with subscription.

AMAZING HEROES. 7563 Lake City Way. Seattle, WA 98115. (206) 524-1967. Fax: (206) 524-2104.
Submissions Editors: Thomas Harrington (stories and features); Mark Thompson (art submissions). Type: comic book-oriented features. Frequency of publication: monthly. Circulation: 10,000. Number of manuscripts accepted per year: 40-50. Payment offered.

Editorial Needs. Nonfiction—comic book-oriented features. **Forms:** book excerpts; book reviews; cartoons; columns; entertaiment reviews; essays; features; fillers; interview/profile.

Initial Contact. Article proposal with subject outline or entire article. SASE required.

Acceptance Policies. Byline given: yes. Publishing rights: first North American serial rights. Payment made: upon publication. Kill fee: no. Expenses: yes. Response time to initial inquiry: 1-6 months. Average time until publication: 3 months. Submit seasonal material 3 months in advance. Simultaneous submissions: no. Disk submissions: yes.

Additional Information. We cover stories about comic book titles, publishers, writers, artists, and characters. Tips: We don't usually print the ordinary "comic-strip" oriented material. Writer's guidelines: none. Sample copy: n/i.

AMERICAN RHODODENDRON SOCIETY JOURNAL. 201 S. State St., A. Bellingham, WA 98225. (206) 733-5409.
Submissions Editor: Sonja Nelson. Type: horticulture. Frequency of publication: quarterly. Circulation: 6500. Number of manuscripts accepted per year: 24. Payment in copies.

Editorial Needs. Nonfiction—horticulture featuring rhododendrums. **Forms:** book reviews (horticulture, gardens); features.

Initial Contact. Query letter or article proposal with subject outline or entire article. SASE required.

Acceptance Policies. Byline given: yes. Publishing rights: n/i. Payment made: in copies. Response time to initial inquiry: 3 weeks. Average time until publication: 6 months. Submit seasonal material 6 months in advance. Simultaneous submissions: no. Disk submissions: no.

Photography Submissions. Format and film: 4x6 prints; transparencies. Photographs should include: captions; identification of subjects; name of photographer. **Payment**: copies. Photographic rights: n/i.

Additional Information. All articles deal with rhododendrons: culture, travel, etc. Writer's guidelines: upon request. Sample copy: upon request.

APPALOOSA JOURNAL. PO Box 8403. Moscow, ID 83843. (208) 882-5578.
Fax: (208) 882-8150. Submissions Editor: Debbie Pitner Moors. Type: horse breed publication for the trade and hobby. Frequency of publication: monthly. Circulation: 14,000. Number of manuscripts accepted per year: 12-15. Payment offered.

Editorial Needs. Nonfiction—pertinent to horse industry. **Forms:** columns; features (horses, owners, breeders, trainers); fillers; how-to (horse health articles); interview/profile (owners, breeders, trainers); photo-features (horse-related); historic pieces. Length and payment varies for all forms.

Initial Contact. Query letter or article proposal with subject outline or entire article. Include photo availability. SASE required.

Acceptance Policies. Byline given: yes. Publishing rights: first rights; work-for-hire assignments. Payment made: upon publication. Response time to initial inquiry: 1 month or less. Average time until publication: 1 month to 1 year. Submit seasonal material 2 months in advance. Simultaneous submissions: inform us. Disk submissions: inquire as to format.

Photography Submissions. Good quality photos needed. Format and film: 3x5, 5x7, or larger black-and-white or color prints; prefer transparencies. Photographs should include: captions; model releases; identification of subjects. **Payment**: varies; cover $200+/-. Photographic rights: n/i.

Additional Information. We are interested in freelancers with knowledge of the horse industry. Tips: Narrow your focus; tie it to Appaloosas. Photos help. Writer's guidelines: SASE. Sample copy: upon request.

ARNAZELLA. Bellevue Community College. 3000 Landerholm Circle SE.
Bellevue, WA 98007. (206) 641-2021. Submissions Editor: Leslie Rogers. Type: literary and arts. Frequency of publication: yearly. Circulation: n/i. Number of manuscripts accepted per year: n/i. Payment in copies.

Editorial Needs. Fiction—Afro-American; avant-garde/experimental; contemporary/modern; erotica; ethnic; fantasy; general; handicapped; Hispanic; humor; Latin American; literary; mainstream; mystery; Native American; new age; science fiction; suspense; women's issues; working people. **Forms:** 1-act plays (3500 words maximum); short stories (3500 words maximum).

Nonfiction—all subjects. **Forms:** cartoons; essays; photo features; poetry.

Initial Contact. Entire article. Include 25-word typed bio. SASE required.

Acceptance Policies. Byline given: yes. Publishing rights: first North American serial rights. Payment made: in copies. Response time to initial inquiry: up to 1 year. Average time until publication: 3 months. Simultaneous submissions: no. Disk submissions: no.

Photography Submissions. Format and film: 8x10 (maximum) black-and-white prints. Photographs should include: n/i. **Payment**: in copies. Photographic rights: first North American serial rights.

Additional Information. *Arnazella* is a student-run publication that comes out once a year. Query response time will be slow. Tips: Please read the magazine before submitting. Writer's guidelines: SASE. Sample copy: back issues upon request; new issue $5.

ARTIST TRUST. 512 The Jones Bldg. 1331 3rd Ave. Seattle, WA 98101. (206) 467-8734. Submissions Editor: Loch Adamson. Type: arts and artist-related issues. Frequency of publication: quarterly. Circulation: 15,000. Number of manuscripts accepted per year: varies. Payment by commission only.

Editorial Needs. Nonfiction—issues on arts on West Coast, particularly Washington State. **Forms:** essays (1000-2000 words); features; interview/profile (artist's profile). Payment varies for all forms.

Initial Contact. Article proposal with subject outline. SASE required.

Acceptance Policies. Byline given: yes. Publishing rights: one-time rights. Payment made: upon publication. Response time to initial inquiry: 1-2 weeks. Average time until publication: 2 months. Submit seasonal material 2 months in advance. Simultaneous submissions: yes. Disk submissions: Macintosh; Microsoft Word.

Photography Submissions. Format and film: 3x5 or 5x7 prints. Photographs should include: captions. **Payment:** n/i. Photographic rights: n/i.

Additional Information. Artist Trust is a statewide nonprofit organization focusing on the arts in Washington. Writer's guidelines: none. Sample copy: upon request.

BAD HAIRCUT. 3115 SW Roxbury St. Seattle, WA 98126. Submissions Editors: Ray and Kim Goforth. Type: politics, human rights, and environmental themes. Frequency of publication: irregular. Circulation: 2000. Number of manuscripts accepted per year: 50. Payment and/or copies offered.

Editorial Needs. Fiction—avant-garde/experimental; contemporary/modern; historical; Latin American; literary; Native American; politics; working people. **Forms:** short stories (500-2000 words; copies, perhaps cash).

Nonfiction—politics; human rights; environmental themes. **Forms:** cartoons (political, copy); columns (2000 words; copy and token cash); essays (2000 words; copy and token cash); interview/profile (5000 words maximum; copy and token cash); poetry (1 page maximum; copy).

Initial Contact. Entire article with cover letter and biography. SASE required.

Acceptance Policies. Byline given: yes. Publishing rights: first North American serial rights. Payment made: upon publication. Response time to initial inquiry: up to 3 months. Average time until publication: 2-12 months. Simultaneous submissions: notify us. Disk submissions: IBM 5 1/4; WordPerfect.

Additional Information. *Bad Haircut* is published by a husband and wife team with the hope that progressive art can positively influence the world. Tips: Read an issue. Writer's guidelines: SASE. Sample copy: $4.

BELLINGHAM REVIEW, THE. (Subsidiary of Signpost Press). 1007 Queen St. Bellingham, WA 98226. (206) 734-9781. Submissions Editor: Susan Hilton. Type: literary. Frequency of publication: 2 times per year. Circulation: 700. Number of manuscripts accepted per year: 70. Payment in copies and subscription.

Editorial Needs. Fiction—avant-garde/experimental; contemporary/modern; general; literary; mainstream. **Forms:** book excerpts; plays; short stories. 5000 word maximum for all forms.

Nonfiction—any subject. **Forms:** poetry (any length).

Initial Contact. Entire article. SASE required.

Acceptance Policies. Byline given: yes. Publishing rights: first North American serial rights. Payment made: in copies and subscription. Response time to initial inquiry: 2-3 months. Average time until publication: 6-12 months. Simultaneous submissions: yes. Disk submissions: no.

Additional Information. Writer's guidelines: SASE. Sample copy: $2.50.

BIKEREPORT. PO Box 8308. Missoula, MT 59807. (406) 721-1776. Fax: (406) 721-8754. Submissions Editor: Daniel D'Ambrosio. Type: bicycle touring (an association publication). Frequency of publication: 9 times per year. Circulation: 20,000. Number of manuscripts accepted per year: 25. Payment offered.

Editorial Needs. Fiction—bicycle touring. **Forms:** short stories (1500 words; $.03 per word).

Nonfiction—bicycle touring. **Forms:** columns (1200 words; payment varies); essays (1500-2000 words; $.03 per word); features (1500-2000; $.03 per word); fillers (200-500 words; $10-$30); interview/profile (1500-2000 words); poetry (any length; payment varies).

Initial Contact. Entire article. Include bio of author. SASE required.

Acceptance Policies. Byline given: yes. Publishing rights: first rights. Payment made: upon publication. Kill fee: no. Expenses: no. Response time to initial inquiry: 4 weeks. Average time until publication: 9 months. Submit seasonal material 4 months in advance. Simultaneous submissions: let us know the name of the other publications. Disk submissions: Macintosh.

Additional Information. Our magazine is the official publication of Bikecentennial, a nonprofit service organization for touring bicyclists. Tips: We like imaginative pieces that use cycling as a starting point to investigate or reveal other topics. Read back issues. Writer's guidelines: upon request. Sample copy: 9x12 SASE, $1 postage.

BRUSSELS SPROUT. PO Box 1551. Mercer Island, WA 98040. (206) 232-3239. Submissions Editors: Francine Porad, editor/publisher; Connie Hutchison, associate editor. Type: haiku poetry. Frequency of publication: 3 times per year. Circulation: 300. Number of manuscripts accepted per year: 450. Payment made in awards.

Editorial Needs. Nonfiction—haiku poetry. **Forms:** book reviews (haiku, senryu, renga; short comments); essays (haiku-related; 200-500 words); poetry (haiku, senryu, renga; 4-12 poems).

Initial Contact. Entire entry. SASE required.

Acceptance Policies. Byline given: yes. Publishing rights: first North American serial rights. Payment made: 3 $10 editor's choice awards made on publication. Response time to initial inquiry: 3 weeks. Average time until publication: 3 months. Simultaneous submissions: no. Disk submissions: no.

Additional Information. Writer's guidelines: SASE. Sample copy: $5.

BUSINESS JOURNAL, THE. PO Box 14490. Portland, OR 97214. (503) 274-8733. Fax: (503) 227-2650. Submissions Editors: Tom Gauntt (news stories); John Knowlton (opinion/editorial). Type: business. Frequency of publication: weekly. Circulation: 15,000. Number of manuscripts accepted per year: 5-10. Payment offered.

Editorial Needs. Nonfiction—business-related. **Forms:** cartoons; columns (20 inches; no payment); features (20 inches; $3 per inch); interview/profile (20 inches).

Initial Contact. Article proposal with subject outline. SASE required.

Acceptance Policies. Byline given: yes. Publishing rights: first North American serial rights; work-for-hire assignments. Payment made: upon publication. Kill fee: no. Expenses: no. Response time to initial inquiry: 10 days. Average time until publication: 1 month. Submit seasonal material 3 months in advance. Simultaneous submissions: if they are not competing publications in our market. Disk submissions: hard copy plus ASCII file.

Photography Submissions. Format and film: 8x10 black-and-white prints. Photographs should include: captions; identification of subjects. **Payment**: $25. Photographic rights: n/i.

Additional Information. Our market is the chief executive, manager, and small business owner in the Portland area. Upper-crust demographics. Writer's guidelines: none. Sample copy: upon request.

CALAPOOYA COLLAGE. PO Box 309. Monmouth, OR 97361. (503) 838-6292. Submissions Editor: T. L. Ferté. Type: literary, primarily poetry. Frequency of publication: yearly. Circulation: 1500. Number of manuscripts accepted per year: 150. Payment in copies.

Editorial Needs. Fiction—Afro-American; avant-garde/experimental; contemporary/modern; ethnic; fantasy; general; Hispanic; Latin American; literary; mainstream; Native American; women's issues. **Forms:** short stories (2000 words).

Nonfiction—literary. **Forms:** book reviews (literary; 200 words); essays (general; 1500 words); poetry (all types and subjects; any length).

Initial Contact. n/i. SASE required.

Acceptance Policies. Byline given: yes. Publishing rights: one-time rights. Payment made: in copies. Response time to initial inquiry: 4-6 weeks. Average time until publication: next annual. Simultaneous submissions: no. Disk submissions: no.

Additional Information. Deadline each year is June 1; each annual issue is published in August. *Calapooya Collage* sponsers the annual $700 Carolyn Kizer Poetry Awards. Writer's guidelines: none. Sample copy: $4.

CANOE. PO Box 3146. Kirkland, WA 98033. (206) 827-636. Submissions Editor: Les Johnson. Associate Editor: Stephen Petit. Type: North America's number one resource for canoeing and kayaking. Frequency of publication: every other month. Circulation: 65,000. Number of manuscripts accepted per year: 35+. Payment offered.

Editorial Needs. Nonfiction—canoeing, kayaking. **Forms:** book excerpts (1000-1500 words); book reviews; essays (1000-1500 words); features (2000-3000 words); fillers (100-300 words); interview/profile (1000+ words). Payment is $5 per inch for all forms.

Initial Contact. Query letter or article proposal with subject outline. SASE required.

Acceptance Policies. Byline given: yes. Publishing rights: all. Payment made: upon publication. Kill fee: no. Expenses: yes. Response time to initial inquiry: 3 weeks. Average time until publication: 6-9 months. Submit seasonal material 6 months in advance. Simultaneous submissions: no. Disk submissions: yes.

Photography Submissions. Format and film: 5x7 or 8x10 black-and-white glossy prints; contact sheets. Photographs should include: captions; model releases; identification of subjects. **Payment**: rates vary with page percentage. Photographic rights: n/i.

Additional Information. This is a national magazine. We receive manuscripts from the United States, Canada, and Europe. Tips: Read our guidelines for photographers and writers. Writer's guidelines: upon request. Sample copy: upon request.

CASCADES EAST. PO Box 5784. Bend, OR 97701. (503) 382-0127. Submissions Editor: Vicki Hill. Type: regional publication for central Oregon. Frequency of publication: quarterly. Circulation: 10,000. Number of manuscripts accepted per year: n/i. Payment offered.

Editorial Needs. Nonfiction—regional. **Forms:** features (history; 1000-2000 words; $.03-$.10 per word); fillers (general recreation); interview/profile (homeowners); photo feature (recreation).

Initial Contact. Entire article. SASE required.

Acceptance Policies. Byline given: yes. Publishing rights: n/i. Payment made: upon publication. Kill fee: no. Expenses: no. Response time to initial inquiry: varies. Average time until publication: varies. Submit seasonal material 9 months in advance. Simultaneous submissions: no. Disk submissions: no.

Photography Submissions. Format and film: black-and-white or color prints; transparencies. Photographs should include: captions; model releases; identification of subjects. **Payment:** varies. Photographic rights: one-time rights.

Additional Information. Tips: Know the central Oregon region. Writer's guidelines: upon request. Sample copy: $3.

CLEANING BUSINESS MAGAZINE. PO Box 1273. Seattle, WA 98111. (206) 622-4241. Submissions Editors: Gerri LaMarche, Jim Saunders. Type: cleaning and maintenance publication for self-employed professionals. Frequency of publication: quarterly. Circulation: 5000. Number of manuscripts accepted per year: 40. Payment offered.

Editorial Needs. Nonfiction—trade specific. **Forms:** cartoons; features (management advice; 2500 words; $10-$90); interview/profile (successful operators; 2500 words; $10-$90).

Initial Contact. Call us or send query letter with synopsis/outline. Include clips. SASE required.

Acceptance Policies. Byline given: yes. Publishing rights: first-time rights or all rights. Payment made: upon publication. Response time to initial inquiry: 1 week. Average time until publication: 3-4 months. Simultaneous submissions: no. Disk submissions: yes.

Photography Submissions. Format and film: 5x7 black-and-white or color prints. Photographs should include: captions. **Payment:** $5 per photo used. Photographic rights: first-time rights.

Additional Information. Tips: Articles should include solid technical advice with a positive, helpful, and friendly slant. Writer's guidelines: upon request. Sample copy: $3.

COLIN'S MAGAZINE. 10254 35th Ave. SW. Seattle, WA 98146. (206) 937-8155. Submissions Editors: Carl Diltz (poetry, general essays); Joseph Keppler (critical articles, book and poetry reviews). Type: literary. Frequency of publication: quarterly. Number of manuscripts accepted per year: 40. Payment in copies.

Editorial Needs. Fiction—literary. **Forms:** plays (2000-3000 words).

Nonfiction—literary. **Forms:** book reviews (technology, poetry, art; 500-2000 words); essays (technology, computers; 500-2000 words); poetry (any subject, any length).

Initial Contact. Entire article. SASE required.

Acceptance Policies. Byline given: yes. Publishing rights: first North American serial rights. Payment made: in copies. Response time to initial inquiry: 2 weeks. Average time until publication: 8-12 weeks. Simultaneous submissions: no. Disk submissions: Macintosh.

Photography Submissions. Format and film: 8x10 or smaller black-and-white prints. Photographs should include: captions. **Payment:** copies. Photographic rights: one-time rights.

Additional Information. Special emphasis on relationship between computer technology and writing. Tips: Writing is thinking and is not personal but communal. Writer's guidelines: none. Sample copy: $5 for writers (usually $7).

COMICS JOURNAL, THE. 7563 Lake City Way NE. Seattle, WA 98115.
(206) 524-1967. Fax: (206) 524-2104. Submissions Editor: Helena Harvilicz. Type: critical trade magazine. Frequency of publication: every other month. Circulation: 14,000. Number of manuscripts accepted per year: 45. Payment offered.

Editorial Needs. Nonfiction—comics; cartooning. **Forms:** book reviews (3000 words); cartoons (1 page; no payment); essays (3000 words); features (5000 words); interview/profile (noted cartoonists; 3000-10,000 words). Payment is $.015 per word for all forms.

Initial Contact. Entire article. Include brief biographical and bibliographical information. SASE required.

Acceptance Policies. Byline given: yes. Publishing rights: one-time rights. Payment made: upon publication. Response time to initial inquiry: 1-6 months. Average time until publication: 3 months. Submit seasonal material 3 months in advance. Simultaneous submissions: no. Disk submissions: Macintosh; Macwrite.

Photography Submissions. Format and film: black-and-white contact sheets. Photographs should include: identification of subjects; time, date, and place of photo. **Payment:** $10. Photographic rights: all rights.

Additional Information. We look at comics, comic strips, and cartoons from a journalistic, critical, and international viewpoint. Tips: Avoid articles on "mature" superheroes. Writer's guidelines: SASE. Sample copy: $4.75 plus $.29 postage.

CONSCIOUS LIVING. PO Box 9. Drain, OR 97435. (503) 836-2358.
Submissions Editor: Dr. Tim Lowenstein. Type: health and fitness, self-improvement, planetary care. Frequency of publication: quarterly. Circulation: 40,000. Number of manuscripts accepted per year: 10. Payment offered.

Editorial Needs. Nonfiction—health and fitness; self-help; world consciousness. **Forms:** book excerpts; book reviews.

Initial Contact. Query letter or article proposal with subject outline or entire article. SASE required.

Acceptance Policies. Byline given: yes. Publishing rights: n/i. Payment made: upon publication. Kill fee: no. Expenses: no. Response time to initial inquiry: 4 weeks. Average time until publication: 16 weeks. Simultaneous submissions: no. Disk submissions: IBM; WordPerfect.

Photography Submissions. Format and film: black-and-white or color prints. Photographs should include: captions; model releases. **Payment:** varies. Photographic rights: n/i.

Additional Information. Writer's guidelines: upon request. Sample copy: upon request.

CRAB CREEK REVIEW. 4462 Whitman N. Seattle, WA 98103. (206) 633-
1090. Submissions Editors: Linda Clifton (general, poetry); Carol Orlock (fiction). Type: literary. Frequency of publication: 3 times per year. Circulation: 500. Number of manuscripts accepted per year: 75. Payment in copies.

Editorial Needs. Fiction—avant-garde/experimental; contemporary/modern; general; Latin American. **Forms:** short stories (4000 words maximum; 2 copies).

Nonfiction—any subject. **Forms:** essays (under 3000 words; 2 copies); poetry (2 copies).

Initial Contact. Entire article. SASE required.

Acceptance Policies. Byline given: yes. Publishing rights: first North American serial rights. Payment made: 2 copies. Response time to initial inquiry: 1-3 months. Average time until publication: 1-2 years. Submit seasonal material 6 months in advance. Simultaneous submissions: absolutely not. Disk submissions: no.

Additional Information. Not seeking mansucripts until 1992. Tips: Read the magazine first. Writer's guidelines: SASE. Sample copy: $3.

CRAFT CONNECTION. PO Box 25124. Seattle, WA 98125-2024. (206) 367-7875. Submissions Editor: Cindy Salazar. Type: crafts. Frequency of publication: every other month. Circulation: 36,000. Number of manuscripts accepted per year: no limit. No payment offered.

Editorial Needs. **Fiction**—holiday. **Forms:** n/i.

Nonfiction—crafting. **Forms:** book reviews; essays (crafting attitudes, trends, projects).

Initial Contact. Article proposal with subject outline. SASE required.

Acceptance Policies. Byline given: yes. Publishing rights: one-time rights. Payment made: none. Response time to initial inquiry: 1-2 weeks. Average time until publication: 2-6 months. Submit seasonal material 4 months in advance. Simultaneous submissions: yes. Disk submissions: Macintosh.

Photography Submissions. Format and film: 5x7 or smaller black-and-white prints. Photographs should include: captions; identification of subjects. **Payment**: none. Photographic rights: none.

Additional Information. Writer's guidelines: none. Sample copy: $2.

CRAFTS REPORT, THE. 87 Wall St. Seattle, WA 98121. (206) 441-3102. Fax: (206) 441-3203. Submissions Editor: Christine Yarrow. Type: trade journal for professional craftspeople. Frequency of publication: monthly. Circulation: 20,000. Number of manuscripts accepted per year: 80. Payment offered.

Editorial Needs. **Nonfiction**—trade oriented. **Forms:** book reviews (500-1000 words); cartoons (no payment); columns (health, photography, finance, computers); features (craft related); fillers (craft related); interview/profile (professional craftspeople). Payment is $1.25 per word for all forms.

Initial Contact. Article proposal with subject outline. SASE required.

Acceptance Policies. Byline given: yes. Publishing rights: first North American serial rights. Payment made: upon publication. Kill fee: depends on length of article. Expenses: no. Response time to initial inquiry: 1 month. Average time until publication: 2-4 months. Submit seasonal material 2 months in advance. Simultaneous submissions: yes. Disk submissions: IBM DOS, Macintosh; Microsoft Word.

Photography Submissions. Format and film: 5x7 prints. Photographs should include: captions; identification of subjects. **Payment**: $25. Photographic rights: none.

Additional Information. We are primarily a business-oriented magazine for professional craftspeople, not hobbyists. Tips: Give us a call to find out what we want. Writer's guidelines: upon request. Sample copy: $2.50.

CUT BANK. c/o Department of English. University of Montana. Missoula, MT 59812. (406) 243-5231. Submissions Editors: Dennis Held, (co-editor); Peter Fong, (co-editor); Claire Davis (fiction); Marnie Bullock (poetry). Type: literary. Frequency of publication: 2 times per year. Circulation: 400. Number of manuscripts accepted per year: 40. Payment in copies.

Editorial Needs. **Fiction**—literary. **Forms:** short stories (40 pages maximum).

Nonfiction—literary. **Forms:** book reviews (regional; 5 pages maximum); interview/profile (10 pages maximum); poetry (any length); art/photos (as illustration).

Initial Contact. Entire article. Submissions are accepted from August to February only. SASE required.

Acceptance Policies. Byline given: yes. Publishing rights: first rights; revert to author upon publication with provision to receive credit. Payment made: in copies. Response time to initial inquiry: 3 months. Average time until publication: 3 months. Simultaneous submissions: yes. Disk submissions: no.

Photography Submissions. Format and film: 5 1/2 x 8 1/2 or 8 1/2 x 11 black-and-white prints. Photographs should include: title or caption. **Payment:** copies. Photographic rights: rights revert to author upon publication with provision for credit.

Additional Information. We actively encourage unknown writers to submit. Tips: Send your best work. Writer's guidelines: SASE. Sample copy: $4.

DOG RIVER REVIEW.
5976 Billings Rd. Parkdale, OR 97041. (503) 352-6494. Submissions Editors: Allove DeVito (poetry); L. Hawkins (fiction). Type: literary. Frequency of publication: 2 times per year. Circulation: 300+. Number of manuscripts accepted per year: 4-8 fiction; 4-8 reviews; 50-60 poetry. Payment in copies.

Editorial Needs. **Fiction**—avant-garde/experimental; humor; literary; Native American; new age; science fiction. **Forms:** book excerpts (3000 words maximum); plays (short); short stories (3000 words maximum).

Nonfiction—literary. **Forms:** book reviews (3000 words maximum); interview/profile (writers and poets; 3000 words maximum); poetry (any length); art/graphics (in black and-white as illustrations).

Initial Contact. Entire article. SASE required.

Acceptance Policies. Byline given: yes. Publishing rights: first North American serial rights. Payment made: in copies. Response time to initial inquiry: 1-2 weeks. Average time until publication: 6-8 months. Submit seasonal material 6-8 months in advance. Simultaneous submissions: yes. Disk submissions: Macintosh.

Photography Submissions. Format and film: black-and-white art/graphics. Photographs should include: identification of subjects. **Payment:** copies. Photographic rights: first rights.

Additional Information. Tips: No experiment is too bold. Writer's guidelines: SASE. Sample copy: $2.

DOUGLAS COUNTY HISTORICAL SOCIETY "UMPQUA TRAPPER."
733 W. Ballf. Roseburg, OR 97470. (503) 673-4572. Submissions Editor: Doris Bacon. Type: local history of Douglas County, Oregon. Frequency of publication: quarterly. Circulation: 300. Number of manuscripts accepted per year: varies. Payment in copies.

Editorial Needs. **Fiction**—historical. **Forms:** n/i.

Nonfiction—historical. **Forms:** features.

Initial Contact. Query letter only. SASE required.

Acceptance Policies. Byline given: yes. Publishing rights: all rights. Payment made: in copies. Response time to initial inquiry: 1 week. Average time until publication: next available space. Simultaneous submissions: n/i. Disk submissions: no.

Photography Submissions. Format and film: 3x5 or larger black-and-white prints. Photographs should include: captions; model releases; identification of subjects. **Payment:** copies. Photographic rights: none.

Additional Information. We are a nonprofit organization. Writer's guidelines: none. Sample copy: upon request.

EASTMAN'S OUTDOORSMEN, MIKE. 1227 Arapahoe. Thermopolis, WY 82443. (307) 864-3405. Submissions Editor: Bertie Eastman. Type: hunting Western big game; instructional and entertaining. Frequency of publication: quarterly. Circulation: 1500. Number of manuscripts accepted per year: 20. Payment in copies.

Editorial Needs. **Nonfiction**—hunting Western big game. **Forms:** cartoons (100 words maximum; $20); columns (500 words maximum; $.08 per word); essays (1000 words maximum; $.08 per word); features (1000 words maximum; $.08 per word); interview/profile ($.08 per word); photo features (payment negotiable); poetry (200 words maximum; $.08 per word); how-to (500 words maximum; $.08 per word).

Initial Contact. Query letter only. Include hunting background and experience. SASE required.

Acceptance Policies. Byline given: yes. Publishing rights: first rights. Payment made: in copies. Response time to initial inquiry: 3 months. Average time until publication: 6 months. Submit seasonal material 3 months in advance. Simultaneous submissions: no. Disk submissions: Macintosh; Ready, Set, Go.

Photography Submissions. Format and film: 4x5 prints; contact sheets. Photographs should include: captions; identification of subjects. **Payment:** copies. Photographic rights: first rights.

Additional Information. Our magazine is read by avid trophy hunters. Tips: You must know trophy hunting and be able to write knowledgeably. Writer's guidelines: none. Sample copy: 9x12 SASE, $1.21 postage.

EMERGENCY LIBRARIAN. Dept. 284, Box C34069. Seattle, WA 98124-1069. (604) 734-0255. Fax: (604) 734-0221. Submissions Editor: varies, send for list. Type: designed specifically for professionals working with children and young adults in school and public libraries. Frequency of publication: 5 times per year. Circulation: 10,000. Number of manuscripts accepted per year: n/i. Payment offered.

Editorial Needs. **Nonfiction**—detailed information given in guidelines. **Forms:** book reviews; cartoons; essays; features.

Initial Contact. Entire article.

Acceptance Policies. Byline given: yes. Publishing rights: all rights. Payment made: honorarium upon publication. Response time to initial inquiry: 6-8 weeks. Average time until publication: varies. Submit seasonal material 6-9 months in advance. Simultaneous submissions: no. Disk submissions: no.

Additional Information. *EL* is one of the largest independent journals offering lively and relevant feature articles that explore current issues. Special sections include professional material in education and librarianship, management, implications of research, microcomputers, paperbacks for children, paperbacks for young adults, best sellers. Writer's guidelines: phone, fax, letter. Sample copy: phone, fax, letter.

EOTU, MAGAZINE OF EXPERIMENTAL FICTION. 1810 W. State, #115. Boise, ID 83702. Fax: (208) 342-4996. Submissions Editor: Larry Dennis. Type: literary. Frequency of publication: every other month. Circulation: 300. Number of manuscripts accepted per year: 80. Payment and copy offered.

Editorial Needs. **Fiction**—avant-garde/experimental; fantasy; horror; humor; science fiction; all genres. **Forms:** novellas (15,000-20,000 words; payment negotiable); short stories (5000 words maximum; $5-$25).

Initial Contact. Entire article. SASE required.

Acceptance Policies. Byline given: yes. Publishing rights: first North American serial rights; other negotiable. Payment made: upon acceptance. Response time to initial inquiry: 2 weeks for query; 2 months for manuscripts. Average time until publication: 4-6 months. Simultaneous submissions: no. Disk submissions: IBM 3 1/2; ASCII or WordPerfect.

Additional Information. We publish experimental fiction. We want new understandings of structure, language, or characterization. Tips: Send for sample copy. Know your market. Writer's guidelines: SASE. Sample copy: $4.

FINE MADNESS. PO Box 31138. Seattle, WA 98103. Submissions Editors: Sean Bentley, Louis Bergsagel, Christine Deavel, John Malek, John Marshall. Type: literary. Frequency of publication: 2 times per year. Circulation: 600. Number of manuscripts accepted per year: 60+/-. Two annual cash awards offered.

Editorial Needs. Fiction—literary. **Forms:** short stories (20 pages; possible annual award).

Nonfiction—poetry. **Forms:** book reviews (poetry, chapbooks; 10 pages maximum); essays (on poetics; 10 pages maximum); poetry (any subject; 5 poems; 20 pages maximum). All forms eligible for annual award.

Initial Contact. Query letter only. SASE required.

Acceptance Policies. Byline given: yes. Publishing rights: anthology rights (not exclusive). Payment made: in an annual award. Response time to initial inquiry: 3 months. Average time until publication: 6-12 months. Simultaneous submissions: no. Disk submissions: no.

Additional Information. We publish mostly poetry, with occasional short stories, essays, and book reviews. Tips: Send us clean, legible copies. Writer's guidelines: SASE. Sample copy: $4.

FLIGHTLINES. Oregon Aeronautics Division. Salem, OR 97310. (503) 378-4880. Submissions Editor: Ed Schoaps. Type: government aviation newsletter. Frequency of publication: quarterly. Circulation: 11,400. Number of manuscripts accepted per year: n/i. No payment offered.

Editorial Needs. Nonfiction—Oregon aviation related. **Forms:** columns; features; interview/profile. Length is 150-500 words for all forms.

Initial Contact. Article proposal with subject outline. SASE required.

Acceptance Policies. Byline given: yes. Publishing rights: author retains copyright. Payment made: none. Response time to initial inquiry: 2 weeks. Average time until publication: varies. Submit seasonal material 4 months in advance. Simultaneous submissions: no. Disk submissions: Macintosh, WordPerfect or Microsoft Word; IBM, WordPerfect.

Additional Information. Our audience is registered Oregon pilots, and our focus is Oregon aviation issues, news, and newsmakers. Writer's guidelines: upon request. Sample copy: upon request.

FREIGHTER TRAVEL NEWS. 3524 Harts Lake Rd. Roy, WA 98580. Submissions Editor: Leland Pledger. Type: newsletter devoted exclusively to freighter travel. Frequency of publication: monthly. Circulation: 1190. Number of manuscripts accepted per year: varies. Payment in copies and subscription.

Editorial Needs. Nonfiction—recent freighter trips. **Forms:** features (100-1000 words; 6-month subscription).

Initial Contact. Entire article. SASE required.

Acceptance Policies. Byline given: yes. Publishing rights: none. Payment made: copies and 6-month subscription. Response time to initial inquiry: 15 days. Average time until publication: 3-6 months. Simultaneous submissions: yes, as long as I can use it also. Disk submissions: no.

Photography Submissions. Format and film: any. Photographs should include: identification of subjects; should accompany story. **Payment**: copies. Photographic rights: none.

Additional Information. Writer's guidelines: none. Sample copy: $2.

FUGUE: LITERARY DIGEST OF THE UNIVERSITY OF IDAHO.
University of Idaho. English Department. Brink Hall, Rm. 200. Moscow, ID 83843. Submissions Editor: address to Executive Editor. Type: literary. Frequency of publication: 3 times per year. Circulation: 200-500. Number of manuscripts accepted per year: 30+. Payment in copies.

Editorial Needs. **Fiction**—any subject. **Forms:** short stories (1000-5000 words); vignettes (1000 words maximum).

Nonfiction—literary. **Forms:** book reviews (contemporary novels only; 1000 words); essays (on contemporary literature; 1500 words); interview/profile (writers, poets; any length); poetry (any premise, any style, any length).

Initial Contact. Entire article. SASE required.

Acceptance Policies. Byline given: yes. Publishing rights: first North American serial rights. Payment made: 1 copy. Response time to initial inquiry: 2 weeks for query; 8-12 weeks for submissions. Average time until publication: 6 months maximum. Submit seasonal material 3 months in advance. Simultaneous submissions: no. Disk submissions: no.

Additional Information. Tips: Above all else, entertain the reader; themes and messages are secondary. Send for guidelines before submitting. Writer's guidelines: SASE. Sample copy: $3.65.

GENERAL AVIATION NEWS AND FLYER. PO Box 98786. Tacoma, WA
98498. (206) 588-1743. Fax: (206) 588-4005. Submissions Editor: Dave Sclair. Type: aviation with travel pieces related to flying. Frequency of publication: 2 times per month. Circulation: 40,000. Number of manuscripts accepted per year: 50. Payment offered.

Editorial Needs. **Nonfiction**—aviation. **Forms:** book reviews (500 words); columns; features (1000-2500 words); interview/profile (1000-2500 words); photo feature. Payment up to $3 per inch for all forms.

Initial Contact. Query letter only. SASE required.

Acceptance Policies. Byline given: yes. Publishing rights: first North American serial rights. Payment made: upon publication. Kill fee: no. Expenses: by agreement. Response time to initial inquiry: 1 month. Average time until publication: 1-3 months. Submit seasonal material 2 months in advance. Simultaneous submissions: no. Disk submissions: Macintosh preferred.

Photography Submissions. Format and film: black-and-white or color prints; transparencies. Photographs should include: captions; identification of subjects. **Payment**: $10 black and white; $30 color. Photographic rights: n/i.

Additional Information. We are a publication for general and business aviation. Tips: Be factual and complete; no "gee whiz" type stuff. Writer's guidelines: SASE. Sample copy: $3 and 10x13 SASE.

GREAT EXPEDITIONS. PO Box 8000-411. Sumas, WA 98295-8000. (604) 852-6170. Submissions Editor: Craig Henderson. Type: travel, adventure. Frequency of publication: 5 times per year. Circulation: 10,000. Number of manuscripts accepted per year: 40. Payment offered.

Editorial Needs. **Nonfiction**—travel. **Forms:** book excerpts (1500 words maximum; $50); book reviews (300 words maximum; $20); features (2000 words maximum; $70).

Initial Contact. Query letter only. SASE required.

Acceptance Policies. Byline given: yes. Publishing rights: first rights; second serial rights; one-time rights. Payment made: upon publication. Kill fee: the offered payment rate. Expenses: no. Response time to initial inquiry: 60 days. Average time until publication: 6-9 months. Simultaneous submissions: yes. Disk submissions: no.

Photography Submissions. Format and film: prints of any size; transparencies. Photographs should include: captions. **Payment:** included in fee for article. Photographic rights: same as article.

Additional Information. Tips: It's best to read a copy of *Great Expeditions* before making a query. Writer's guidelines: SASE. Sample copy: $4.

GROWING EDGE, THE. PO Box 1027. Corvallis, OR 97339. (503) 757-0027. Fax: (503) 757-0028. Submissions Editor: Don Parker. Type: home and garden. Frequency of publication: quarterly. Circulation: n/i. Number of manuscripts accepted per year: 25. Payment offered.

Editorial Needs. **Nonfiction**—high-tech gardening. **Forms:** features (any length; $.075 per word); fillers (any length; $.075 per word); interview/profile (any length; $.075 per word); photo feature (any length; $10-$25 per photo).

Initial Contact. Article proposal with subject outline. SASE required.

Acceptance Policies. Byline given: yes. Publishing rights: first rights; second serial rights. Payment made: upon publication. Kill fee: no. Expenses: yes. Response time to initial inquiry: 1 month. Average time until publication: 3 months. Submit seasonal material 6 months in advance. Simultaneous submissions: no. Disk submissions: Macintosh preferred.

Photography Submissions. Format and film: black-and-white or color contact sheets; transparencies. Photographs should include: captions; model releases; identification of subjects. **Payment:** $10-$25. Photographic rights: first and reprint rights.

Additional Information. *Growing Edge* covers the emerging high-tech world of gardening. Tips: We are interested in any story that shows examples and techniques of controlled-environment gardening. Writer's guidelines: SASE. Sample copy: $6.50.

HOUSEWIFE-WRITER'S FORUM. PO Box 780. Lyman, WY 82937. (307) 786-4513. Submissions Editors: Diane Wolverton; Lindy Capel, assistant. Type: magazine for women writers. Frequency of publication: every other month. Circulation: 1200. Number of manuscripts accepted per year: 100. Payment and copies offered.

Editorial Needs. **Fiction**—humor; women's issues; writing life. **Forms:** short stories (2000 words maximum; $.01 per word).

Nonfiction—varies. **Forms:** book reviews (writing, organization; 500 words); cartoons (housewife/writer humor); features (tips on writing; 500-2000 words); fillers; interview/profiles (writers, how they did it; 1000 words); poetry. Payment is $.01 per word for all forms.

Initial Contact. Entire article. SASE required.

Acceptance Policies. Byline given: yes. Publishing rights: one-time rights. Payment made: upon acceptance. Kill fee: no. Expenses: no. Response time to initial inquiry: 6-8 weeks. Average time until publication: 2-4 months. Submit seasonal material 6 months in advance. Simultaneous submissions: notify us if manuscript is purchased elsewhere. Disk submissions: no.

Photography Submissions. Format and film: 5x7 black-and-white prints. Photographs should include: captions; identification of subjects. **Payment:** $3. Photographic rights: one-time rights.

Additional Information. This magazine is for and by women (and men) who share a commitment to writing while juggling home life and family responsibility. Tips: We look for clear, concise, and vivid language. Style should be lucid and to the point. Writer's guidelines: upon request. Sample copy: $4.

IDAHO WILDLIFE. Idaho Department of Fish and Game. PO Box 25. Boise, ID 83707. (208) 334-3748. Fax: (208) 334-2114. Submissions Editor: Diane Ronayne. Type: fish, wildlife, conservation. Frequency of publication: every other month. Circulation: 30,000. Number of manuscripts accepted per year: 2. Payment in copies.

Editorial Needs. Nonfiction—fish; wildlife; conservation. **Forms:** book reviews (200-500 words); features (600-1500 words).

Initial Contact. Query letter only. SASE required.

Acceptance Policies. Byline given: yes. Publishing rights: one-time rights. Payment made: in copies. Response time to initial inquiry: 3 weeks. Average time until publication: 2 months. Submit seasonal material 6 months in advance. Simultaneous submissions: yes. Disk submissions: WordPerfect or ASCII.

Photography Submissions. Format and film: color transparencies. Photographs should include: identification of subjects. **Payment:** $35 inside; $60 cover. Photographic rights: one-time rights.

Additional Information. Submissions must be written by people with credentials and experience in fish/wildlife management or be a first-person account of wildlife contacts in Idaho. Writer's guidelines: upon request. Sample copy: send request to Diane Ronayne.

IMAGO: COMIX/ART DIGEST OF SCIENCE FICTION/FANTASY. Figment Press. PO Box 3566. Moscow, ID 838430-0477. Submissions Editor: J. C. Hendee. Type: science fiction, fantasy. Frequency of publication: quarterly. Circulation: n/i. Number of manuscripts accepted per year: 10-20. Payment offered.

Editorial Needs. Nonfiction—science fiction; fantasy. **Forms:** cartoons; poetry. Payment is $2-$5 for all forms.

Initial Contact. Article proposal with subject outline or entire article. SASE required.

Acceptance Policies. Byline given: yes. Publishing rights: first North American serial rights. Payment made: within 30 days of acceptance. Kill fee: no. Expenses: no. Response time to initial inquiry: 2 weeks. Average time until publication: 3-6 months. Submit seasonal material 6 months in advance. Simultaneous submissions: no. Disk submissions: no.

Additional Information. We are primarily a comics/art digest looking for potential short scripts. Tips: Submission should be in proper comics script form. Writer's guidelines: SASE. Sample copy: SASE.

JEOPARDY. 132 College Hall. Western Washington University. Bellingham, WA 98225. (206) 676-3118. Submissions Editors: Scott Payton, Teresa de Bellis. Type: literary. Frequency of publication: yearly. Circulation: 4000. Number of manuscripts accepted per year: 65. Payment in copies.

Editorial Needs. Fiction—contemporary/modern; literary. **Forms:** book excerpts; plays; short stories. Length is 20 pages maximum for all forms.

Nonfiction—literary. **Forms:** essays (15 pages maximum); photo feature (5 photos); poetry (10 pages maximum).

Initial Contact. Entire article. SASE required.

Acceptance Policies. Byline given: yes. Publishing rights: first rights. Payment made: 2 copies. Response time to initial inquiry: 3 weeks. Average time until publication: 2-3 months. Simultaneous submissions: let us know. Disk submissions: no.

Photography Submissions. Format and film: black-and-white or color prints; transparencies. Photographs should include: captions. **Payment:** 2 copies. Photographic rights: first rights.

Additional Information. Writer's guidelines: upon request. Sample copy: $2 back issue; $4 current issue.

LAVENDAR NETWORK, THE. PO Box 5421. Eugene, OR 97405. (503) 485-7285. Submissions Editors: Bob Mattiazzi, Kate Hibbard (literary); Vicki Silvers, John Darcy (arts, entertainment). Type: gay, lesbian, bisexual. Frequency of publication: monthly. Circulation: 10,000. Number of manuscripts accepted per year: 75. Payment in copies.

Editorial Needs. Fiction—anything with a gay/lesbian slant. **Forms:** book excerpts; novellas; serialized fiction; short stories. Length is 1200 words for all forms.

Nonfiction—gay/lesbian. **Forms:** any (800-2000 words).

Initial Contact. Query letter or article proposal with subject outline or entire article. Advise whether multiple submission. SASE required.

Acceptance Policies. Byline given: yes. Publishing rights: none. Payment made: in copies. Response time to initial inquiry: 2-4 months. Average time until publication: 1-4 months. Submit seasonal material 2 months in advance. Simultaneous submissions: okay if not to other Oregon publications. Disk submissions: prefer Macintosh 3 1/2; Microsoft Word.

Additional Information. Writer's guidelines: SASE. Sample copy: $1.50 postage.

LESBIAN CONTRADICTION: A JOURNAL OF IRREVERENT FEMINISM. 1007 N. 47th St. Seattle, WA 98103. Submissions Editors: Jan Adams, Rebecca Gordon, Jane Meyerding. Type: for feminist women (lesbian and non-lesbian). Frequency of publication: quarterly. Circulation: 2000. Number of manuscripts accepted per year: 24. Payment in copies.

Editorial Needs. Nonfiction—feminist. **Forms:** book reviews (analysis of feminist theory, women's lives); cartoons; essays (personal experience, theory, opinion); interview/profile (activist women); photo feature. Length is 2500 words maximum for all forms.

Initial Contact. Entire article. Include brief bio and address. SASE preferred.

Acceptance Policies. Byline given: yes. Publishing rights: none. Payment made: in copies. Response time to initial inquiry: 1 week. Average time until publication: 3-6 months. Submit seasonal material 4-6 months in advance. Simultaneous submissions: no. Disk submissions: Macintosh.

Additional Information. Tips: Request a sample and read it. Writer's guidelines: upon request. Sample copy: $1.50.

LIGHTHOUSE FICTION COLLECTION. PO Box 1377. Auburn, WA 98071-1377. Submissions Editor: Lorraine Clinton. Type: literary. Frequency of publication: every other month. Circulation: 300. Number of manuscripts accepted per year: 66. Payment and copies offered.

Editorial Needs. Fiction—children's/young adult; contemporary/modern; general (any race, any class, anywhere); handicapped; historical; holiday; humor; mainstream; mystery; romance; science fiction; sports; suspense; Western; working people. **Forms:** short stories (5000 words maximum; $50 maximum plus 1 copy).

Initial Contact. Entire manuscript. SASE required.

Acceptance Policies. Byline given: yes. Publishing rights: first North American serial rights; first rights. Payment made: upon publication. Response time to initial inquiry: 1-2 months. Average time until publication: 1 year. Simultaneous submissions: no. Disk submissions: no.

Additional Information. All materials must be G-rated. Tips: Make sure material fits our guidelines before submitting it. Writer's guidelines: SASE, or included with sample copy. Sample copy: $3.

LITE FLYER NEWSLETTER. 939 S. 3rd Ave. Walla Walla, WA 99362. (509) 522-0158. Fax: (509) 525-3929. Submissions Editor: LeBaron W. Amacker. Type: for the sports enthusiast who is oriented to ultralight and very light aircraft. Frequency of publication: 5 issues per year. Circulation: 1245. Number of manuscripts accepted per year: 24. Payment or copies offered.

Editorial Needs. Nonfiction—flight safety; building, etc. **Forms:** columns (1500 words maximum); features (3000 words); interview/profile (3000 words); photo feature (4 pages). Payment is $15-$25 per half page, $45 per full page for all forms.

Initial Contact. Article proposal with subject outline. SASE required.

Acceptance Policies. Byline given: yes. Publishing rights: all. Payment made: upon acceptance. Kill fee: yes. Expenses: by arrangement. Response time to initial inquiry: 30 days. Average time until publication: 60 days. Submit seasonal material 2 months in advance. Simultaneous submissions: no. Disk submissions: no.

Photography Submissions. Format and film: 3x5, 5x7, 8x10 black-and-white prints (preferred) or contact sheets. No negatives or transparencies. Photographs should include: captions; identification of subjects. Detailed information to be found in guidelines. **Payment:** $3.50-$7.50. Photographic rights: all.

Additional Information. *LFN* is one of only three sport flying publications in the United States and is sold internationally. We are independent and not a subsidiary of any sport flying organization, albeit a member of EAA, NRFA, and others. No paid advertising is accepted. Tips: I'm particularly interested in a weight shift trike column by experienced trike pilot. (*LFN* has the only space dedicated to powered parachutes in any sport flying publication). Writer's guidelines: SASE. Sample copy: $1 postage.

LOVE MAGAZINE. c/o Patrick McCabe. PO Box 87817. Seattle, WA 98145-1817. Submissions Editor: Patrick McCabe. Type: literary. Frequency of publication: varies. Circulation: varies. Number of manuscripts accepted per year: n/i. Payment in copies.

Editorial Needs. Nonfiction—love. **Forms:** cartoons; essays; interview/profile; photo feature; poetry. Length should be brief for all forms.

Initial Contact. Entire article. SASE required.

Acceptance Policies. Byline given: yes. Publishing rights: one-time rights. Payment made: in copies. Response time to initial inquiry: varies. Average time until publication: varies. Simultaneous submissions: inform us. Disk submissions: no.

Photography Submissions. Format and film: prints only. Photographs should include: captions; identification of subjects. **Payment:** copies. Photographic rights: one-time rights.

Additional Information. *Love Magazine* is a nonfiction, purely evocative collection. Tips: Be real. Base your material on true-life experiences. Be brief. Writer's guidelines: none. Sample copy: upon request.

MONTANA MAGAZINE. PO Box 59604. Helena, MT 59601. (406) 443-2842.
Fax: (406) 443-5480. Submissions Editor: Carolyn Cunningham. Type: regional, travel. Frequency of publication: every other month. Circulation: 50,000. Number of manuscripts accepted per year: 60. Payment offered.

Editorial Needs. Nonfiction—regional; travel. **Forms:** columns (800-1000 words; $75); features (2000-2500 words; $125-$400); interview/profile (800-1000 words; $75-$15); photo feature (payment negotiable).

Initial Contact. Article proposal with subject outline. SASE required.

Acceptance Policies. Byline given: yes. Publishing rights: one-time rights. Payment made: upon publication. Kill fee: negotiable. Expenses: by agreement in advance. Response time to initial inquiry: 3-6 weeks. Average time until publication: varies. Submit seasonal material 4 months in advance. Simultaneous submissions: if submitted outside of region. Disk submissions: yes.

Photography Submissions. Format and film: black-and-white or color prints; transparencies. Photographs should include: captions; model releases; identification of subjects. **Payment:** $50. Photographic rights: one-time rights.

Additional Information. Tips: Look at the last two years of the magazine. Writer's guidelines: upon request. Sample copy: call us.

MONTANA, THE MAGAZINE OF WESTERN HISTORY. Montana
Historical Society. 225 N. Roberts St. Helena, MT 59620. (406) 444-4708. Fax: (406) 444-2696. Submissions Editor: Charles E. Rankin. Type: historical. Frequency of publication: quarterly. Circulation: 8500. Number of manuscripts accepted per year: 50. Payment made.

Editorial Needs. Nonfiction—history. **Forms:** book excerpts (5000 words); book reviews (450-500 words); essays (5000 words); interview/profile (3000 words).

Initial Contact. Query letter only. SASE required.

Acceptance Policies. Byline given: yes. Publishing rights: all rights. Payment made: upon acceptance of solicited manuscripts. Kill fee: no. Expenses: no. Response time to initial inquiry: 6 weeks. Average time until publication: 1 year. Submit seasonal material 12 months in advance. Simultaneous submissions: no. Disk submissions: WordPerfect 5.0 or ASCII format.

Photography Submissions. Format and film: black-and-white prints or photocopies of prints. Photographs should include: identification of subjects. **Payment:** $10. Photographic rights: one-time rights.

Additional Information. We are looking for a good narrative that will contribute to Montana or Western history, based on new research or new interpretation. Tips: Look at previous issues of magazine. Writer's guidelines: call or write. Sample copy: call or write.

MR. COGITO. Pacific University. UC Box 627. Forest Grove, OR 97116. (503) 226-4135. Submissions Editors: Robert A. Davies, John M. Gogol. Type: literary. Frequency of publication: 2-3 times per year. Circulation: 500. Number of manuscripts accepted per year: 40. Payment in copies.

Editorial Needs. Nonfiction—varied topics in translation or in English. **Forms:** poetry (any length).

Initial Contact. 4-5 poems. SASE required.

Acceptance Policies. Byline given: yes. Publishing rights: anthology rights; first rights. Payment made: in copies. Contest offers prize money. Response time to initial inquiry: 1-8 weeks. Average time until publication: 6 months. Simultaneous submissions: yes. Disk submissions: no.

Photography Submissions. Format and film: must fit 4 1/4 x 11 page. Photographs should include: n/i. **Payment:** 1 copy. Photographic rights: anthology; first rights.

Additional Information. Tips: Poems should have a clear subject and should be moving. Send 4-5 poems and try often. We do offer money to contest winners. Writer's guidelines: none. Sample copy: $3.

MUSHING MAGAZINE. PO Box 149. Ester, AK 99725. (907) 479-0454. Submissions Editors: Todd Hoener, editorial; Carey Brink, associate editor. Type: nonfiction information or entertainment about all dog-driving sports. Frequency of publication: every other month. Circulation: 6000. Number of manuscripts accepted per year: 36. Payment offered.

Editorial Needs. Nonfiction—dog; dog driving. **Forms:** book excerpts (500 words); book reviews; cartoons; columns; essays; features; interview/profile.

Initial Contact. Query letter or article proposal with subject outline or entire article. SASE required.

Acceptance Policies. Byline given: yes. Publishing rights: first North American serial rights; second serial rights; work-for-hire assignments. Payment made: upon publication. Kill fee: 50%. Expenses: yes. Response time to initial inquiry: 1 month. Average time until publication: 2 months. Submit seasonal material 4 months in advance. Simultaneous submissions: no. Disk submissions: Macintosh; DOS.

Photography Submissions. Format and film: black-and-white prints; color prints for cover. Photographs should include: captions; model releases; identification of subjects. **Payment:** $15-$150 (color cover). Photographic rights: same as article.

Additional Information. Dog driving is sledding, carting, skijoring, packing, weight-pulling. Writer's guidelines: upon request. Sample copy: $4.

MYSTERY TIME. PO Box 1870. Hayden, ID 83835. (208) 772-6184. Submissions Editor: Linda Hutton. Type: mystery and suspense. Frequency of publication: yearly. Circulation: 100. Number of manuscripts accepted per year: 8. Payment offered.

Editorial Needs. Fiction—mystery; suspense. **Forms:** short stories (1500-2000 words; $.025 per word).

Nonfiction—mystery; suspense. **Forms:** poetry (12 lines; $.25 per line).

Initial Contact. Entire article. No cover letters. SASE required.

Acceptance Policies. Byline given: yes. Publishing rights: first North American serial rights; first rights; second serial rights; one-time rights; simultaneous rights. Payment made: upon acceptance. Kill fee: no. Expenses: no. Response time to initial inquiry: 2 weeks. Average time until publication: 6 months. Submit seasonal material 6 months in advance. Simultaneous submissions: inform us. Disk submissions: no.

Additional Information. A touch of humor is always welcome. Tips: Follow *Writer's Digest* manuscript mechanics. Writer's guidelines: #10 SASE. Sample copy: $3.50.

NATIONAL BOYCOTT NEWS. 6506 28th Ave. NE. Seattle, WA 98115.
(206) 523-0421. Submissions Editor: Todd Putnam. Type: consumer, public interest, news, politics, economics, social/sociology. Frequency of publication: irregular. Circulation: 7000+. Number of manuscripts accepted per year: n/i. Payment negotiable and in copies.

Editorial Needs. Nonfiction—business/government, social change, consumerism, alternative economics. **Forms:** book excerpts (200-2000 words); book reviews (200-2000 words); cartoons; columns; entertainment reviews (movies on issues of corporate power, social control; 200-2000 words); features (corporate irresponsibility; 200-2000 words); fillers (corporate irresponsibility; 50-200 words); interview/profile (consumerism, boycotts, social change, alternative economics; 1000-3000 words); photo feature (boycotts, bumper stickers, corporate irresponsibility, social commentary; any length).

Initial Contact. Article proposal with subject outline. SASE required.

Acceptance Policies. Byline given: yes. Publishing rights: negotiable. Payment made: in copies; some cash payments may be negotiable. Response time to initial inquiry: 2-3 weeks. Average time until publication: 4 months. Simultaneous submissions: yes. Disk submissions: PC.

Photography Submissions. Format and film: black-and-white prints. Photographs should include: captions; identification of subjects. **Payment:** negotiable. Photographic rights: negotiable.

Additional Information. Our focus is consumer empowerment and responsiblity and the use of economic power as political power. Tips: Nothing preachy. Fair, even-handed coverage. Opinions okay. Writer's guidelines: yes. Sample copy: $3.50 or request with intial contact.

NORTHWEST ETHNIC NEWS. 144 NE 54th St., #6. Seattle, WA 98105.
(206) 522-2188. Fax: (206) 762-7932. Submissions Editor: Kent Chadwick. Type: ethnic news, arts, features, reviews, and poetry. Frequency of publication: monthly. Circulation: n/i. Number of manuscripts accepted per year: 50. Payment in copies and subscription.

Editorial Needs. Nonfiction—ethnic news, arts, history. **Forms:** book excerpts (1000 words); book reviews (1000 words); columns (1000 words); entertaiment/reviews (1000 words); essays (1000-2000 words); features (1000-2000 words); fillers (500 words); interview/profile (people involved with the news, arts, etc.; 1000 words); poetry (any length).

Initial Contact. Query letter only, or phone. Give your background and reason for interest in our publication. SASE required.

Acceptance Policies. Byline given: yes. Publishing rights: first North American serial rights. Payment made: in copies and subscription. Response time to initial inquiry: 1 month. Average time until publication: 2 months. Submit seasonal material 2 months in advance. Simultaneous submissions: inform us. Disk submissions: MS DOS, ASCII, Macintosh Word, Macwrite.

Photography Submissions. Format and film: 3x5 black-and-white prints. Photographs should include: captions; model releases; identification of subjects. **Payment**: $5 per photo. Photographic rights: first publication rights.

Additional Information. We are a multicultural advocate covering all the communities and cultures of the Northwest. Tips: Call and discuss your article idea. Writer's guidelines: none. Sample copy: $1.

NORTHWEST MAGAZINE. 1320 SW Broadway. Portland, OR 97201.

(503) 221-8228. Fax: (503) 227-5306. Submissions Editors: Ellen Heltzel (cover stories); Kevin Murphy (health and fitness); Barry Johnson (profiles, humor); Beth Erickson (food, home). Type: Sunday supplement of *The Sunday Oregonian*; contemporary life in the Northwest. Frequency of publication: weekly. Circulation: 400,000. Number of manuscripts accepted per year: 200. Payment offered.

Editorial Needs. Nonfiction—regional. **Forms**: features (lifestyle; 1000-2000 words; $250-$500); features (regional issues; 3000 words); interview/profile (movers and shakers; 2000-3000 words; up to $800); photo feature ($175 per piece).

Initial Contact. Query letter first has the best chance of a quick response. SASE required.

Acceptance Policies. Byline given: yes. Publishing rights: first North American serial rights. Payment made: upon acceptance. Response time to initial inquiry: 2-4 weeks. Average time until publication: 2-4 months. Submit seasonal material 3 months in advance. Simultaneous submissions: as long as they're not in Oregon and Washington. Disk submissions: contact us for procedure.

Photography Submissions. Format and film: color transparencies; see our guidelines for specifics. Photographs should include: captions; model releases; identification of subjects. **Payment**: $75-$500. Photographic rights: included with article unless for files.

Additional Information. You should assume a fairly sophisticated audience and write with substance, high quality, and in a contemporary style. Tips: We are looking for stories that entertain and inform by combining fiction techniques and journalistic acumen. Writer's guidelines: upon request. Sample copy: upon request.

NORTHWEST REVIEW. 369 PLC. University of Oregon. Eugene, OR 97403.

Submissions Editors: John Witte (poetry); Cecelia Hagen (fiction). Type: literary and arts. Frequency of publication: 3 times per year. Circulation: 1150. Number of manuscripts accepted per year: 80. Payment in copies.

Editorial Needs. Fiction—Afro-American; avant-garde/experimental; contemporary/modern; ethnic; general; handicapped; Hispanic; Latin American; literary; Native American; women's issues; all serious literature. **Forms**: short stories (40 pages maximum).

Nonfiction—contemporary literature. **Forms**: book reviews (3-5 pages); columns (3-15 pages); essays (5-25 pages); interview profile (10-15 pages); poetry (1-40 pages).

Initial Contact. Entire article. SASE required.

Acceptance Policies. Byline given: yes. Publishing rights: first North American serial rights. Payment made: 3 copies. Response time to initial inquiry: 10 weeks. Average time until publication: 2-3 months. Simultaneous submissions: no. Disk submissions: WordPerfect after acceptance.

Additional Information. Tips: Familiarize yourself with a sample copy. Persist. Writer's guidelines: SASE. Sample copy: $3.

NORTHWEST TRAVEL. (Also publishes *Oregon Coast* and *Oregon Coast Getaway Guide*.) PO Box 18000. Florence, OR 97439. 1-800-727-8401. Fax: (503) 997-1124. Submissions Editors: Dave Peden (correspondence, queries, submissions); Judy Fleagle (articles). Type: regional. Frequency of publication: every other month. Circulation: 40,000. Number of manuscripts accepted per year: 60+. Payment and copies offered.

Editorial Needs. Nonfiction—Northwest topics. **Forms:** book reviews; features (travel, profiles, historical, nature; 1200-2000 words; $100-$250); fillers (brief historical items, short travel notes; $50-$75); interview/profile (interesting people working in the Northwest; 1200-2000 words; $100-$250).

Initial Contact. Query letter only. Include clips. SASE required.

Acceptance Policies. Byline given: yes. Publishing rights: one-time rights. Payment made: upon publication. Kill fee: 1/3 for assigned articles. Expenses: no. Response time to initial inquiry: 3-4 weeks. Average time until publication: 3-4 months. Submit seasonal material 6 months in advance. Simultaneous submissions: no. Disk submissions: ASCII accompanied by hard copy.

Photography Submissions. Format and film: 35mm color slides or larger. Photographs should include: captions; model releases (if necessary); identification of subjects; credit. **Payment:** $150 cover; $50 full-page; $100 calendar. Photographic rights: one-time rights only.

Additional Information. If the article does not pertain to the Pacific Northwest, it will be returned. Tips: Study a copy of our older publication, *Oregon Coast*. Writer's guidelines: SASE. Sample copy: $3.50.

NORWESTING. PO Box 1027. Edmonds, WA 98020. (206) 776-3138. Submissions Editor: Thomas F. Kincaid. Type: recreational boating. Frequency of publication: monthly. Circulation: 11,000. Number of manuscripts accepted per year: 30. Payment offered.

Editorial Needs. Nonfiction—recreational boating. **Forms:** cartoons ($25); columns (1000 words; $100); features ($100); interview/profile (1000-2000 words; $100); photo feature (1000-2000 words; $100).

Initial Contact. Query letter only. SASE required.

Acceptance Policies. Byline given: yes. Publishing rights: first North American serial rights. Payment made: upon publication. Kill fee: no. Expenses: no. Response time to initial inquiry: 30 days. Average time until publication: 90 days. Submit seasonal material 3 months in advance. Simultaneous submissions: no. Disk submissions: ASCII.

Photography Submissions. Format and film: any size prints. Photographs should include: captions; identification of subjects. **Payment:** $75. Photographic rights: same as article.

Additional Information. Strong Northwest bias. Writer's guidelines: upon request. Sample copy: write or call.

OLD OREGON. 101 Chapman Hall. University of Oregon. Eugene, OR 97403. (503) 346-5047. Fax: (503) 346-2537. Submissions Editors: Tom Hager; Mike Lee, associate editor (University-related news and features). Type: alumni magazine. Frequency of publication: quarterly. Circulation: 90,000. Number of manuscripts accepted per year: 8. Payment offered.

Editorial Needs. Nonfiction—University of Oregon-related articles. **Forms:** features (related research; 2500 words; $.10 per word); interview/profile (alumni, professors; 1500 words; $.10 per word); photo feature (campus; payment varies).

Initial Contact. Article proposal with subject outline. SASE required.

Acceptance Policies. Byline given: yes. Publishing rights: first rights; second serial rights. Payment made: upon publication. Kill fee: 33% of contract. Expenses: yes. Response time to initial inquiry: 30 days. Average time until publication: 60 days. Submit seasonal material 4 months in advance. Simultaneous submissions: if sent to non-Oregon publications. Disk submissions: IBM or Macintosh only; ASCII.

Photography Submissions. Format and film: contact sheets. Photographs should include: captions; identification of subjects. **Payment:** varies. Photographic rights: one-time rights.

Additional Information. Writer's guidelines: upon request. Sample copy: upon request.

PACIFIC FISHING. 1515 NW 51st. Seattle, WA 98107. (206) 789-5333. Fax: (206) 784-5545. Submissions Editor: Steve Shapiro. Type: trade and commercial fishing on Pacific Coast of United States and Canada. Frequency of publication: monthly. Circulation: 10,000. Number of manuscripts accepted per year: 50. Payment offered.

Editorial Needs. Nonfiction—trade and commercial fishing. **Forms:** columns (first-person anecdotes; 500-700 words; $100); features (technical how-to, economics of the industry, in-depth analysis of issues affecting industry; 2000-3000 words; $.10-$.15 per word); industry news (500-1500 words; $.15 per word); interview/profile (fishermen, processor, or company); photo feature.

Initial Contact. Query letter and article proposal with subject outline. SASE required.

Acceptance Policies. Byline given: yes. Publishing rights: first North American serial rights. Payment made: upon publication. Kill fee: $50. Expenses: sometimes. Response time to initial inquiry: 2-4 weeks. Average time until publication: 1-2 months. Simultaneous submissions: no. Disk submissions: no.

Photography Submissions. Format and film: prefer 35mm color slides. Photographs should include: captions; identification of subjects. **Payment:** Varies from $10 to $150 (cover). Photographic rights: one-time rights.

Additional Information. Our audience is primarily commercial fishermen from San Diego to Alaska and secondarily seafood processors, distributors, and brokers. Tips: Good quality photos will often sway us towards acceptance. Read the magazine and be familiar with West Coast fishing. Writer's guidelines: upon request. Sample copy: SASE.

PACIFIC NORTHWEST MAGAZINE. 701 Dexter Ave. N., Ste. 101. Seattle, WA 98109. (206) 284-1750. Fax: (206) 284-2550. Submissions Editors: Jo Brown (travel); John Doerper (food, wine, and dining out); Kate Roosevelt (outdoor recreation, events). Type: regional consumer magazine. Frequency of publication: monthly. Circulation: 100,000. Number of manuscripts accepted per year: 60+. Payment offered.

Editorial Needs. Nonfiction—regional. **Forms:** features (2000 words maximum; $350+); interview/profile (regional newsmakers; 1500 words; $350+).

Initial Contact. Query letter only. SASE required.

Acceptance Policies. Byline given: yes. Publishing rights: first North American serial rights. Payment made: upon publication. Kill fee: 30%. Expenses: per contract. Response time to initial inquiry: 3 weeks. Average time until publication: 4 months. Submit seasonal material 6-8 months in advance. Simultaneous submissions: inform us in query letter. Disk submissions: WordPerfect.

Photography Submissions. Send sample of work to art director. **Payment:** $150+. Photographic rights: first North American serial rights.

Additional Information. We cover Washington, Oregon, Idaho, Western Montana, Northern California, Alaska, and British Columbia. Tips: We are now looking for material beyond the I-5 corridor. Writer's guidelines: upon request. Sample copy: $4.

PALOUSE JOURNAL. PO Box 9362. Moscow, ID 83843. (208) 882-0888.
Submissions Editors: Phil Druker, Ed Hughes. Type: Northwest, Northwest interior. Frequency of publication: 5 times per year. Circulation: 11,000. Number of manuscripts accepted per year: many. Payment offered.

Editorial Needs. Fiction—regional. **Forms:** short stories (2000 words maximum; $75).

Nonfiction—regional. **Forms:** book reviews (150 words; $10); cartoons ($20); entertainment/reviews (700 words; $35); features (Inland Northwest; 1500 words; $100); interview/profile (1400 words; $75).

Initial Contact. Query letter and article proposal with subject outline. SASE required.

Acceptance Policies. Byline given: yes. Publishing rights: first North American serial rights. Payment made: upon publication. Kill fee: no. Expenses: no. Response time to initial inquiry: 2-4 weeks. Average time until publication: 2 months. Submit seasonal material 3 months in advance. Simultaneous submissions: yes. Disk submissions: DOS; WordPerfect 4.2. Include hard copy.

Photography Submissions. Format and film: any size black-and-white or color prints. Photographs should include: identification of subjects. **Payment:** $25; generally included with article payment. Photographic rights: one-time rights.

Additional Information. This is a regional magazine. We cover Eastern Washington; Northern Idaho, and Western Montana only. Tips: Don't send it if it doesn't deal with our region. Writer's guidelines: SASE. Sample copy: $2.

PARSLEY, SAGE AND TIME. 1931 First Ave. Seattle, WA 98103. (206)
728-2773. Submissions Editor: Constance Pedersen. Type: issues for senior citizens. Frequency of publication: monthly. Circulation: n/i. Number of manuscripts accepted per year: n/i. No payment offered.

Editorial Needs. Fiction—seniors. **Forms:** short stories (100-300 words).

Nonfiction—seniors. **Forms:** cartoons (1-3 panels); poetry (any subject; 50-100 words).

Initial Contact. Entire submission. SASE required.

Acceptance Policies. Byline given: yes. Publishing rights: none. Payment made: none. Response time to initial inquiry: 1-2 months. Average time until publication: 1 month. Submit seasonal material 1 month in advance. Simultaneous submissions: n/i. Disk submissions: inquire.

Photography Submissions. Format and film: black-and-white prints. Photographs should include: identification of subjects. **Payment:** none. Photographic rights: none.

Additional Information. We are a nonprofit corporation working to assist homeless and low-income seniors in downtown Seattle. Tips: Be sensitive to the issues of the homeless and the low-income as they apply to the elderly. Writer's guidelines: none. Sample copy: upon request.

PERCEPTIONS. 1317 Johnson. Missoula, MT 59801. Submissions Editor: Temi
Rose. Type: women's, literary. Frequency of publication: 3 times per year. Circulation: 100. Number of manuscripts accepted per year: varies. Payment in copies.

Editorial Needs. Fiction—we rarely print fiction because of space limitions.

Nonfiction—any subject. **Forms:** poetry (1-2 pages).

Initial Contact. Query letter with poems. SASE required.

Acceptance Policies. Byline given: yes. Publishing rights: none. Payment made: 1 copy. Response time to initial inquiry: 1-2 months. Average time until publication: varies. Simultaneous submissions: yes. Disk submissions: yes.

Additional Information. We publish mostly poetry, mostly by women. Always interested in personal perspectives. Writer's guidelines: upon request. Sample copy: $3.

PERMAFROST. Department of English. University of Alaska. Fairbanks, AK 99775-0640. (907) 474-5237. Submissions Editors: Dave Howell, Karen Sylte. Type: literary. Frequency of publication: 2 times per year. Circulation: 500. Number of manuscripts accepted per year: 50. Payment in copies.

Editorial Needs. Fiction—Afro-American; avant-garde/experimental; contemporary/modern; erotica; ethnic; folklore; handicapped; Hispanic; historical; Latin American; literary; Native American; new age; science fiction; sports; women's issues; working people. **Forms:** book excerpts; novellas; plays. Length is 7500 words in all forms.

Nonfiction—any subject. **Forms:** creative nonfiction (7500 words); essays (7500 words); poetry (no epics).

Initial Contact. Entire article. SASE required.

Acceptance Policies. Byline given: yes. Publishing rights: rights revert to author upon publication. Payment made: 2 copies. Response time to initial inquiry: 1-3 months. Average time until publication: 4-6 months. Simultaneous submissions: yes. Disk submissions: no.

Photography Submissions. Format and film: black-and-white prints. Photographs should include: identification of subjects. **Payment:** copies. Photographic rights: revert to author upon publication.

Additional Information. We print high-quality literary material only—fiction, poetry, creative nonfiction. Tips: Send your best work. We are not looking specifically for Alaskan topics. Writer's guidelines: SASE. Sample copy: $4.

POETIC SPACE: POETRY AND FICTION. PO Box 11157. Eugene, OR 97440. Submissions Editor: Don Hildenbrand. Type: literary. Frequency of publication: quarterly. Circulation: 600. Number of manuscripts accepted per year: 10%. Payment in copies.

Editorial Needs. Fiction—Afro-American; avant-garde/experimental; contemporary/modern; erotica; ethnic; handicapped; Hispanic; Latin American; literary; Native American. **Forms:** short stories (1500 words).

Nonfiction—literary. **Forms:** book reviews (poetry, fiction; 600-800 words); interview/profile (writers; 500-600 words); poetry (contemporary; short to medium length); art (black-and-white drawings as illustrations).

Initial Contact. Entire article. SASE required.

Acceptance Policies. Byline given: yes. Publishing rights: one-time anthology rights. Payment made: 1 copy. Response time to initial inquiry: 1-3 months. Average time until publication: 1-3 months. Simultaneous submissions: no. Disk submissions: no.

Additional Information. We accept black-and-white drawings. Tips: Send us clean, typed copy with your name and address on every page. Writer's guidelines: SASE. Sample copy: $3, SASE.

POETS. PAINTERS. COMPOSERS. 10254 35th Ave. SW. Seattle, WA 98146. (206) 937-8155. Submissions Editors: Carl Diltz; Jim Andrews (poetry and audio). Type: literary. Frequency of publication: yearly. Circulation: 300. Number of manuscripts accepted per year: 50. Payment in copies.

Editorial Needs. Nonfiction—any subject. **Forms:** book reviews (500-2000 words); essays (1000-3000 words); poetry (any length).

Initial Contact. Entire article. SASE required.

Acceptance Policies. Byline given: yes. Publishing rights: first rights. Payment made: in copies. Response time to initial inquiry: 2 weeks. Average time until publication: depends on project. Simultaneous submissions: no. Disk submissions: Macintosh.

Photography Submissions. Format and film: black-and-white prints. Photographs should include: captions. **Payment:** copies. Photographic rights: one-time use.

Additional Information. Writer's guidelines: none. Sample copy: see publication in library at better universities.

PORTABLE WALL, THE. 215 Burlington. Billings, MT 59101. (406) 256-3588. Submissions Editor: Daniel R. Strockman. Type: literary. Frequency of publication: 2 times per year. Circulation: 200. Number of manuscripts accepted per year: 100. Payment in copies.

Editorial Needs. Fiction—avant-garde/experimental; contemporary/modern; folklore; general; literary; Native American; women's issues; working people. **Forms:** book excerpts (250-500 words); short stories (500-1000 words).

Nonfiction—any subject. **Forms:** book reviews (500 words maximum); cartoons; essays (1000 words); features (1500 words); poetry (any length).

Initial Contact. Article proposal with subject outline. SASE required.

Acceptance Policies. Byline given: yes. Publishing rights: first rights. Payment made: in copies. Response time to initial inquiry: 2 weeks. Average time until publication: 1 year. Submit seasonal material 12 months in advance. Simultaneous submissions: no. Disk submissions: no.

Additional Information. This is a small magazine striving for high quality in its execution. Tips: Be brief. Writer's guidelines: none. Sample copy: $5.

PORTLAND FAMILY CALENDAR. 600 NW 14th Ave. Portland, OR 97209. (503) 226-8335. Submissions Editor: Peggy J. Coquet. Type: family health, children's crafts, reviews (book, tape, video). Frequency of publication: monthly. Circulation: 14,000. Number of manuscripts accepted per year: 12+. Payment offered.

Editorial Needs. Nonfiction—family-related subjects. **Forms:** book reviews (parenting, children's, family; 500 words; $20); columns (family health, safety, crafts, how-to's; 500 words; $30); features (local resources, parenting; 750 words; $30); interview/profile (local authors, parenting authorities; 500-750 words; $30).

Initial Contact. Query letter only. SASE required.

Acceptance Policies. Byline given: yes. Publishing rights: one-time rights. Payment made: upon publication. Kill fee: no. Expenses: no. Response time to initial inquiry: 30 days. Average time until publication: 30-60 days. Submit seasonal material 3 months in advance. Simultaneous submissions: outside Portland metro area. Disk submissions: MS DOS; ASCII.

Photography Submissions. Format and film: 3x4 or larger black-and-white prints. Photographs should include: captions; identification of subjects. **Payment:** $10. Photographic rights: first rights.

Additional Information. This Portland metro area parenting magazine offers resources and activities for families. Tips: Be concrete and factual; offer useful information; shorter is better. Writer's guidelines: none. Sample copy: call or write.

PORTLAND REVIEW, THE. PO Box 751. Portland, OR 97207. (503) 725-4533. Submissions Editor: Max Provino. Type: literary. Frequency of publication: 3 times per year. Circulation: 400. Number of manuscripts accepted per year: 1500. Payment in copies.

Editorial Needs. Fiction—Afro-American; avant-garde/experimental; contemporary/modern; fantasy; folklore; handicapped; Hispanic; historical; humor; Latin American; literary; Native American; new age; romance; science fiction; women's issues. **Forms:** book excerpts; novellas; plays; serialized fiction; short stories. Length is 2500 words maximum for all forms.

Nonfiction—literary. **Forms:** cartoons; essays (5 pages); photo features; photos/art work; poetry.

Initial Contact. Entire article. Include bio. SASE required.

Acceptance Policies. Byline given: yes. Publishing rights: none. Payment made: in copies. Response time to initial inquiry: 2 months. Average time until publication: 1 1/2 months. Simultaneous submissions: yes. Disk submissions: Macintosh.

Photography Submissions. Format and film: send appropriate size prints for a 9x12 magazine; contact sheets. Photographs should include: name of photographer and permission to use. **Payment:** copies. Photographic rights: none.

Additional Information. We are looking for creative perspectives and signs of life, intelligence, and thought to provoke our readers. Writer's guidelines: SASE (with submission). Sample copy: $5.

PRINTER'S DEVIL, THE. PO Box 66. Harrison, ID 83833-0066. (208) 689-3738. Submissions Editor: Joe M. Singer (poet-in-residence for Mother of Ashes Press handles all editorial duties). Type: graphic arts for the small press (publishing and printing). Frequency of publication: 3 times per year. Circulation: 200+. Number of manuscripts accepted per year: 30. Payment in copies.

Editorial Needs. Nonfiction—graphic arts; publishing. **Forms:** book reviews (100-1000 words); cartoons; columns (by invitation only); essays (1000-5000 words); interview/profile; fillers (100 words); photo feature.

Initial Contact. Article proposal with subject outline or entire article. SASE required.

Acceptance Policies. Byline given: yes. Publishing rights: prefer first use but will reprint exceptional material. Payment made: in copies. Response time to initial inquiry: 2-3 weeks. Average time until publication: within 4 months. Simultaneous submissions: inform us. Disk submissions: no.

Photography Submissions. Format and film: contact sheets. Photographs should include: identification of subjects. **Payment:** copies. Photographic rights: one-time use.

Additional Information. This is a practical how-to journal for small press publishers. Tips: Know something about graphic arts for the small press. Writer's guidelines: #10 SASE. Sample copy: $2.

PROWOMAN MAGAZINE. PO Box 6957. Portland, OR 97228-6957. (503) 221-1298. Submissions Editor: Judy Henderson. Type: women's professional issues, health and fitness, arts and entertainment. Frequency of publication: every other month. Circulation: 15,000. Number of manuscripts accepted per year: n/i. Payment in copies and perks.

Editorial Needs. Nonfiction—women's issues. **Forms:** book excerpts (skills for professional women; 1500-2000 words); essays (women's rights, opportunities, economic equity, political, community issues in Oregon; 1000-2000 words); features (issues, health, arts, careers; 1000-2000 words); interview/profile (successful women; 1000-2000 words).

Initial Contact. Query letter or article proposal with subject outline. SASE required.

Acceptance Policies. Byline given: yes. Publishing rights: first North American serial rights. Payment made: in copies and subscriptions or tickets to arts events. Response time to initial inquiry: 2-3 weeks. Average time until publication: 2-4 months. Submit seasonal material 4 months in advance. Simultaneous submissions: noncompeting region. Disk submissions: DOS preferred; Macintosh okay.

Photography Submissions. Format and film: black-and-white or color contact sheets. Photographs should include: captions; model releases; identification of subjects. **Payment:** varies. Photographic rights: first-time rights.

Additional Information. We are feminist oriented for well-educated, involved women. Tips: Write a short, interesting query. Know our Oregon subjects of interest. Writer's guidelines: SASE. Sample copy: $5.

PULPHOUSE: A WEEKLY MAGAZINE. PO Box 1227. Eugene, OR 97440. (503) 344-6742. Submissions Editor: Dean Wesley Smith. Type: slick science fiction, fantasy, and horror fiction publication. Frequency of publication: weekly. Circulation: n/i. Number of manuscripts accepted per year: 50+. Payment offered.

Editorial Needs. Fiction—avant-garde/experimental; contemporary/modern; fantasy; folklore; horror; literary; mainstream; suspense. **Forms:** novellas (length varies; payment negotiable); serialized fiction; short stories (7500 words; $.03-$.06 per word).

Nonfiction—science fiction; fantasy; horror fiction. **Forms:** book reviews (payment negotiable); columns (assigned); essays (any subject; 3000-5000 words; $.03-$.06 per word); interview/profile (writers; 3000-5000 words; $.03-$.06 per word).

Initial Contact. Query letter only for nonfiction; entire article for fiction. SASE required.

Acceptance Policies. Byline given: yes. Publishing rights: first North American serial rights. Payment made: upon acceptance. Kill fee: no. Expenses: no. Response time to initial inquiry: 1 month. Average time until publication: n/i. Submit seasonal material 6 months in advance. Simultaneous submissions: no. Disk submissions: no.

Photography Submissions. We only use portraits of writers. Format and film: black-and-white contact sheets. Photographs should include: model releases. **Payment:** $100 for cover. Photographic rights: one-time use.

Additional Information. Tips: Be familiar with the publication. Writer's guidelines: upon request. Sample copy: $3.

RHYME TIME. PO Box 1870. Hayden, ID 83835. (208) 772-6184. Submissions Editor: Linda Hutton. Type: poetry. Frequency of publication: every other month. Circulation: n/i. Number of manuscripts accepted per year: n/i. Payment in copies.

Editorial Needs. Nonfiction—any subject. **Forms:** poetry (rhymed preferred; 16 lines maximum).

Initial Contact. Entire submission. #10 SASE required.

Acceptance Policies. Byline given: yes. Publishing rights: revert to author upon publication. Payment made: 1 copy. Response time to initial inquiry: 2-3 weeks. Average time until publication: 2-4 months. Simultaneous submissions: yes. Disk submissions: no.

Photography Submissions. Illustrations are welcome.

Additional Information. We do not use haiku, avant-garde, or sugary poetry. Tips: Rhyme and meter must be consistent. Follow our guidelines. Writer's guidelines: SASE. Sample copy: #10 SASE, 2 first class stamps.

Rocky Mountain Game & Fish *see* **WASHINGTON-OREGON GAME & FISH.**

RURALITE. PO Box 558. Forest Grove, OR 97116. (503) 357-2105. Fax: (503) 365-8615. Submissions Editor: R. O'Dell. Type: general interest, Northwest region. Frequency of publication: monthly. Circulation: 260,000. Number of manuscripts accepted per year: 30+. Payment offered.

Editorial Needs. Nonfiction—regional; general interest. **Forms:** cartoons; essays; features (Northwest activities, travel locations, unique personalities, current issues vital to Northwest; 1800 words; $100-$400); photo feature (Northwest locations, current issues).

Initial Contact. Query letter only. SASE required.

Acceptance Policies. Byline given: yes. Publishing rights: first North American serial rights; one-time rights; work-for-hire assignments. Payment made: upon acceptance. Kill fee: yes. Expenses: no. Response time to initial inquiry: 3-4 weeks. Average time until publication: 1-6 months. Submit seasonal material 3-6 months in advance. Simultaneous submissions: no. Disk submissions: IBM or Macintosh.

Photography Submissions. Format and film: any size prints; contact sheets; transparencies. Photographs should include: captions; model releases; identification of subjects. **Payment:** $25-$400. Photographic rights: all.

Additional Information. We have a strong Northwest orientation with a focus on electric or energy issues. Writer's guidelines: upon request. Sample copy: $1, SASE.

SEA KAYAKER. 6327 Seaview Ave. NW. Seattle, WA 98107. (206) 789-1326. Fax: (206) 789-6392. Submissions Editors: Christopher Cunningham, editor; Deborah Davis, associate editor. Type: sea kayaking. Frequency of publication: quarterly. Circulation: n/i. Number of manuscripts accepted per year: 40. Payment offered.

Editorial Needs. Fiction—relating to sea kayaking.

Nonfiction—sea kayaking. **Forms:** book excerpts (1000-2000 words); book reviews (videos also; 2000-4000 words); cartoons; columns (2000-4000 words); essays (2000-4000 words). Payment is $.05-$.10 per word for all forms.

Initial Contact. Article proposal with subject outline. SASE required.

Acceptance Policies. Byline given: yes. Publishing rights: first North American serial rights. Payment made: upon publication. Kill fee: 10%. Expenses: yes. Response time to initial inquiry: 2 months. Average time until publication: 6 months. Submit seasonal material 6 months in advance. Simultaneous submissions: inform us. Disk submissions: Macintosh; Microsoft Word.

Photography Submissions. Format and film: any size black-and-white or color prints; transparencies. Photographs should include: captions; identification of subjects. **Payment:** $15-$50. Photographic rights: first North American serial rights.

Additional Information. Tips: We look for clear writing and technical accuracy on all topics related to sea kayaking. Writer's guidelines: SASE. Sample copy: call with Visa or Mastercard, or send check for $4.60.

SEATTLE REVIEW, THE. Padelford Hall, GN-30. University of Washington. Seattle, WA 98195. (206) 543-9865. Submissions Editors: Charles Johnson (fiction); Colleen McElroy (poetry); Irene Wanner (essays and interviews). Type: literary. Frequency of publication: 2 times per year. Circulation: 800. Number of manuscripts accepted per year: varies. Payment offered.

Editorial Needs. Fiction—Afro-American; contemporary/modern; ethnic; folklore; handicapped; humor; Latin American; literary; science fiction; women's issues; working people. **Forms:** book excerpts; plays; short stories. Length is 20 pages maximum and payment varies for all forms.

Nonfiction—literary. **Forms:** essays (craft of writing); features (occasional folktales); interview/profile (Northwest writers); poetry; artwork (must reproduce well in black and white). Length is 20 pages maximum and payment varies for all forms.

Initial Contact. Entire article with brief cover letter. SASE required.

Acceptance Policies. Byline given: yes. Publishing rights: one-time rights. Payment made: upon publication. Response time to initial inquiry: 3-4 months. Average time until publication: 3-12 months. Submit seasonal material 6 months in advance. Simultaneous submissions: writer must notify us of acceptance immediately. Disk submissions: no.

Photography Submissions. Format and film: 3x5 black-and-white prints; transparencies. Photographs should include: captions; identification of subjects. **Payment:** varies. Photographic rights: one-time rights.

Additional Information. Editors have a wide variety of interests and are looking first at the quality of the writing. Tips: Send clear, double-spaced copy only. Writer's guidelines: upon request. Sample copy: $3.

SEATTLE WEEKLY. 1931 Second Ave. Seattle, WA 98101. (206) 441-5555. Fax: (206) 441-6213. Submissions Editor: Manuscripts Editor. Type: investigative journalism, political commentary, arts criticism, life and news of the city and the region. Frequency of publication: weekly. Circulation: 35,000. Number of manuscripts accepted per year: n/i. Payment offered.

Editorial Needs. Nonfiction—regional. **Forms:** news stories (Seattle and region; 800-1500 words); features (political commentary, arts; 1500-2000 words); cover stories (3000-5000 words); art criticism (750 words). Payment is $.10 per word for all forms.

Initial Contact. Query letter first. Include short bio and resumé if not previously published by us. SASE required.

Acceptance Policies. Byline given: yes. Publishing rights: first North American serial rights; rights to use stories for promotional purposes in all our publications; all other rights revert back to author. Payment made: upon publication. Kill fee: yes, under certain conditions. Response time to initial inquiry: 3 weeks. Average time until publication: 2-3 months. Submit seasonal material 3 months in advance. Simultaneous submissions: no. Disk submissions: yes, but check with us first.

Photography Submissions. Will be considered, but usually superseded by staff-generated photography.

Additional Information. We look for articles that stem from considerable familiarity with a topic, argue challenging theses, and negotiate complexities with grace. Tips: We only return material with SASE. Writer's guidelines: upon request. Sample copy: $2.

SHAPING THE LANDSCAPE JOURNAL. Alaska State Writing Consortium. Department of Education. PO Box F. Juneau, AK 99811. (907) 465-2841. Submissions Editor: Editor. Type: literary for teacher/writers. Frequency of publication: yearly. Circulation: n/i. Number of manuscripts accepted per year: 30+\-. Payment in copies.

Editorial Needs. Fiction—any subject. **Forms:** short stories.

Nonfiction—any subject. **Forms:** essays; intervew/profile; poetry. Length varies for all forms.

Initial Contact. Entire article. Include where your Alaska teaching assignment is located. SASE required.

Acceptance Policies. Byline given: yes. Publishing rights: one-time rights. Payment made: 1 copy. Response time to initial inquiry: 1 week. Average time until publication: next annual issue. Simultaneous submissions: no. Disk submissions: Macintosh compatible.

Additional Information. This is a journal for Alaskan teacher/writers. Writer's guidelines: none. Sample copy: $5.

SIGN OF THE TIMES, A CHRONICLE OF DECADENCE IN THE ATOMIC AGE. 3819 NE 15th. Portland, OR 97212. (206) 323-6764. Submissions Editor: Mark Souder. Type: avant-garde, controversial. Frequency of publication: 2 times per year. Circulation: 1000. Number of manuscripts accepted per year: 20. Payment in copies.

Editorial Needs. Fiction—avant-garde/experimental; erotica; gay/lesbian. **Forms:** plays (500-2500 words); short stories (500-2500 words).

Nonfiction—avant-garde; controversial. **Forms:** cartoons (humor, decadence); essays (humor, decadence; 500-2500 words); photo feature (decadence).

Initial Contact. Entire article. SASE required.

Acceptance Policies. Byline given: yes. Publishing rights: first North American serial rights; anthology rights. Payment made: in copies. Response time to initial inquiry: 8 weeks. Average time until publication: 3 months. Submit seasonal material 12 months in advance. Simultaneous submissions: no. Disk submissions: IBM PC or Macintosh.

Photography Submissions. Format and film: 5x7 or 8x10 black-and-white prints. Photographs should include: captions. **Payment:** copies. Photographic rights: first rights; anthology rights.

Additional Information. Stories should be short enough for quality bathroom reading. Tips: Write what you know. Writer's guidelines: SASE. Sample copy: $4.

SIGNPOST FOR NORTHWEST TRAILS. 1305 Fourth Ave., #512. Seattle, WA 98101. (206) 625-1367. Submissions Editor: Ann Marshall. Type: sports, recreation, health and fitness. Frequency of publication: monthly. Circulation: 3000. Number of manuscripts accepted per year: 12-20. Payment and copies offered.

Editorial Needs. Nonfiction—sports; recreation; health and fitness. **Forms:** book excerpts (hiking guides, nature study, personal experience; 500-1500 words); book reviews (climbing, personal experiences, hiking, skiing, world travel, nature study; 100-300 words); essays (philosophy of outdoors management of public lands, land use; 500-1500 words); features (backcountry experiences, new equipment, safety, minimum impact; 500-2000 words; $10-$25); fillers (equipment reviews, recipes, wilderness travel hints).

Initial Contact. Entire article. SASE required.

Acceptance Policies. Byline given: yes. Publishing rights: first North American serial rights; second serial rights; one-time rights. Payment made: upon publication. Most of our material is written and donated to us by subscribers. We do buy freelance manuscripts but pay only $10-$25 and copies. Response time to initial inquiry: 2-8 weeks. Average time until publication: 1-12 months. Submit seasonal material 6-12 months in advance. Simultaneous submissions: yes. Disk submissions: no.

Photography Submissions. Format and film: 5x7 (minimum) black-and-white glossy prints. Photographs should include: captions; identification of subjects. **Payment**: copies; $25 cover photo. Photographic rights: one-time use.

Additional Information. We focus on non-motorized, backcountry recreation, primarily in the Pacifc Northwest, but also cover any areas of the world of interest to our readers. Tips: Familiarity with our informal, conversational style would help an author "fit in." Remember our focus. Get a sample copy of our magazine. Writer's guidelines: SASE. Sample copy: call or write.

SIGNS OF THE TIMES. PO Box 7000. Boise, ID. (208) 465-2577. Fax: (208) 465-2531. Submissions Editor: send to editor. Type: devotional. Frequency of publication: monthly. Circulation: 285,000. Number of manuscripts accepted per year: 50. Payment offered.

Editorial Needs. Nonfiction—Christian focus. **Forms:** columns (today's issues; 700 words; $150); features (of spiritual or inspirational value; 2000 words; $300).

Initial Contact. Entire article. SASE required.

Acceptance Policies. Byline given: yes. Publishing rights: first North American serial rights; first rights; second serial rights. Payment made: upon acceptance. Kill fee: $100. Expenses: yes. Response time to initial inquiry: 2 weeks. Average time until publication: 4-6 months. Submit seasonal material 6 months in advance. Simultaneous submissions: yes. Disk submissions: no.

Additional Information. We are a Christian publication seeking to help the general public solve problems by using Biblical principles. Tips: Keep it focused, use anecdotes, try the light touch, and write memorable leads. Writer's guidelines: upon request. Sample copy: large manilla SASE.

SLIGHTLY WEST. The Evergreen State College. CRC 306. Olympia, WA 98505. (206) 866-6000, ext. 6879. Submissions Editor: Editorial Board. Type: college literary arts. Frequency of publication: 2 times per year. Circulation: 2000. Number of manuscripts accepted per year: 3. Payment in copies.

Editorial Needs. Fiction—Afro-American; avant-garde/experimental; contemporary/modern; erotica; ethnic; folklore; general; handicapped; Hispanic; Latin American; literary; Native American. **Forms:** book excerpts; novellas; plays; serialized fiction; short stories. Length is 1-10 pages for all forms.

Nonfiction—literary; general subject matter. **Forms:** book excerpts (literary, work in progress; 1-10 pages); book reviews (1-10 pages); cartoons; essays (literary; 1-10 pages); poetry; photo/art features (single photos reprintable in black and white).

Initial Contact. n/i. SASE required.

Acceptance Policies. Byline given: yes. Publishing rights: rights revert to author. Payment made: in copies, if requested. Response time to initial inquiry: 1 month. Average time until publication: 4-6 weeks. Simultaneous submissions: no. Disk submissions: IBM or Macintosh.

Photography Submissions. Format and film: black-and-white prints to fit in space 7 1/4 x 10 1/2, including white space. Photos can be reduced as long as it does not detract from image. Photographs should include: captions; identification of subjects. **Payment**: copies. Photographic rights: returned to author.

Additional Information. Writer's guidelines: SASE. Sample copy: SASE, $2 postage.

SNAKE RIVER ECHOES. PO Box 244. Rexburg, ID 83440. (208) 356-9101. Submissions Editors: Ralph Thompson, editor; Louis Clements, director. Type: historical. Frequency of publication: annually. Circulation: 1000. Number of manuscripts accepted per year: 20. Payment in copies.

Editorial Needs. Nonfiction—history. **Forms:** book reviews (Idaho history; 5 pages maximum); features (East Idaho history; 5 pages maximum).

Initial Contact. Query letter only, with description of article. SASE required.

Acceptance Policies. Byline given: yes. Publishing rights: none. Payment made: in copies. Response time to initial inquiry: 1 week. Average time until publication: 3 months. Submit seasonal material by April 1. Simultaneous submissions: no. Disk submissions: no.

Additional Information. Writer's guidelines: none. Sample copy: look in the library.

SNAKE RIVER REFLECTIONS. 1863 Bitterroot Dr. Twin Falls, ID 83301-3561. Submissions Editor: Bill White. Type: literary. Frequency of publication: 10 times per year. Circulation: 150-200. Number of manuscripts accepted per year: 50. Payment in copies.

Editorial Needs. Fiction—avant-garde/experimental; contemporary/modern; ethnic; fantasy; folklore; general; holiday; horror; humor; literary; mainstream; mystery; romance; science fiction; suspense; Western; working people. **Forms:** short stories (1500 words maximum).

Nonfiction—on writing. **Forms:** articles (1 page maximum); cartoons; essays (1500 words maximum); features (1500 words maximum); fillers; poetry (30 lines maximum).

Initial Contact. Entire article. Include previous publications and writer's interests. SASE required.

Acceptance Policies. Byline given: yes. Publishing rights: first North American serial rights. Payment made: in copies. Response time to initial inquiry: 3 weeks. Average time until publication: 3-4 weeks. Submit seasonal material 1 month in advance. Simultaneous submissions: no. Disk submissions: IBM compatible, 5 1/4, low density (360K); WordPerfect 4.2 or 5.0.

Additional Information. Writer's guidelines: #10 SASE. Sample copy: SASE, 1 first class stamp.

SNEAK PREVIEW, THE. PO Box 639. Grants Pass, OR 97526. Or 1530 Windsor. Ashland, OR 97520. (503) 482-0368, 474-3044. Submissions Editor: Claire Pennington. Type: literary. Frequency of publication: weekly. Circulation: n/i. Number of manuscripts accepted per year: 15. Payment in copies.

Editorial Needs. Fiction—humor; satire. **Forms:** short stories (500-1000 words).

Nonfiction—general. **Forms:** poetry (short).

Initial Contact. Entire article. SASE required.

Acceptance Policies. Byline given: yes. Publishing rights: one-time rights. Payment made: in copies. Response time to initial inquiry: 2 weeks. Average time until publication: 3 months. Simultaneous submissions: no. Disk submissions: no.

Additional Information. *The Sneak Preview* is a free, local, weekly arts, news, and entertainment publication. Tips: We like light-hearted, humorous pieces and prefer unrhymed poetry. Writer's guidelines: SASE. Sample copy: SASE (manila), $.65 postage.

SPINDRIFT. Shoreline Community College. 16101 Greenwood Ave. N. Seattle, WA 98133. (206) 546-4101. Submissions Editor: C. Orlock, faculty advisor. Type: literary and art. Frequency of publication: yearly. Circulation: 500. Number of manuscripts accepted per year: 30. Payment in copies.

Editorial Needs. Fiction—Afro-American; avant-garde/experimental; contemporary/modern; ethnic; fantasy; folklore; general; handicapped; Hispanic; historical; humor; literary; mainstream; working people. **Forms:** book excerpts (4500 words maximum); short stories (4500 words maximum).

Nonfiction—any subject. **Forms:** book excerpts (4500 words maximum); essays (4500 words maximum).

Initial Contact. Entire article. SASE required.

Acceptance Policies. Byline given: yes. Publishing rights: first North American serial rights. Payment made: 1 copy. Response time to initial inquiry: 6 months. Average time until publication: 3 months. Simultaneous submissions: yes. Disk submissions: no.

Photography Submissions. Format and film: 5x7 or 8x10 black-and-white or color prints. Photographs should include: brief bio of photographer. **Payment:** copies. Photographic rights: one-time use.

Additional Information. Art and literary magazine of Shoreline Community College, publishing writers and artists from the college and elsewhere. Writer's guidelines: SASE. Sample copy: $5.

STYLIST AND SALON. PO Box 1117. Portland, OR 97207-1117. (503) 226-2461. Fax: (503) 226-2461. Submissions Editor: David Porter. Type: trade paper to all salons and shops in the Pacific Northwest. Frequency of publication: monthly. Circulation: 10,000 (Oregon, Idaho); 6500 (Washington). Number of manuscripts accepted per year: 15-25. Payment offered.

Editorial Needs. Nonfiction—salon; fashion. **Forms:** book reviews (200-500 words; payment varies); cartoons ($10-$15); photo feature (any length; payment varies).

Initial Contact. Article proposal with subject outline or entire article. Include black-and white photos, if possible. SASE required.

Acceptance Policies. Byline given: yes. Publishing rights: one-time rights. Payment made: upon publication. Kill fee: yes, if on assignment. Expenses: yes. Response time to initial inquiry: 2-4 weeks. Average time until publication: 1-3 months. Submit seasonal material 3 months in advance. Simultaneous submissions: inform us. Disk submissions: IBM compatible.

Photography Submissions. Format and film: 3x5, 5x7, or 8x10 black-and-white prints (no negatives or transparencies). Photographs should include: captions; model releases; identification of subjects. **Payment:** varies. Photographic rights: first rights.

Additional Information. We are strictly a trade publication for salon owners and employees. Writer's guidelines: none. Sample copy: upon request.

TABLE ROCK SENTINEL. Southern Oregon Historical Society. 106 N. Central Ave. Medford, OR 97501. (503) 773-6536. Fax: (503) 776-7994. Submissions Editor: Natalie Brown. Type: regional, Western, Northwestern history (prefer Southern Oregon and Northern California). Frequency of publication: every other month. Circulation: 2500. Number of manuscripts accepted per year: 15. Payment offered.

Editorial Needs. Nonfiction—regional; Northwestern or Western history. **Forms:** book excerpts ($75-$200); book reviews ($10-$50); features ($75-$200); fillers ($10-$50); photo feature ($75-$200); poetry ($10-$50).

Initial Contact. Query letter and article proposal with subject outline. Include clips and short bio. SASE required.

Acceptance Policies. Byline given: yes. Publishing rights: one-time rights; work-for-hire assignments. Payment made: upon acceptance. Kill fee: no. Expenses: only if we solicit an article. Response time to initial inquiry: 1 month. Average time until publication: varies. Submit seasonal material 6 months in advance. Simultaneous submissions: yes. Disk submissions: no.

Photography Submissions. Format and film: black-and-white prints or negatives. Photographs should include: captions; identification of subjects. **Payment**: $10-$50. Photographic rights: one-time use.

Additional Information. Besides being accurate, stories must be readable. Endnotes required and will be verified. Tips: Query or call for story ideas. Writer's guidelines: call or write. Sample copy: call or write.

TECHNICAL ANALYSIS OF STOCKS AND COMMODITIES.

3517 SW Alaska St. Seattle, WA 98126. (206) 938-0570. Fax: (206) 938-1307. Submissions Editors: Thom Hartle, editor; John Sweeney, technical editor. Type: technical trading of stocks and commodities. Frequency of publication: monthly. Circulation: 25,000. Number of manuscripts accepted per year: 150. Payment offered.

Editorial Needs. **Nonfiction**—how-to articles on technical trading of stocks and commodities. **Forms**: book reviews (investments, trading, computer techniques; 1000 words; $50+); cartoons (investment humor; $10-$50); features (use of technical analysis in trading; 1000-3000 words; $100-$500).

Initial Contact. Article proposal with subject outline or entire article.

Acceptance Policies. Byline given: yes. Publishing rights: all rights; however, second serial (reprint) rights revert to author, provided proper copyright credit is given. Payment made: upon publication. Kill fee: 50%. Expenses: no. Response time to initial inquiry: 3-4 weeks. Average time until publication: 3-6 months. Simultaneous submissions: no. Disk submissions: yes.

Photography Submissions. Format and film: 5x7 black-and-white glossy prints. Photographs should include: captions; model releases; identification of subjects. **Payment**: $20-$150. Photographic rights: one-time and reprint rights.

Additional Information. Describe how to use technical analysis, charting, or computer work in day-to-day trading in stocks and commodities. Tips: Completeness and accuracy are more important than writing style. Writer's guidelines: #10 SASE. Sample copy: $5.

TIMBER/WEST. PO Box 610. Edmonds, WA 98020. (206) 778-3388.

Fax: (206) 771-3623. Submissions Editor: John Nederlee. Type: trade publication for Pacific Northwest and Northern California logging industry. Frequency of publication: monthly. Circulation: 10,000. Number of manuscripts accepted per year: 24. Payment offered.

Editorial Needs. **Nonfiction**—regional logging. **Forms**: features (1500 words; $200); photo feature (1500 words; $200).

Initial Contact. Query letter or phone. SASE required.

Acceptance Policies. Byline given: no. Publishing rights: all rights. Payment made: upon publication. Kill fee: no. Expenses: yes. Response time to initial inquiry: 10 days. Average time until publication: 30-60 days. Simultaneous submissions: no. Disk submissions: Macintosh or IBM PC if program compatible.

Additional Information. Our readers are loggers, log truckers, and forest road builders. Tips: On-the-job field articles about logging or road building in the forest sell. Writer's guidelines: write, fax, phone. Sample copy: phone; write or fax and include one piece of your work.

TRANSFORMATION TIMES. PO Box 425. Beavercreek, OR 97004.
(503) 632-7141. Submissions Editor: Connie Faubel. Type: new age. Frequency of publication: 10 times per year. Circulation: 8000. Number of manuscripts accepted per year: 25. Payment offered.

Editorial Needs. Nonfiction—new age; metaphysical. **Forms:** cartoons ($10); features (1000 words; $.01-$.03 per word); fillers (100-300 words; $.01 per word); interview/profile (1000 words; $.01-$.03 per word).

Initial Contact. Entire article. SASE required.

Acceptance Policies. Byline given: yes. Publishing rights: one-time rights. Payment made: upon publication. Kill fee: no. Expenses: no. Response time to initial inquiry: 2 months. Average time until publication: 1-3 months. Submit seasonal material 2 months in advance. Simultaneous submissions: yes, if submitted outside of Oregon. Disk submissions: IBM 5 1/4 or 3 1/2; WordPerfect.

Photography Submissions. Format and film: black-and-white prints. Photographs should include: captions; identification of subjects. **Payment:** $5-$10. Photographic rights: one-time use.

Additional Information. Our publication is dedicated to expanding awareness of physical, mental, and spiritual resources. Writer's guidelines and sample copy: $1 for both.

VICTORY MUSIC REVIEW. PO Box 7515. Bonney Lake, WA 98390.
(206) 863-6617. Submissions Editor: Chris Lunn. Type: folk, traditional jazz, jazz, old-time dance, string band, bluegrass, and acoustic music. Frequency of publication: monthly. Circulation: 5200. Number of manuscripts accepted per year: n/i. Payment in copies.

Editorial Needs. Nonfiction—music, as described above. **Forms:** entertainment reviews.

Initial Contact. Query letter or call.

Acceptance Policies. Byline given: yes. Publishing rights: one-time rights. Payment made: in copies. Response time to initial inquiry: 2 weeks. Average time until publication: 30-60 days. Simultaneous submissions: yes on reviews; no on cover features. Disk submissions: Macintosh.

Additional Information. Support music for Northwest musicians and songwriters in the areas of folk, jazz, acoustic, blues, etc. Tips: Call us first. Writer's guidelines: call. Sample copy: $1.25 for back issues.

VILLAGE IDIOT, THE. PO Box 66. Harrison, ID 83833-0066. (208) 689-3738.
Submissions Editor: Joe M. Singer. Type: general interest. Frequency of publication: 3 times per year. Circulation: 300. Number of manuscripts accepted per year: n/i. Payment in copies.

Editorial Needs. Nonfiction—general interest. **Forms:** any form.

Initial Contact. Query letter. SASE required.

Acceptance Policies. Byline given: yes. Publishing rights: one-time rights. Payment made: in copies. Response time to initial inquiry: n/i. Average time until publication: n/i. Simultaneous submissions: no. Disk submissions: no.

Photography Submissions. Format and film: black-and-white prints. Photographs should include: captions; model releases; identification of subjects. **Payment:** copies. Photographic rights: one-time rights.

Additional Information. This is a general interest magazine insofar as my interests are general. Writer's guidelines: none. Sample copy: $3.

VIRTUE MAGAZINE. PO Box 850. Sister, OR 97759. (503) 549-8261.

Fax: (503) 549-0153. Submissions Editors: Marlee Alex (profiles, fiction, features, interviews); Holly Halverson (poetry, book and music reviews, products and trends). Type: women's. Frequency of publication: every other month. Circulation: 175,000. Number of manuscripts accepted per year: n/i. Payment offered.

Editorial Needs. Fiction—Afro-American; contemporary/modern; general; handicapped; Hispanic; holiday; humor; Latin American; literary; mainstream; Native American; romance; women's issues; working people. **Forms:** book excerpts; short stories (1000-2000 words).

Nonfiction—women; families; Christianity; contemporary issues. **Forms:** book excerpts; book reviews; cartoons; columns; essays; features; interview/profile; photo feature; poetry. Payment is $.15-$.25 per word for all forms.

Initial Contact. Article proposal with subject outline. Include clips. SASE required.

Acceptance Policies. Byline given: yes. Publishing rights: first North American serial rights; second serial rights. Payment made: upon acceptance. Kill fee: yes. Expenses: negotiable. Response time to initial inquiry: 6-8 weeks. Average time until publication: varies greatly. Submit seasonal material 6 months in advance. Simultaneous submissions: inform us. Disk submissions: WordPerfect 5.0.

Photography Submissions. Photos on assignment only.

Additional Information. We aim to be inspirational rather than preachy. Writer's guidelines: SASE. Sample copy: $3.

VISIONS. 19600 NW Von Neumann Dr. Beaverton, OR. (503) 690-1066.

Fax: (503) 690-1029. Submissions Editor: Steve Dodge. Type: science and technology. Frequency of publication: 3 times per year. Circulation: 20,000. Number of manuscripts accepted per year: 10-15. Payment offered.

Editorial Needs. Fiction—science fiction. **Forms:** short stories (2000-3000 words; $250-$400).

Nonfiction—science and technology. **Forms:** book reviews (500-1000 words; $150-$200); cartoons; essays (education, business, science, technology; 1000-2000 words; generally no payment); features (science, technology; 2000-3000 words; $250-$400); fillers (science briefs; 200 words; $25-$75); interview/profile (science personalities; 1000-2000 words; $150-$250); photo features (photomicrography, science photo essay; $150-$350); will consider humorous nonfiction relating to science.

Initial Contact. Query letter only. Include clips.

Acceptance Policies. Byline given: yes. Publishing rights: first North American serial rights; second serial rights; one-time rights; simultaneous rights (will consider). Payment made: upon acceptance. Kill fee: no. Expenses: by prior arrangement. Response time to initial inquiry: 6-8 weeks. Average time until publication: 3-12 months. Submit seasonal material 6 months in advance. Simultaneous submissions: if not in direct competition. Disk submissions: prefer Macintosh 3 1/2; Microsoft Word; can convert IBM disks.

Photography Submissions. Format and film: 4x5 or larger black-and-white prints; transparencies; 35mm. Photographs should include: captions; model releases; identification of subjects. **Payment:** $25-$150 per photo; $350 for photo essay. Photographic rights: one-time rights.

Additional Information. Write for free guidelines. Sample article must be nontechnical and in journalistic style. Tips: Science briefs, short profiles (1000-2000 words) are best way to break in. Writer's guidelines: call or write. Sample copy: 9x12 SASE.

WASHINGTON-OREGON GAME & FISH. PO Box 741. Marietta, GA 30061. (404) 953-9222. Fax: (404) 933-9510. Submissions Editor: Burt Carey. Type: hunting and fishing. Frequency of publication: monthly. Circulation: n/i. Number of manuscripts accepted per year: 96. Payment offered.

Editorial Needs. Nonfiction—where to hunt or fish. **Forms:** features (1500-2000 words; $125-$250).

Initial Contact. Query letter only. Include about 6 transparencies. SASE required.

Acceptance Policies. Byline given: yes. Publishing rights: first North American serial rights. Payment made: 2 1/2 months prior to publication. Kill fee: no. Expenses: no. Response time to initial inquiry: 3-4 weeks. Average time until publication: 6 months. Submit seasonal material 8 months in advance. Simultaneous submissions: no. Disk submissions: no.

Photography Submissions. Format and film: 8x10 black-and-white prints; color transparencies. Photographs should include: photographer's name and address. **Payment:** $75 per published 4-color; $25 per published black-and-white. Photographic rights: one-time rights.

Additional Information. Focus stories on where, when, and how for the best fishing/hunting in your state. Tips: Don't expect the first query to be accepted. Send a "laundry list." Writer's guidelines: SASE. Sample copy: $2.50, SASE.

WASHINGTON WILDFIRE. PO Box 45187. Seattle, WA 98145. (206) 633-1992. Submissions Editors: Virginia Baker or Chris Carrel. Type: environmental. Frequency of publication: every other month. Circulation: 1500. Number of manuscripts accepted per year: n/i. Payment in copies.

Editorial Needs. Nonfiction—environmental topics. **Forms:** book excerpts; book reviews; cartoons; columns; essays; features; interview/profile; photo feature (short).

Initial Contact. Query letter only.

Acceptance Policies. Byline given: yes. Publishing rights: none. Payment made in complimentary copy to author. Response time to initial inquiry: 2 weeks. Average time until publication: 1-2 months. Submit seasonal material 3 months in advance. Simultaneous submissions: list other submissions. Disk submissions: Macintosh; Microsoft Word 3.5.

Photography Submissions. Format and film: prints; reasonable actuals. Photographs should include: identification of subjects. **Payment:** none. Photographic rights: none.

Additional Information. We are interested specifically in old growth forests, wilderness areas, streams, etc. Tips: Make sure your information is current and accurate. Writer's guidelines: none. Sample copy: SASE.

WESTERN MILLS TODAY. PO Box 610. Edmonds, WA 98020. (206) 778-3388. Fax: (206) 771-3623. Submissions Editor: John Nederlee. Type: trade publication for mill operators in Western United States and Canada. Frequency of publication: monthly. Circulation: 10,000. Number of manuscripts accepted per year: 24. Payment offered.

Editorial Needs. Nonfiction—sawmills; plywood; paper. **Forms:** features (1500-2000 words, $200+); photo feature (1500-2000 words; $200+).

Initial Contact. Query letter or phone. SASE required.

Acceptance Policies. Byline given: no. Publishing rights: all rights. Payment made: upon publication. Kill fee: no. Expenses: yes. Response time to initial inquiry: 10 days. Average time until publication: 30-60 days. Simultaneous submissions: no. Disk submissions: Macintosh or IBM PC if program compatible.

Additional Information. Tips: Relate to Western United States in articles about wood products, manufacturing, machinery, techniques, and electronics. We prefer on-the-job articles. Writer's guidelines: write or fax. Sample copy: write or fax, include one sample of your work.

WESTERN RV NEWS. 1350 SW Upland Dr., Ste. B. Portland, OR 97221. (503) 222-1255. Fax: (503) 222-1255. Submissions Editor: Jim Schumock. Type: recreational vehicles. Frequency of publication: monthly. Circulation: 16,000. Number of manuscripts accepted per year: 25-30. Payment offered.

Editorial Needs. Nonfiction—RVs. **Forms:** book reviews (250-500 words; $25-$50); cartoons ($5-$35); features (250-1500 words; $25-$150); fillers (25-100 words; $5-$25); interview/profile (250-750 words; $25-$75).

Initial Contact. Entire article. Include which rights and photos are available. SASE required.

Acceptance Policies. Byline given: sometimes. Publishing rights: first North American serial rights; second serial rights; one-time rights; work-for-hire. Payment made: upon publication. Kill fee: no. Expenses: no. Response time to initial inquiry: 3 weeks. Average time until publication: 2-6 months. Submit seasonal material 2 months in advance. Simultaneous submissions: inform us in cover letter. Disk submissions: no.

Photography Submissions. Format and film: 3x5 black-and-white glossy prints. Photographs should include: captions; identification of subjects. **Payment:** $5-$15. Photographic rights: one-time rights.

Additional Information. We want RV lifestyle and camping slant only; no folksy, generic writing. Tips: Make sure your articles are well written, thoroughly researched, and accurate. Articles concerning new products, new or improved equipment, and innovative ways to utilize an RV to enhance a particular lifestyle are most sought. Writer's guidelines: SASE. Sample copy: request with guidelines.

WILLOW SPRINGS. MS-1. Eastern Washington University. Cheney, WA 99004. (509) 458-6429. Submissions Editor: Nance Van Winckel. Type: literary. Frequency of publication: 2 times per year. Circulation: n/i. Number of manuscripts accepted per year: 60. Payment and copies offered.

Editorial Needs. Fiction—avant-garde/experimental; contemporary/modern; ethnic; literary; Native American. **Forms:** book excerpts (6-25 pages; payment varies); short stories (6-25 pages; payment varies).

Nonfiction—literary. **Forms:** book excerpts (literary nonfiction; 5-20 pages); book reviews (recent poetry and fiction; 2-5 pages); poetry. Payment varies for all forms.

Initial Contact. Entire article. SASE required.

Acceptance Policies. Byline given: yes. Publishing rights: first rights. Payment made: upon publication. Kill fee: no. Response time to initial inquiry: 2-3 months. Average time until publication: 6 months. Simultaneous submissions: no. Disk submissions: no.

Photography Submissions. Format and film: any size prints. Photographs should include: identification of subjects. **Payment:** varies. Photographic rights: first rights.

Additional Information. We're a nationally recognized literary journal with awards from The National Endowment for the Arts, GE Foundation, and CLMP. We don't accept submissions in June, July, and August. Tips: Read copies of our journal before submitting. Writer's guidelines: SASE. Sample copy: $4.

WRITERS' OPEN FORUM. PO Box 516. Tracyton, WA 98393. Submissions Editor: Sandra E. Haven. Type: writer's magazine. Frequency of publication: every other month. Circulation: n/i. Number of manuscripts accepted per year: 30+. Payment offered.

Editorial Needs. **Fiction**—children's/young adult; contemporary/modern; fantasy; general; historical; holiday; humor; mainstream; mystery; new age; romance; science fiction; sports; suspense; Western; women's issues; working people. **Forms:** book excerpts (2000 words maximum; $5 minimum); short stories (2000 words maximum; $5 minimum).

Nonfiction—any subject. **Forms:** book excerpts (2000 words maximum; $5 minimum); cartoons (3 copies); essays (2000 words maximum, $5 minimum); features (2000 words maximum; $5 minimum).

Initial Contact. Entire article. Include brief bio. SASE required.

Acceptance Policies. Byline given: yes. Publishing rights: one-time rights. Payment made: upon publication. Kill fee: yes. Expenses: no. Response time to initial inquiry: 6 weeks. Average time until publication: 2 months. Submit seasonal material 4 months in advance. Simultaneous submissions: no. Disk submissions: no.

Additional Information. *Writers' Open Forum* is a critique and information exchange for writers. Readers send in critiques, some are published, but all are redirected to the author. Tips: Fiction needs tight story line (no slice-of-life); nonfiction, a distinct purpose developed to a conclusion. Writer's guidelines: SASE. Sample copy: $2 (includes guidelines).

WYOMING: THE HUB OF THE WHEEL . . . A JOURNEY FOR UNIVERSAL SPOKESMEN. PO Box 9. Saratoga, WY 82331. (307) 326-5214. Submissions Editors: Dawn Senior, managing editor; Lenore A. Senior; founding and consulting editor. Type: literary. Frequency of publication: yearly. Circulation: 300. Number of manuscripts accepted per year: 80. Payment in copies.

Editorial Needs. **Fiction**—Afro-American; ethnic; fantasy; folklore; general; Hispanic; humor; Latin American; literary; mainstream; Native American; women's issues. **Forms:** short stories (2500 words maximum).

Nonfiction—humanist emphasis. **Forms:** essays (2500 words); poetry (humanist, nature; 80 lines); artwork.

Initial Contact. Query letter. SASE required.

Acceptance Policies. Byline given: yes. Publishing rights: first North American serial rights. Payment made: in copies. Response time to initial inquiry: 2 weeks. Average time until publication: varies. Simultaneous submissions: inform us at time of submission. Disk submissions: no.

Photography Submissions. Format and film: 5x7 black-and-white preferred; 3 1/2 x 5, 8x10 okay. Photographs should include: title. **Payment:** copy. Photographic rights: first North American serial rights.

Additional Information. Write to us for information about projected themes for future issues. Tips: Suggest brief query letter. Writer's guidelines: SASE. Sample copy: discount available on samples, but prices vary. Write for information.

ZERO HOUR. PO Box 766. Seattle, WA 98111. (206) 323-3648. Submissions Editor: Jim Jones. Type: literary. Frequency of publication: 2 times per year. Circulation: 3000. Number of manuscripts accepted per year: 20. Payment in copies.

Editorial Needs. Fiction—avant-garde/experimental; contemporary/modern; literary. **Forms:** book excerpts (1500 words maximum); short stories (1500 words maximum).

Nonfiction—each issue centers on a different topic. **Forms:** book excerpts; book reviews; cartoons; columns; entertainment reviews; essays; features; fillers; interview/profile; photo feature; poetry (200 words). Length is 1500 words for all forms except poetry.

Initial Contact. Entire article. SASE required.

Acceptance Policies. Byline given: yes. Publishing rights: one-time rights. Payment made: 4 copies. Response time to initial inquiry: 3 weeks. Average time until publication: up to 6 months. Simultaneous submissions: yes. Disk submissions: WordPerfect 5.0.

Photography Submissions. Format and film: any size prints. Photographs should include: model releases; identification of subjects; title, if any. **Payment:** 4 copies. Photographic rights: none.

Additional Information. Each issue is theme oriented, dealing with fringe culture. Tips: Keep it short. Writer's guidelines: upon request. Sample copy: $4.

Newspapers

Many writers first break into print with a published column in a local newspaper. While the pay may be nominal, writing for a newspaper provides an opportunity to learn about writing within editorial requirements, targeting specific markets, and meeting deadlines.

How to Use the Information in This Section

Our listings are divided into sections by state and alphabetized by the name of the newspaper or by the area serviced. We felt the listings would be more useful this way since writers are often writing for a specific audience in a specific area. If the name of the area is in parenthesis, do not include it when sending material to the newspaper; it is for your use in determining the geographical area served by that publication.

The entry first provides the name of the publication, its location, and phone number.

Freelance submissions: If the text indicates that the newspaper accepts freelance submissions, write to the editor to request writer's guidelines and information about the editorial needs of the newspaper's special sections. For papers that do not accept freelance submissions, only this item and the circulation are included.

Submissions Editor: Direct your initial contact to the appropriate editor.

Book Review Editor: Send review copies and press releases about your book to this individual.

Travel Editor: Most newspapers use travel material in the form of articles or columns. We have included the names of travel editors whenever specific names were provided.

Circulation: This number helps you judge the size of your market.

Partial Listings

Some newspapers failed to provide information by press time. We retained these listings for a more comprehensive coverage and added the comment, "No information returned." Contact these papers directly to request submission information.

Alaska

ANCHORAGE DAILY NEWS. PO Box 149001. Anchorage, AK 99514-9001. (907) 257-4200. Freelance Submissions: yes. Submissions Editors: Stan Jones (general); Jim Macknicki (book review and travel). Circulation: 57,976 daily; 74,857 Sunday.

ANCHORAGE TIMES. PO Box 100040. Anchorage, AK 99510-0040. (907) 263-9000. Freelance Submissions: limited. Submissions Editor: J. Randolph Murray (general, book review, and travel). Circulation: 45,000.

(ANCHORAGE) TUNDRA TIMES. PO Box 104480. Anchorage, AK 99510-4480. (907) 274-2512. Freelance Submissions: yes. Submissions Editor: Alexandra McClanahan (general, book review, and travel). Circulation: 4000.

(BETHEL) TUNDRA DRUMS. PO Box 868. Bethel, AK 99559. (907) 543-3551. No information returned.

(EAGLE RIVER) CHUGIAK-EAGLE RIVER STAR. 16941 N. Eagle River Loop. Eagle River, AK 99577. (907) 694-2719. Freelance Submissions: rarely; local only. Submissions Editor: Lee Jordan (general). Circulation: 4500.

FAIRBANKS DAILY NEWS-MINER. PO Box 70710. Fairbanks, AK 99707-0710. (907) 456-6661. Freelance Submissions: yes. Submissions Editors: Dan Joling (general); Eric Troyer (book review and travel). Circulation: 19,000.

HOMER NEWS, THE. 3482 Landings St. Homer, AK 99603. (907) 235-7767. Freelance Submissions: yes. Submissions Editor: Karen Higley (general, book review, and travel). Circulation: 4550.

(JUNEAU) CAPITAL CITY WEEKLY. 8365 Old Dairy Rd. Juneau, AK 98901. (907) 789-4144. Freelance Submissions: yes. Submissions Editor: address to editor. Circulation: 16,000.

JUNEAU EMPIRE. 3100 Channel Dr. Juneau, AK 99801-7814. (907) 586-3740. Freelance Submissions: rarely. Submissions Editor: Carl Sampson (general, book review, and travel). Circulation: 7500.

(KETCHIKAN) ISLAND NEWS. PO Box 19430. Thorne Bay, AK 99919. (907) 828-3377. Freelance Submissions: seldom; unpaid only. Submissions Editor: Bill MacCannell (general, book review, and travel). Circulation: 1600.

KODIAK DAILY MIRROR. 1419 Selig. Kodiak, AK 99615. (907) 486-3227. Freelance Submissions: yes; local only. Submissions Editor: Cecil Ranney (general, book review, and travel). Circulation: 4000.

NOME NUGGET, THE. PO Box 610. Nome, AK 99762. (907) 443-5235. Freelance Submissions: seldom. Submissions Editor: Nancy McGuire (general, book review, and travel). Circulation: 3000.

(SITKA) DAILY SITKA SENTINEL. PO Box 799. Sitka, AK 99835. (907) 747-3219. Freelance Submissions: seldom. Submissions Editor: Sandy Poulson (general, book review, and travel). Circulation: 2600.

Idaho

(BLACKFOOT) MORNING NEWS. 27 NW Main St. PO Box 70. Blackfoot, ID 83221. (208) 785-1100. Freelance Submissions: yes. Submissions Editor: John Miller (general, book review, and travel). Circulation: 5000.

(BOISE) IDAHO BUSINESS REVIEW. PO Box 7193. Boise, ID 83707. (208) 336-3768. Freelance Submissions: yes. Submissions Editor: Carl A. Miller (general, book review, and travel). Circulation: 2200.

(BOISE) IDAHO STATESMAN, THE. PO Box 40. Boise, ID 83707. (208) 377-6200. Freelance Submissions: yes. Submissions Editor: Bill Roberts, features editor (general, book review, and travel). Circulation: 100,000.

BUHL HERALD. 126 S. Broadway. Buhl, ID 83316-0312. (208) 543-4335. Freelance Submissions: rarely. Submissions Editor: David Lewis (general, book review, and travel). Circulation: 3300.

(BURLEY) SOUTH IDAHO PRESS. 230 E. Main St. PO Box 190. Burley, ID 83318. (208) 678-2201. Freelance Submissions: rarely. Submissions Editor: Ralph Berenger (general). Circulation: 6500.

COEUR D'ALENE PRESS. Second and Lakeside. Coeur d'Alene, ID 83814. (208) 664-8176. Freelance Submissions: yes. Submissions Editor: Roy Wellman (general, book review, and travel). Circulation: 25,000.

(GRANGEVILLE) IDAHO COUNTY FREE PRESS. PO Box 690. Grangeville, ID 83530. (208) 983-1070. Freelance Submissions: seldom. Submissions Editor: David Medel (general, book review, and travel). Circulation: 8000.

(IDAHO FALLS) POST REGISTER, THE. PO Box 1800. Idaho Falls, ID 83403. (208) 522-1800. Freelance Submissions: yes. Submissions Editors: Roger Plothow (general); Paul Menser (book review and travel). Circulation: 27,000.

(JEROME) NORTH SIDE NEWS. PO Box 468. Jerome, ID 83338. (208) 324-3391. Freelance Submissions: no. Circulation: 2200.

(KELLOGG) SHOSHONE NEWS-PRESS. 401 Main St. Kellogg, ID 83837. (208) 783-1107. Freelance Submissions: yes. Submissions Editor: Ed McDonald (general). Circulation: 5100.

(LEWISTON) MORNING TRIBUNE. 505 C St. Lewiston, ID 83501. (208) 743-9411. Freelance Submissions: yes. Submissions Editors: Sandy Lee, city editor (general); John McCarthy (book review); Jeanne DePaul (travel). Circulation: 26,000.

(MOUNTAIN HOME) NEWS. 195 S. Third E. PO Box Drawer 1330. Mountain Home, ID 83647. (208) 587-3331. Freelance Submissions: seldom. Submissions Editor: Kelly Everitt (general, book review, and travel). Circulation: 4000.

(NAMPA) IDAHO PRESS TRIBUNE. PO Box 9399. Nampa, ID 83652-9399. (208) 467-9251. Freelance Submissions: rarely. Submissions Editor: B. Rick Koffman (general, book review, and travel). Circulation: 19,000.

(POCATELLO) IDAHO STATE JOURNAL. 305 S. Arthur. Pocatello, ID 83204. (208) 232-4161. Freelance Submissions: yes. Submissions Editors: Lyle Olson (general); Joy Morrison (book review and travel). Circulation: 20,000.

POST FALLS TRIBUNE. PO Box 39. Post Falls, ID 83854. (208) 773-7502. Freelance Submissions: rarely. Submissions Editor: Robert Dorroh (general, book review, and travel). Circulation: 2000.

REXBURG STANDARD JOURNAL. PO Box 10. Rexburg, ID 83440. Freelance Submissions: rarely; local only. Submissions Editor: Cathy Koon (general, book review, and travel). Circulation: 9200.

(RUPERT) NEWS JOURNAL, THE. PO Box 395. Rupert, ID 83350. (208) 436-1129. Freelance Submissions: yes. Submissions Editor: Tanya Enger (general and book review). Circulation: 16,000.

(TWIN FALLS) TIMES-NEWS, THE. PO Box 548. Twin Falls, ID 83308. (208) 733-0931. Freelance Submissions: occasionally; local only. Submissions Editor: address to editor. Circulation: 22,000.

Montana

ANACONDA LEADER. 121 Main St. Anaconda, MT 59711. (406) 563-5283. Freelance Submissions: yes. Submissions Editor: Dick Crockford (general). Circulation: 3900.

(BELGRADE) HIGH COUNTRY INDEPENDENT PRESS. 220 S. Broadway. Belgrade, MT 59714-1019. (406) 388-6762. Freelance Submissions: no. Circulation: 6000.

BILLINGS GAZETTE, THE. PO Box 36300. Billings, MT 59107-6300. (406) 657-1200. Freelance Submissions: seldom; local only. Submissions Editors: Gary Svee (general); Chris Meyers (travel). Circulation: 60,000.

BOZEMAN DAILY CHRONICLE. PO Box 1188. Bozeman, MT 59715. (406) 587-4491. Freelance Submissions: rarely. Submissions Editor: address to feature editor. Circulation: 14,000.

(COLUMBIA FALLS) HUNGRY HORSE NEWS. PO Box 189. Columbia Falls, MT 59912. (406) 892-2151. Freelance Submissions: yes. Submissions Editor: Brian Kennedy (general). Circulation: 7500.

(COLUMBUS) STILLWATER COUNTY NEWS. PO Box 659. Columbus, MT 59019. (406) 322-5212. Freelance Submissions: yes. Submissions Editor: Larry Eanglen (general). Circulation: 2250.

(DEER LODGE) SILVER STATE POST. PO Box 271. Deer Lodge, MT 59722. (406) 846-2424. Freelance Submissions: yes. Submissions Editor: Aubrey Larson.

DILLON TRIBUNE-EXAMINER. PO Box 911. Dillon, MT 59725. (406) 683-2331. Freelance Submissions: local only. Submissions Editor: John Barrows (general). Circulation: 6000.

(FORSYTH) INDEPENDENT ENTERPRISE, THE. PO Box 106. Forsyth, MT 59327. (406) 356-2149. Freelance Submissions: yes. Submissions Editor: Pat Corley (general). Circulation: 2000.

(GLENDIVE) RANGER REVIEW. PO Box 61. Glendive, MT 59330. (406) 365-3303. Freelance Submissions: yes. Submissions Editor: Tana Reinhardt (general). Circulation: 3700.

GREAT FALLS TRIBUNE. PO Box 5468. Great Falls, MT 59403. (406) 791-1444. Freelance Submissions: yes. Submissions Editor: address to attention of type of editor, i.e., book review editor, travel editor. Circulation: 34,000 daily; 41,000 Sunday.

(HARDIN) BIG HORN COUNTY NEWS. 204 N. Center. Hardin, MT 59034. (406) 665-1008. Freelance Submissions: yes. Submissions Editor: Richard Bowler (general). Circulation: 4000.

(HELENA) INDEPENDENT-RECORD. PO Box 4249. Helena, MT 59604. (406) 442-7190. Freelance Submissions: occasionally; mostly local. Submissions Editors: Charles Wood (general); David Shors (book review and travel). Circulation: 14,000.

(KALISPELL) DAILY INTER LAKE. PO Box 8. Kalispell, MT 59903. (406) 755-7000. Freelance Submissions: no. Circulation: 13,500.

LEWISTOWN NEWS-ARGUS. PO Box 900. Lewistown, MT 59457-0900. (406) 538-3401. Freelance Submissions: seldom. Submissions Editor: Lee James (general). Circulation: 5000.

(LIBBY) WESTERN NEWS. PO Box 1377. Libby, MT 59923. (406) 293-4124. No information returned.

LIVINGSTON ENTERPRISE. PO Box 665. Livingston, MT 59047. (406) 222-2000. Freelance Submissions: yes. Submissions Editors: Tom Shands, managing editor (general); Al Knauber (book review); Meredith Thompson (travel). Circulation: 3850.

MISSOULIAN. 500 S. Higgins. PO Box 8029. Missoula, MT 59807. (406) 523-5200. Freelance Submissions: seldom. Submissions Editors: Theresa Johnson, feature editor (general and travel); Ginny Merriam (book review). Circulation: 30,000.

SIDNEY HERALD, THE. 121 N. Central Ave. Sidney, MT 59270. (406) 482-2403. Freelance Submissions: rarely. Submissions Editor: Berney A. Fox (general). Circulation: 4200.

(WOLF POINT) HERALD-NEWS, THE. PO Box 639. Wolf Point, MT 59201. (406) 653-2222. Freelance Submissions: no. Circulation: 3400.

Oregon

ALBANY DEMOCRAT-HERALD. 138 Sixth Ave. SW. PO Box 130. Albany, OR 97321-0041. (503) 926-2211. Freelance Submissions: rarely. Submissions Editor: Graham Kislingbury (general). Circulation: 21,000.

(ASHLAND) DAILY TIDINGS, THE. PO Box 7. Ashland, OR 97520. (503) 482-3456. Freelance Submissions: rarely. Submissions Editor: Ken O'Toole (general, book review, and travel). Circulation: 6500; 10,000 on Tuesday and Thursday.

(ASTORIA) DAILY ASTORIAN, THE. PO Box 210. Astoria, OR 97103. (503) 325-3211. Freelance Submissions: yes. Submissions Editor: Steve Forrester (general, book review, and travel). Circulation: 10,000.

BAKER CITY HERALD. PO Box 807. Baker City, OR 97814. (503) 523-3673. Freelance Submissions: yes. Submissions Editor: Dean Brickey (general, book review, and travel). Circulation: 3500.

(BEND) BULLETIN. 1526 NW Hill St. Bend, OR 97701. (503) 382-1811. Freelance Submissions: yes. Submissions Editor: address to department, i.e., managing editor, travel editor. Circulation: 23,000.

(BROOKINGS) CURRY COASTAL PILOT. PO Box 700. Brookings, OR 97415. (503) 469-3123. Freelance Submissions: yes. Submissions Editor: Will Sampson (general, book review, and travel). Circulation: 8000.

(BROWNSVILLE) TIMES, THE. PO Box 278. Brownsville, OR 97327. (503) 466-5311. Freelance Submissions: yes. Submissions Editor: Ralph Sand (general). Circulation: 2000.

BURNS TIMES-HERALD. 355 N. Broadway. PO Box 473. Burns, OR 97720. (503) 573-2022. Freelance Submissions: yes. Submissions Editor: Polleen Braymen (general). Circulation: 3400.

CANBY HERALD, THE. PO Box 1108. Canby, OR 97013. (503) 266-6831. Freelance Submissions: rarely. Submissions Editor: Tom Lawrence (general). Circulation: 6800.

(CAVE JUNCTION) ILLINOIS VALLEY NEWS, THE. PO Box M. Cave Junction, OR 97523. (503) 592-2541. Freelance Submissions: yes. Submissions Editor: Bob Rodriguez (general). Circulation: 3300.

CLACKAMAS COUNTY REVIEW. PO Box 1520. Clackamas, OR 97015. (503) 656-4101. Freelance Submissions: yes. Submissions Editor: Ron Oberg (general). Circulation: 12,000.

(COOS BAY) WORLD, THE. PO Box 1840. Coos Bay, OR 97420-0147. (503) 269-1222. Freelance Submissions: yes. Submissions Editor: Charlie Kocher, managing editor (general). Circulation: 17,000.

CORVALLIS GAZETTE-TIMES, THE. PO Box 368. Corvallis, OR 97339. (503) 753-2641. Freelance Submissions: rarely. Submissions Editor: Barbara Curtin (general, book review, and travel). Circulation: 13,500.

(DALLES) POLK COUNTY ITEMIZER-OBSERVER. PO Box 108. Dalles, OR 97338. (503) 623-2373. Freelance Submissions: rarely. Submissions Editor: Paul Apfelbeck. Circulation: 5000.

DRAIN ENTERPRISE, THE. 309 1st St. Drain, OR 97435. (503) 836-2241. Freelance Submissions: yes; unpaid only. Submissions Editor: Lowell Anderson (general, book review, and travel). Circulation: 1400.

(ENTERPRISE) WALLOWA COUNTY CHIEFTAN. PO Box 338. Enterprise, OR 97828. (503) 426-4567. Freelance Submissions: rarely. Submissions Editor: Rick Swart (general). Circulation: 3800.

(EUGENE) REGISTER-GUARD, THE. PO Box 10188. Eugene, OR 97440-2188. (503) 485-1234. Freelance Submissions: yes. Submissions Editor: Jim Godbold (general, book review, and travel). Circulation: 70,000.

(FLORENCE) SIUSLAW NEWS. PO Box 10. Florence, OR 97439. (503) 997-3441. Freelance Submissions: rarely. Submissions Editor: Bob Serra (general and travel). Circulation: 6130.

FOREST GROVE NEWS TIMES. PO Box 408. Forest Grove, OR 97116. (503) 357-3181. Freelance Submissions: yes. Submissions Editor: Jim Hart (general). Circulation: 5000.

(GOLD BEACH) CURRY COUNTY REPORTER. PO Box 766. Gold Beach, OR 97444. (503) 247-6643. Freelance Submissions: local only. Submissions Editor: Bob Van Leer (general). Circulation: 3300.

GRANTS PASS DAILY COURIER. PO Box 1468. Grants Pass, OR 97526. (503) 474-3700. Freelance Submissions: yes. Submissions Editor: Dennis Roler (general). Circulation: 20,000.

GRESHAM OUTLOOK, THE. PO Box 747. Gresham, OR 97030. (503) 665-2181. Freelance Submissions: yes. Submissions Editor: Lloyd Woods (general). Circulation: 13,000.

(HERMISTON) HERALD, THE. PO Box 46. Hermiston, OR 97838. (503) 567-6457. Freelance Submissions: yes. Submissions Editor: Pat Moser (general). Circulation: 13,500.

HILLSBORO ARGUS. 150 SE Third. Hillsboro, OR 97123. (503) 648-1131. Freelance Submissions: seldom. Submissions Editor: Hess Val, managing editor (general). Circulation: 15,000.

HOOD RIVER NEWS. PO Box 390. Hood River, OR 97031. (503) 386-1234. Freelance Submissions: no. Circulation: 6000.

(JOHN DAY) BLUE MOUNTAIN EAGLE, THE. PO Box 69. John Day, OR 97845-0069. (503) 575-0710. Freelance Submissions: yes. Submissions Editor: Loren Russell (general). Circulation: 3900.

KEIZERTIMES. 680 Chemawa Rd. NE. Keizer, OR 97303. (503) 390-1051. Freelance Submissions: yes. Submissions Editor: Scotta Callister (general). Circulation: 4000.

(KLAMATH FALLS) HERALD AND NEWS. PO Box 788. Klamath Falls, OR 97601. (503) 885-4410. Freelance Submissions: rarely. Submissions Editors: Tom Hottman (general); Rita Backa (travel). Circulation: 19,000.

(LA GRANDE) OBSERVER, THE. PO Box 3170. La Grande, OR 97850. (503) 963-3161. Freelance Submissions: no. Circulation: 7400.

LAKE OSWEGO REVIEW. PO Box 548. Lake Oswego, OR 97034. (503) 635-8811. Freelance Submissions: seldom. Submissions Editor: Rick Crone (general and book review). Circulation: 9000.

(LAKEVIEW) LAKE COUNTY EXAMINER. PO Box 271. Lakeview, OR 97630. (503) 947-3379. Freelance Submissions: rarely; not for pay. Submissions Editor: Sharon Liddycoat (general, book review, and travel). Circulation: 3000.

LEBANON EXPRESS. PO Box 459. Lebanon, OR 97355. (503) 258-3151. Freelance Submissions: local only. Submissions Editor: Aaron Knox (general). Circulation: 4200.

(LINCOLN CITY) NEWS GUARD, THE. PO Box 848. Lincoln City, OR 97367. (503) 994-2178. Freelance Submissions: no; occasionally book reviews by local authors. Submissions Editor: Pam Geddes. Circulation: 6000.

MADRAS PIONEER, THE. PO Box 4. Madras, OR 97741. (503) 475-2275. Freelance Submissions: seldom. Submissions Editor: Susan Mantheny (general). Circulation: 3800.

(MC MINNVILLE) NEWS-REGISTER. PO Box 727. Mc Minnville, OR 97128. (503) 472-5114. Freelance Submissions: yes; not for pay. Submissions Editor: Nanda McAlister (general). Circulation: 21,000.

(MEDFORD) MAIL TRIBUNE, THE. PO Box 1108. Medford, OR 97501. (503) 776-4411. Freelance Submissions: rarely. Submissions Editors: Bob Hunter, managing editor (general); Cleve Twitchell (book review and travel). Circulation: 30,000.

NEWBERG GRAPHIC. PO Box 110. Newberg, OR 97132. (503) 538-2181. Freelance Submissions: rarely. Submissions Editor: John Wenos (general and travel). Circulation: 6000.

(NEWPORT) NEWS-TIMES. PO Box 965. Newport, OR 97365. (503) 265-8571. Freelance Submissions: no; reviews of local books and authors only. Submissions Editor: Leslie O'Donnell. Circulation: 10,500.

(ONTARIO) ARGUS OBSERVER. PO Box 130. Ontario, OR 97914. (503) 889-5387. Freelance Submissions: yes; usually not paid. Submissions Editor: Chris Moore (general). Editor does book reviews monthly. Circulation: 1800.

(PENDELTON) EAST OREGONIAN. PO Box 1089. Pendelton, OR 97801. (503) 276-2211. Freelance Submissions: rarely. Submissions Editor: Hal McCune (general). Circulation: 13,500.

(PORTLAND) OREGONIAN, THE. 1320 SW Broadway. Portland, OR 97201. (503) 221-8327. Freelance Submissions: yes. Submissions Editor: address to general editor. Circulation: 344,000.

(PRINEVILLE) CENTRAL OREGONIAN. 558 N. Main St. Prineville, OR 97754. (503) 447-6205. Freelance Submissions: seldom; local only. Submissions Editor: Tony Ahern (general). Circulation: 4100.

REDMOND SPOKESMAN, THE. PO Box 788. Redmond, OR 97756-0181. (503) 548-1284. No information returned.

(ROSEBURG) NEWS REVIEW, THE. PO Box 1248. Roseburg, OR 97470. (503) 672-3321. Freelance Submissions: no. Circulation: 22,500.

(ST. HELENS) CHRONICLE/SENTINEL MIST. PO Box 1153. St. Helens, OR 97051. (503) 397-0116. Freelance Submissions: rarely. Submissions Editor: Greg Cohen (general). Circulation: 6200.

(SALEM) CAPITAL PRESS. PO Box 2048. Salem, OR 97308. (503) 364-4431. Freelance Submissions: yes; strictly agricultural and forestry in Pacific Northwest. Submissions Editor: Carolyn Homan (general). Circulation: 35,000.

(SALEM) TAKE FIVE and **WEST SIDE.** (West Side Publishing). PO Box 5027. Salem, OR 97304. (503) 362-8987. Freelance Submissions: yes. Submissions Editors: Tim Hinshaw (general); Randall Lawrence (book review and travel). Circulation: 15,000 (*Take Five*, entertainment focus); 10,000 (*West Side*).

(SCAPPOSE) SPOTLIGHT, THE. PO Box C. Scappose, OR 97056. (503) 543-6387. Freelance Submissions: no. Circulation: 4000.

SEASIDE SIGNAL. PO Box 848. Seaside, OR 97138. (503) 738-5561. Freelance Submissions: rarely; local only. Submissions Editor: Fred Bassett (general). Circulation: 4500.

(SILVERTON) APPEAL-TRIBUNE, THE. PO Box 35. Silverton, OR 97381. (503) 873-8385. Freelance Submissions: rarely. Submissions Editor: Tom Mann (general). Circulation: 5900.

SPRINGFIELD NEWS, THE. PO Box 139. Springfield, OR 97477. (503) 746-1671. Freelance Submissions: no. Circulation: 11,000.

THE DALLES CHRONICLE. PO Box 902. The Dalles, OR 97058. (503) 296-2141. Freelance Submissions: rarely; local only. Submissions Editor: Austin Abrahms (general). Circulation: 1500.

(TILLAMOOK) HEADLIGHT-HERALD. PO Box 444. Tillamook, OR 97141. (503) 842-7535. Freelance Submissions: rarely. Submissions Editor: Carl Anderson (general). Travel and book reviews are accepted on an irregular basis. Circulation: 8000.

West Side *see* **(SALEM) TAKE FIVE.**

Washington

ABERDEEN DAILY WORLD. PO Box 269. Aberdeen, WA 98520. (206) 532-4000. Freelance Submissions: rarely. Submissions Editor: Bill Lindstrom, city editor (general). Circulation: 18,400.

ANACORTES AMERICAN. PO Box 39. Anacortes, WA 98221. (206) 293-3122. Freelance Submissions: no. Circulation: 4850.

ARLINGTON TIMES. PO Box 67. Arlington, WA 98223. (206) 435-5757. Freelance Submissions: yes. Submissions Editors: Andy Turner (general); Cindi Delaney (book review and travel). Circulation: 14,000.

BAINBRIDGE ISLAND REVIEW, THE. 7689 Day Rd. Bainbridge Island, WA 98040. (206) 842-8305. Freelance Submissions: yes. Submissions Editor: Suzanne Downing (general). Circulation: 6500.

(BELLEVUE) JOURNAL AMERICAN. PO Box 90130. Bellevue, WA 98009-9230. (206) 455-2222. Freelance Submissions: yes. Submissions Editors: Carl Thunemann (editorial); Liz Enbysk (features and travel). Circulation: 35,000.

BELLINGHAM HERALD. 1155 North State St. Bellingham, WA 98225. (206) 676-2600. Freelance Submissions: no. Circulation: 30,000.

(BREMERTON) CENTRAL KITSAP REPORTER. (Kitsap Publishing Group). PO Box 2588. Bremerton, WA 98310. (206) 373-7969. Freelance Submissions: yes. Submissions Editor: Julie Siebert (general, book review, and travel). Circulation: 15,000.

BREMERTON SUN. 545 Fifth St. Bremerton, WA 98310. (206) 377-3711. Freelance Submissions: yes. Submissions Editor: Ann Strosnidee (general). Circulation: 40,000.

BREWSTER QUAD-CITY HERALD. PO Box 37. Brewster, WA 98812. (509) 689-2507. Freelance Submissions: possible. Submissions Editor: Ike Vallance (general). Circulation: 2500.

(BURIEN) HIGHLINE TIMES AND DES MOINES NEWS. 207 SW 150th St. Burien, WA 98166. (206) 242-0100. Freelance Submissions: no. Circulation: 35,000.

CAMAS-WASHOUGAL POST-RECORD. PO Box 1013. Camas, WA 98607. (206) 892-2000. Freelance Submissions: no. Circulation: 9200.

CHELAN VALLEY MIRROR. PO Box 249. Chelan, WA 98816. (509) 682-2213. Freelance Submissions: no. Circulation: 3300.

CHEWALAH INDEPENDENT, THE. PO Box 5. Chewalah, WA 99109. (509) 935-8422. Freelance Submissions: yes. Submissions Editor: Liz Rily (general). Circulation: 2200.

COLFAX GAZETTE. PO Box 770. Colfax, WA 99111. (509) 397-4333. Freelance Submissions: yes. Submissions Editor: Jerry Jones (general, book review, and travel). Circulation: 4500.

(COLVILLE) STATESMAN-EXAMINER. PO Box 271. Colville, WA 99114. (509) 684-4567. Freelance Submissions: no. Circulation: 13,620.

CONCRETE HERALD. PO Box 407. Concrete, WA 98237. (206) 853-8800. Freelance Submissions: yes. Submissions Editor: Mae Falavolito (general, book review, and travel).

(CONNELL) FRANKLIN COUNTY GRAPHIC. PO Box 160. Connell, WA 99326. (509) 234-3181. Freelance Submissions: yes; unpaid only. Submissions Editor: Duane Ruser (general, book review, and travel). Circulation: 2200.

DAYTON CHRONICLE. PO Box 6. Dayton, WA 99328. (509) 382-2221. Freelance Submissions: rarely. Submissions Editor: Jack Williams (general, book review, and travel). Circulation: 1800.

(DEER PARK) TRIBUNE. PO Box 400. Deer Park, WA 99006. (509) 276-5043. Freelance Submissions: yes. Submissions Editor: Shannon Vinson (general, book review, and travel). Circulation: 7100.

(EASTSOUND) ISLAND'S SOUNDER, THE. PO Box 758. Eastsound, WA 98245. (206) 376-4500. Freelance Submissions: very seldom; local only, concerning community and San Juan Islands. Submissions Editor: Monica Woelfel (general, book review, and travel). Circulation: 4600.

ELLENSBURG DAILY RECORD. PO Box 248. Ellensburg, WA 98926. (509) 925-1414. Freelance Submissions: yes. Submissions Editor: John Ludtka (general, book review, and travel). Circulation: 6000.

ENUMCLAW COURIER-HERALD. PO Box 157. Enumclaw, WA 98022. (206) 825-2555. Freelance Submissions: yes. Submissions Editor: Jack Darnton (general, book review, and travel). Circulation: 15,000.

EVERETT HERALD, THE. PO Box 930. Everett, WA 98206. (206) 339-3030. Freelance Submissions: yes. Submissions Editor: Stan Strick (general, book review, and travel). Circulation: 56,000.

FERNDALE WESTSIDE RECORD JOURNAL. 2008 Main St. Ferndale, WA 98248-0038. (206) 384-1411. Freelance Submissions: no. Circulation: 10,000.

FORKS FORUM AND PENINSULA HERALD. PO Box 300. Forks, WA 98331. (206) 374-2281. Freelance Submissions: rarely. Submissions Editor: Robert Rochon (general, book review, and travel). Circulation: 5100.

(FRIDAY HARBOR) JOURNAL OF THE SAN JUAN ISLAND, THE. PO Box 519. Friday Harbor, WA 98250. (206) 378-4191. Freelance Submissions: yes. Submissions Editor: attention editor. Circulation: 7000.

(GOLDENDALE) SENTINEL. 117 W. Main St. Goldendale, WA 98620. (509) 773-3777. Freelance Submissions: only within the area. Submissions Editor: Alan Bowhill (general). Circulation: 3000.

(GRAND COULEE) STAR, THE. PO Box 150. Grand Coulee, WA 99133-0150. (509) 633-1350. Freelance Submissions: yes. Submissions Editor: Judy Sprankle (general, book review, and travel). Circulation: 2000.

GRANDVIEW HERALD, THE. 107 Division. Grandview, WA 98930. (509) 882-3712. Freelance Submissions: yes. Submissions Editor: Tom McCrady (general, book review, and travel). Circulation: 2700.

ISSAQUAH PRESS. PO Box 1328. Issaquah, WA 98027-1328. (206) 392-6434. Freelance Submissions: rarely. Submissions Editor: Linda Thielke. Circulation: 18,000.

(KENT) VALLEY DAILY NEWS. PO Box 130. Kent, WA 98035-0130. (206) 872-6600. Freelance Submissions: rarely. Submissions Editor: Dean Radford (general, book review, and travel). Circulation: 33,000.

LONGVIEW DAILY NEWS. PO Box 189. Longview, WA 98632. (206) 577-2500. Freelance Submissions: seldom. Submissions Editors: Ted Natt (general); Joan Kropf (book review and travel). Circulation: 24,000.

(LYNNWOOD) ENTERPRISE AND COMMUNITY NEWS. PO Box 977. Lynnwood, WA 98047. (206) 775-7521. Freelance Submissions: yes. Submissions Editor: Randall Dodd (general, book review, and travel). Circulation: 57,145.

MERCER ISLAND REPORTER. PO Box 38. Mercer Island, WA 98040. (206) 232-1215. Freelance Submissions: yes. Submissions Editor: Virginia Smyth (general, book review, and travel). Circulation: 5000.

(MOSES LAKE) COLUMBIA BASIN HERALD. PO Box 910. Moses Lake, WA 98837. (509) 765-4561. Freelance Submissions: rarely. Submissions Editor: Dan Black (general, book review, and travel). Circulation: 23,000.

NEWPORT MINER AND GEM STATE MINER. PO Box 349. Newport, WA 99156. (509) 447-2433. Freelance Submissions: seldom. Submissions Editor: Don Gronning (general, book review, and travel). Circulation: 5300.

(OAK HARBOR) WHIDBEY NEWS TIMES. PO Box 10. Oak Harbor, WA 98277. (206) 675-6611. Freelance Submissions: yes. Submissions Editors: Fred Obee (general); Ellen Slater (book review and travel). Circulation: 18,000.

(OLYMPIA) GRANGE NEWS, THE. PO Box 1186. Olympia, WA 98507-1186. (206) 943-9911. Freelance Submissions: no. Circulation: 46,650.

OMAK-OKANOGAN COUNTY CHRONICLE. PO Box 553. Omak, WA 98841-0553. (509) 826-1110. Freelance Submissions: yes. Submissions Editor: Dee Camp (general, book review, and travel). Circulation: 6500.

(PASCO) TRI-CITY HERALD. PO Box 2608. Pasco, WA 99302. (509) 582-1500. Freelance Submissions: yes. Submissions Editors: Rick Larson (general); Skip Card (book review and travel). Circulation: 35,000 daily; 38,000 Sunday.

(PORT ANGELES) PENINSULA NEWS. 305 W. First St. Port Angeles, WA 98362. (206) 452-2345. Freelance Submissions: yes, pre-approved only. Submissions Editor: John McCartney, managing editor (general, book review, and travel). Circulation: 14,500 daily; 15,000 Sunday.

PORT ORCHARD INDEPENDENT. PO Box 27. Port Orchard, WA 98366. (206) 876-4414. Freelance Submissions: yes. Submissions Editor: Mike Shepard (general, book review, and travel). Circulation: 17,000.

PORT TOWNSEND/JEFFERSON COUNTY LEADER. PO Box 552. Port Townsend, WA 98368. (206) 385-2900. Freelance Submissions: yes. Submissions Editor: Scott Wilson, managing editor (general, book review, and travel). Circulation: 9000.

PROSSER RECORD BULLETIN. (Valley Publishing Co.) PO Box 750. Prosser, WA 99350. (509) 786-1711. Freelance Submissions: no. Circulation: 3250.

PULLMAN DAILY NEWS. 107 S. Grand, Ste. B. Pullman, WA 99163. (509) 334-6397. Freelance Submissions: seldom. Submissions Editors: Kristen Moulton (general); Vera White (book review and travel). Circulation: 3500. (Many of the same sections are used in *The Idahoan*, a sister paper, bringing the circulation to 9000.)

(PUYALLUP) PIERCE COUNTY HERALD. PO Box 517. Puyallup, WA 98371-1070. (206) 841-2481. Freelance Submissions: rarely. Submissions Editor: Theresa Chebultar (general, book review, and travel). Circulation: 16,000.

QUINCY VALLEY POST-REGISTER. PO Box 217. Quincy, WA 98848. (509) 787-4511. Freelance Submissions: seldom. Submissions Editor: Gary Lindbergh (general, book review, and travel). Circulation: 2000.

(REDMOND) SAMMAMISH VALLEY NEWS. PO Box 716. Redmond, WA 98073. (206) 883-7187. Freelance Submissions: yes. Submissions Editor: Frank Parchman (general, book review, and travel). Circulation: 18,400.

(SEATTLE) BEACON HILL NEWS. (Pacific Media Group). 2314 3rd Ave. Seattle, WA 98121. (206) 723-1300. Freelance Submissions: only on request. Submissions Editor: address to editor. Circulation: 22,000.

(SEATTLE) CAPITOL HILL TIMES. (Pacific Media Group). 2314 3rd Ave. Seattle, WA 98121. (206) 723-1300. Freelance Submissions: yes. Submissions Editor: address to editor. Circulation: 17,000.

(SEATTLE) FACTS NEWSPAPER. PO Box 22015. Seattle, WA 98122. (206) 324-0552. Freelance Submissions: yes. Submissions Editor: Fitzgerald Beaver (general, book review, and travel). Circulation: 50,000.

(SEATTLE) FEDERAL WAY NEWS. PO Box 3007. Federal Way, WA 98063. (206) 839-0700. Freelance Submissions: rarely. Submissions Editors: Brad Broberg (general); Melodie Steiger (living). Circulation: 110,000.

(SEATTLE) FILIPINO-AMERICAN HERALD. 508 Maynard Ave., S. PO Box 14240. Seattle, WA 98166. (206) 725-6606. Freelance Submissions: yes. Submissions Editor: E. Francisco. Circulation: 7000.

(SEATTLE) JEWISH TRANSCRIPT. (Jewish Federation). 2031 Third Ave., Ste. 200. Seattle, WA 98121. (206) 441-4553. Freelance Submissions: yes. Submissions Editors: Craig Degginger (general); Diana Brement (book review and travel). Circulation: 4000.

SEATTLE MEDIUM, THE. PO Box 22047. Seattle, WA 98122. (206) 323-3070. Freelance Submissions: yes. Submissions Editor: Connie Cameron (general, book review, and travel). Circulation: 37,500.

(SEATTLE) NEW TIMES, THE. PO Box 51186. Seattle, WA 98115-1186. (206) 524-9071. Freelance Submissions: yes; payment in subscription only. Submissions Editor: Krysta Gibson (general, book review, and travel). Circulation: 30,000.

(SEATTLE) NORTH CENTRAL OUTLOOK. (Pacific Media Group). 2314 3rd Ave. Seattle, WA 98121. (206) 723-1300. Freelance Submissions: yes. Submissions Editor: Andra Addison (general, book review, and travel). Circulation: 17,000.

(SEATTLE) NORTHWEST ETHNIC NEWS. 3123 Eastlake Ave., E. Seattle, WA 98102. (206) 762-7932. Freelance Submissions: n/i. Submissions Editor: Chadwick Kent (general).

SEATTLE POST-INTELLIGENCER. 101 Elliott Ave., W. Seattle, WA 98119. (206) 464-2121. Freelance Submissions: seldom. Submissions Editors: Don Smith (news); Chris Beringer (book review); Janet Grimley (travel).

(SEATTLE) PUGET SOUND BUSINESS JOURNAL. 101 Yesler Way, Ste. 200. Seattle, WA 98104. (206) 583-0701. Freelance Submissions: yes. Submissions Editor: Larry Liebman (general, book review, and travel). Circulation: 16,000.

(SEATTLE) QUEEN ANNE/MAGNOLIA NEWS. 225 W. Galer. Seattle, WA 98119. (206) 282-0900. Freelance Submissions: seldom. Submissions Editor: Todd Davidson (general, book review, and travel). Circulation: 21,000.

(SEATTLE) SOUTH DISTRICT JOURNAL. (Pacific Media Group). 2314 3rd Ave. Seattle, WA 98121. (206) 723-1300. Freelance Submissions: yes. Submissions Editor: address to editor. Circulation: 10,000.

SEATTLE TIMES. PO Box 70. Seattle, WA 98111. (206) 464-2111. Freelance Submissions: yes. Submissions Editors: Kathy Andrisevic (Pacific Magazine Department); Donn Fry (book review); John MacDonald (travel). Circulation: 240,000.

(SEATTLE) WEEKLY. 1931 Second Ave. Seattle, WA 98101. (206) 441-5555. Freelance Submissions: yes. Submissions Editor: address all submissions to manuscripts editor. Circulation: 34,000.

(SEATTLE) WESTERN VIKING. 2405 NW Market St. Seattle, WA 98107. (206) 784-4617. Freelance Submissions: yes. Submissions Editor: Alf L. Knudsen, Ph.D. (general, book review, and travel). Circulation: 3000.

(SEATTLE) WEST SEATTLE HERALD. PO Box 16069. Seattle, WA 98116. (206) 932-0300. Freelance Submissions: yes. Submissions Editor: Dan Portman (general, book review, and travel). Circulation: 37,000.

SEQUIM GAZETTE. PO Box 1750. Sequim, WA 98382. (206) 683-3311. Freelance Submissions: yes. Submissions Editor: Jim Manders (general, book review, and travel). Circulation: 11,000.

SHELTON-MASON COUNTY JOURNAL. Third and Cota Sts. PO Box 430. Shelton, WA 98584. (206) 426-4412. Freelance Submissions: no. Circulation: 8965.

SNOHOMISH COUNTY TRIBUNE. PO Box 499. Snohomish, WA 98290. (206) 568-4121. Freelance Submissions: rarely. Submissions Editor: Leslie Hynes (general, book review, and travel). Circulation: 9000.

SNOQUALMIE VALLEY RECORD. PO Box 300. Snoqualmie, WA 98065. (206) 888-2311. Freelance Submissions: yes. Submissions Editor: Paul Weideman (general, book review, and travel). Circulation: 5600.

SPOKANE CHRONICLE. PO Box 2160. Spokane, WA 99210. (509) 459-5000. No information returned.

(SPOKANE) INLAND REGISTER. PO Box 48. Spokane, WA 99210-0048. (509) 456-7140. Freelance Submissions: yes. Submissions Editor: Eric Meisfjord (general, book review, and travel). Circulation: 8500.

(SPOKANE) JOURNAL OF BUSINESS. S. 104 Division St. Spokane, WA 99202. (509) 456-5257. Freelance Submissions: yes; business topics. Submissions Editor: Norman Thorpe (general, book review, and travel). Circulation: 16,200.

(SPOKANE) OUTDOOR PRESS. N. 2012 Ruby St. Spokane, WA 99207-2281. (509) 328-9392. Freelance Submissions: yes. Submissions Editor: Fred. C. Peterson, Jr. (general, book review, and travel).

(SPOKANE) SENIOR TIMES. 7802 E. Mission Ave. Spokane, WA 99212-2598. (509) 928-1677. Freelance Submissions: yes; unpaid only. Submissions Editor: Jim Osman. Circulation: 25,000.

SPOKANE VALLEY HERALD. PO Box 141268. Spokane, WA 99214. (509) 924-2440. Freelance Submissions: seldom. Submissions Editor: Mike Ulahovich (general, book review, and travel). Circulation: 20,000.

WENATCHEE DAILY WORLD. PO Box 1511. Wenatchee, WA 98807. (509) 663-5161. Freelance Submissions: rarely. Submissions Editors: Steve Lachowicz (general); Dave Kraft (book review and travel). Circulation: 30,000.

Wyoming

(AFTON) STAR VALLEY INDEPENDENT. PO Box 129. Afton, WY 83110-0158. (307) 886-5727. Freelance Submissions: rarely. Submissions Editor: Dan Dockstader (general, book review, and travel). Circulation: 3200.

BUFFALO BULLETIN. PO Box 730. Buffalo, WY 82834. (307) 684-2223. Freelance Submissions: rarely. Submissions Editor: Jim Hicks (general, book review, and travel). Circulation: 3650.

(CASPER) JOURNAL. 2000 Fairground Rd. Casper, WY 82604. (307) 265-3870. Freelance Submissions: no. Circulation: 3500.

CASPER STAR-TRIBUNE. 170 Star Lane. PO Box 80. Casper, WY 82602. (307) 266-0500. Freelance Submissions: seldom. Submissions Editors: Anne Mackinnon (editorial); Charles Levendosky (opinion). Circulation: 50,000.

(CHEYENNE) WYOMING EAGLE. 702 W. Lincoln Way. Cheyenne, WY 82001. (307) 634-3361. Contact (Mr.) Kerry Drake for information.

(CHEYENNE) WYOMING STATE TRIBUNE. 702 W. Lincoln Way. Cheyenne, WY 82001. (307) 634-3361. Freelance Submissions: yes. Submissions Editor: Don Davis (general, book review, and travel).

(CHEYENNE) WYOMING TRIBUNE-EAGLE. 702 W. Lincoln Way. Cheyenne, WY 82001. (307) 634-3361. Freelance Submissions: yes. Submissions Editors: (Mr.) Kerry Drake (daily); Betty Rata (Sunday).

CODY ENTERPRISE. PO Box 1090. Cody, WY 82414. (307) 587-2231. Freelance Submissions: seldom. Submissions Editor: Bruce McCormack (general, book review, and travel). Circulation: 5000.

(EVANSTON) UINTA COUNTY HERALD. PO Box 210. Evanston, WY 82930-0021. (307) 789-6560. Freelance Submissions: yes. Submissions Editor: Chad Baldwin (general, book review, and travel). Circulation: 5000.

(GILLETTE) NEWS RECORD, THE. 1201 W. Second St. PO Box 3006. Gillette, WY 82717. (307) 682-9306. Freelance Submissions: yes. Submissions Editor: Ron Franscell (general, book review, and travel). Circulation: 13,000.

JACKSON HOLE GUIDE. PO Box 648. Jackson, WY 83001. (307) 733-2430. Freelance Submissions: local only; must query for approval prior to submission. Submissions Editor: Dave Stump. Circulation: 8000.

JACKSON HOLE NEWS. PO Box 7445. Jackson, WY 83001. (307) 733-2047. Freelance Submissions: yes. Submissions Editor: Ann Gordon (general, book review, and travel). Circulation: 8000.

LARAMIE DAILY BOOMERANG. 314 S. Fourth St. Laramie, WY 82070. (307) 742-2176. Freelance Submissions: seldom; only with prior approval. Submissions Editor: Bob Wilson (general, book review, and travel). Circulation: 8200.

(RAWLINS) DAILY TIMES. PO Box 370. Rawlins, WY 82301. (307) 324-3411. Freelance Submissions: no. Circulation: 3800.

RIVERTON RANGER, THE. PO Box 993. Riverton, WY 82501. (307) 856-2244. Freelance Submissions: pre-approved only. Submissions Editor: Dave Perry (general, book review, and travel). Circulation: 6800.

(RIVERTON) RANGER REVIEW, THE. 421 E. Main St. Riverton, WY 82501. (307) 856-2244. Freelance Submissions: yes. Submissions Editor: Dave Perry (general, book review, and travel). Circulation: 6500.

(ROCK SPRINGS) DAILY ROCKET-MINER. PO Box 98. Rock Springs, WY 82902-0098. (307) 362-3736. Freelance Submissions: yes; unpaid only. Submissions Editor: Linda Linn. Circulation: 8000.

SHERIDAN PRESS. 144 Grinnell. PO Box 2006. Sheridan, WY 82801. (307) 672-2431. Freelance Submissions: no. Circulation: 7600.

(WORLAND) NORTHERN WYOMING DAILY NEWS. PO Box 508. Worland, WY 82401. (307) 347-3241. Freelance Submissions: seldom. Submissions Editor: Sandy Collins (general, book review, and travel). Circulation: 4600.

Literary Agents

There is no law which says that a writer must have an agent. However, for some writers the benefits of having an agent are well worth the 10 to 15 percent commission charged. For example, some publishers simply refuse to consider unagented manuscripts. The specific services and charges vary from agent to agent, but they usually include the following:

Before sale—Evaluates your manuscript, advises on the preparation of your proposal, talks to editors, sends out your submissions, and informs you of results.

During sale—Negotiates contract with publisher and reviews the terms with you, after which you must decide to sign or not sign.

After sale—Receives and examines your royalty statements and payments, deducts the appropriate commission, and sends you the remainder. Pursues the sale of subsidiary rights retained by you in your contract.

Merely writing to one agent does not guarantee you will be accepted as a client, so expect the search to involve several contacts. The following information has been gathered and organized to help you in contacting an agency located in the Northwest.

Because a limited number of agents are based in this area, you may need to expand your search to include additional resources, such as the *Literary Market Place* (LMP), available in most libraries, or *California and Hawaii Publishing Marketplace* and *Southwest Publishing Marketplace*, available from Writers Connection. Or write to Author Aid/Research Associates International, 430 East 52nd Street, New York, NY 10022, for information on their directory of *Literary Agents of America*. See also the Books for Writers section of this book.

How to Use the Information in This Section

The first paragraph of each entry gives the basic contact information and identifies the agent to whom you should address your query.

Subjects of Interest

We've included information on the type of material the agent prefers to handle. Your chances of a positive response to your initial inquiry improve when you approach an agent who is already interested in your subject matter. Books that the agent has previously sold indicate the contacts and success the agent has had. However, some agents prefer to keep this type of information confidential.

Initial Contact

Never send a complete manuscript unless requested by the agent. An initial query letter may include no more than an outline or brief summary of your story and idea. For nonfiction, include your qualifications. Always include a SASE.

Commissions and Fees

Most agents charge between 10 and 15 percent of your writing income as their commission for representing you. You alone must decide if it is worth it to you to market your book yourself or pay an agent to do it.

Many agents charge additional fees to cover "out-of-pocket" expenses, such as long-distance phone calls, photocopying, express mail, etc. Some also charge reading fees, often to first-time writers only. These fees do not guarantee the agent will accept your work. If you decide to pay a reading fee, you should find out if the fee will be refunded or applied against the commission due if the agent accepts you as a client and sells your work.

Agency Policies

Many agents will handle new writers only if they have been referred by current clients, editors, or other professional colleagues. Other agents will gladly encourage new writers and are eager to represent well-written manuscripts.

Agents who do not handle all forms of subsidiary rights often will work in conjunction with other agents to get you the best deal possible. Agents will also work closely with their counterparts in Europe for sales of foreign rights or in Hollywood for sales of dramatization, motion picture, and broadcast (performance) rights.

Agents try to respond to your submissions or queries in a reasonable length of time; make it easier for them by including a SASE.

Additional Information

This section lists any other information the agent expects you to know, or wants you to know, about the agency.

CATALOG, THE. PO Box 2964. Vancouver, WA 98668. (206) 694-8531. Agent: Douglas Storey.

Subjects of Interest. Books—Fiction: mainstream with strong sales potential (100,000 or more); juvenile (middle and upper grades). Nonfiction: business; health; money; science; women's interests; hobbies; how-to; self-help; technical; textbooks. Representative titles: *In the Mouth of the Dragon* (Avery); *Your Child's Dental Care* (Insight); *Doctors Who Rape* (Longwood Academic). Do not want: poetry; plays; scripts; articles; short stories; genre fiction.

Initial Contact. Query with synopsis or proposal.

Commission and Fees. 15% commission for books sold in United States; 20% foreign. Fees: handling fee which covers postage, photocopying, and telephone.

Initial Contact. Query with synopsis or proposal.

Commission and Fees. 15% commission for books sold in United States; 20% foreign. Fees: handling fee which covers postage, photocopying, and telephone.

Agency Policies. Previously unpublished authors: yes. Response time to initial query: 3 weeks. Subsidiary rights: all.

Additional Information. We have special expertise in science, electronics, and computers. We also do book publicity.

NATASHA KERN LITERARY AGENCY, INC. PO Box 2908. Portland, OR 97208-2908. (503) 226-2221. Agent: Natasha Kern.

Subjects of Interest. Books—Fiction: commercial and literary romances, Westerns, action and adventure, historical, high-tech and medical thrillers, mysteries; middle grade, young adult novels. Nonfiction: health; science; parenting; psychology; how-to; self-help; cook books; current issues; gardening; true crime; celebrity bios; business; controversial; women's issues. Representative titles: *How to Raise a Hyper-Active Child* (St. Martins); *The Asian Mind Game* (Macmillan); *Rugged Splendor* (Avon). Do not want: sports; scholarly; short stories; poetry; articles; scripts; software.

Initial Contact. Query letter only.

Commission and Fees. 15% commission. Fees: $35 reading fee. Authorized overseas phone calls.

Agency Policies. Previously unpublished authors: yes. Response time to initial query: 4-6 weeks. Subsidiary rights: first serialization; second serialization; dramatization, motion picture and broadcast; direct mail or direct sales; translation and foreign; computer and other magnetic and electronic rights; commercial rights; English language publication outside the United States and Canada. Foreign rights: Alexandria Chapman (France); Lenart Sane (Scandinavia, Spain, Portugal, South America).

Additional Information. In 1989 successfully sold manuscripts for twelve first-time authors and sold the movie rights on two first-time books. Sold foreign rights to Sweden, France, Italy, etc.

LEVANT AND WALES LITERARY AGENCY, INC. 108 Hayes St. Seattle, WA 98109. (206) 284-7114. Fax: (206) 286-1025. Agents: Elizabeth Wales, Dan Levant.

Subjects of Interest. Books—Fiction and nonfiction: mainstream. Representative titles: *Writing in a Convertible with the Top Down* (Warner); *Aftermath: A Survivor's Rape Story* (Prentice Hall); *Catfish* (Ten Speed).

Initial Contact. Query with proposal for nonfiction; query with writing sample for fiction.

Commission and Fees. 15% commission. Fees: photocopy of manuscripts; express mail; overseas phone calls.

Agency Policies. Previously unpublished authors: yes. Response time to initial query: 5 weeks. Subsidiary rights: all. Foreign rights: we use subagents on a project basis.

Additional Information. We prefer clients from the Pacific Northwest: Washington, Oregon, Montana, Idaho, Alaska, and Hawaii.

Professional Organizations

Membership in one or more professional organizations can enhance your resumé, expand your network of professional contacts, and be a source of industry information and news. No two organizations are exactly alike, as you'll see from reading this section. Membership criteria, dues, and activities vary, as does the contact information.

Some organizations maintain an office where you can request information; others use branch members' homes or work addresses and phone numbers. A few organizations prefer that queries be directed to their national headquarters. In any case, with dozens to choose from, you are sure to find one that's right for your writing field and geographic area.

How to Use the Information in This Section

The first paragraph of each entry identifies the name of the organization, address and phone number of its headquarters, and name and/or title of a contact person. When available, we've listed the date when the organization was founded, number of members, and annual dues.

Members: This figure represents the number of members of the organization at the time it was surveyed.

Dues: While some organizations with local chapters or branches require only national *or* branch dues, others require dues to be paid at both levels. Still others require a one-time processing fee in addition to the dues. When information on branch dues was supplied, we included it with the branch information.

Purpose: Most of the organizations we surveyed listed a statement of purpose, which often emphasized the organization's role in the pursuit of excellence in writing, advancement of members' career goals and communication skills, and dissemination of information.

Membership criteria: Some organizations list only an interest in writing and payment of dues as their criteria for membership; others offer several types of membership and require different levels of professional achievement as criteria.

Meetings: Most organizations hold regular or monthly meetings, often with guest speakers.

Activities: Many organizations sponsor seminars, critique group sessions, and/or annual conferences. If an organization lists conferences as one of its activities, there may be additional information in the Conferences section. Some organizations sponsor conferences in a different state each year.

Benefits: Some chapters offer many benefits, including local programs, monthly newsletters, a membership directory, medical insurance, legal representation, a lending library of books or tapes, and more. Others offer networking at regular meetings.

Newsletters: In addition to providing information to its members, some organizations' newsletters accept freelance material (though usually not for pay) and publish book reviews and/or press releases of events or news.

Whenever information was available, we specified the editor of the newsletter, the frequency (newsletter publication schedule), and submission policies (types of written material the publication accepts).

Additional publications: Some organizations produce a variety of publications or resources. Those publications, other than newsletters, are listed here.

Local Chapters

For national organizations with local chapters, we've listed at least the name and address and/or phone number of the local contact person whenever possible. Not all established local chapters are listed since new groups often form where sufficient interest insures participation, and annual elections also render published information inaccurate. For these reasons, some organizations prefer all inquiries to be directed to their national headquarters. In such cases, chapter listings may be omitted or be quite concise. Other organizations supplied detailed information about chapter activities. These more comprehensive entries may include any of the previously listed items.

AMERICAN MEDICAL WRITERS ASSOCIATION. 9650 Rockville Pike. Bethesda, MD 20814. (301) 493-0003. Executive Director, Lillian Sablack. Founded: 1940. Members: 3300 (national). Dues: $65.

Purpose: To further clarity in medical communications. Membership criteria: interest in medical communications. Meetings: 8-10 times annually (chapter); annually (national). Activities: meetings, chapter events, workshops/seminars, conferences. Benefits: curriculum of workshops leading to a certificate in specialty area of medical communications; networking; annual conference (location varies); medical and life insurance.

Chapter Newsletter: *The Pacemaker*. Editor: Judith Windt. Frequency: 8 times annually. Submissions: articles for quarterly journal only. Additional publications: freelance directory, quarterly journal.

AMERICAN SOCIETY FOR TRAINING AND DEVELOPMENT.
National office: (703) 683-8100. Founded: 1946. Members: 23,000 (national). National dues: $120.

Purpose: To provide leadership, service, and education for the training and development of individuals, organizations, and the community. Membership criteria: Any person who is interested in the training and development of individuals is eligible for membership. Benefits: membership directory.

MONTANA
Big Sky Chapter (Billings). Contact person: Linda Garner. (406) 657-7917.

OREGON
Portland Metro Chapter. Contact person: Paula Myers. (503) 225-0850.

WASHINGTON
Columbia Basin Chapter (Richland). Contact person: Sylvia Zavaletta. (509) 943-2649.

Inland Northwest Chapter (Spokane). Contact person: Dave Zimmerman. (509) 489-0500.

Nisqually Valley Chapter (Tacoma). Contact person: Jo Dee Owens. (206) 565-2053.

Puget Sound Chapter (Seattle). Contact person: Mary Ann Alderson. (206) 286-7678.

AMERICAN SOCIETY OF INDEXERS. 1700 18th St., NW. Washington, DC 20009. (202) 328-7110 (phone and leave message). Founded: 1968. Members: 700 (national). Dues: $40.

Purpose: To improve the quality of indexes, increase awareness of indexing among publishers and public. Membership criteria: interest in indexing. Meetings: bimonthly. Activities: meetings, workshops/seminars, conferences, trade shows, potluck informal gatherings. Benefits: informative newsletter, publications, and conferences; medical, life, and disability insurance; membership directory.

Newsletter: *ASI Newsletter*. Frequency: quarterly. Submissions: letters to the editor, articles, press releases. Additional publications: register of freelance indexers, many aids to indexers (national level).

AMERICAN SOCIETY OF JOURNALISTS & AUTHORS, INC. 1501 Broadway, Ste. 302. New York, NY 10036. (212) 977-0947. Executive Director, Alexandra Cantor; President, Florence Isaacs. Founded: 1948. National dues: $120.

Purpose: to establish high ethical standards and to further pursuit of excellence in writing nonfiction. Membership criteria: professional published nonfiction writers. Benefits: medical benefits package, dial-a-writer referral service, membership directory. Branch-level activities: meetings, workshops, seminars, annual conference, discussion groups, networking with professionals. Refer all requests for information to national office.

Newsletter: *ASJA Newsletter*. Frequency: monthly. Additional publications: *Tools of the Writer's Trade, The Complete Guide to Writing Nonfiction, The ASJA Handbook.*

ASIAN AMERICAN JOURNALISTS ASSOCIATION. 1765 Sutter St., Room 1000. San Francisco, CA 94115. (415) 346-2051. Executive Director, Diane Yen-Mei Wong. Founded: 1981. Members: 900 (national). Dues: $36 (paid at branch level).

Purpose: to increase employment of Asian/American (A/A) journalists; to assist students pursuing journalism careers; to encourage fair and accurate news coverage of A/A issues; to provide support for A/A journalists. Membership criteria: includes categories for professional members, full members (journalists), associate members (non-journalists, retired, or part-time), student members. Meetings: two times annually; chapters meet monthly. Activities: workshops, seminars, conferences. Benefits: reduced rates for organization conventions, job bank.

Newsletter: *Asian/American Journalists Association.* Frequency: quarterly. Submissions: press releases, articles. Additional publications: periodic studies and handbook.

ASSOCIATED BUSINESS WRITERS OF AMERICA *see* NATIONAL WRITERS CLUB.

CLARION WEST. 340 15th Ave. E., Ste. 350. Seattle, WA 98112. (206) 322-9083. Contact Person: Linda Jordan. Founded: 1984. Members: 100. Dues: $25.

Purpose: to promote the literary arts. Meetings: Seattle area. Activites: workshops/seminars; public readings; outreach program to local schools; conference. Benefits: notice of and discounts to events; information network among writers.

Newsletter: *The Seventh Week.* Editor: Adam Bridge. Frequency: 3 times per year. Submissions: press releases, articles (from members).

COSMEP, THE INTERNATIONAL ASSOCIATION OF INDEPENDENT PUBLISHERS. PO Box 703. San Francisco, CA 94101. (415) 922-9490. Executive Director, Richard Morris. Founded: 1968. Members: 1500. Dues: $60.

Purpose: trade association of small publishers. Membership criteria: must be publishers of books or periodicals; self-publishers are eligible to join. Benefits: information available on request; medical and life insurance offered.

Newsletter: *COSMEP Newsletter.* Editor: Richard Morris. Frequency: monthly. Submissions: press releases.

FICTIONEERS. Fremont Library. 4712 Highway 20. Concrete, WA 98237. President, Thelma Schiller. (206) 853-8596.

Purpose: to support and encourage writers. Membership criteria: interest in writing and publishing. Meetings: third Saturday of each month. Place: Fremont Library, Seattle, Washington. Activities: meetings and speakers. Benefits: readings, critiques, slants toward markets, newsletter.

FRIENDS OF MYSTERY. PO Box 8251. Portland, OR 97207. (503) 241-0759. Contact Person: Jay Margulies. Founded: 1982. Members: 100. Dues: $15.

Purpose: to promote interest and knowledge of mystery and detective literatures, both fact and fiction. Membership criteria: interest. Meetings: fourth Thursday, every other month, at the Northwest Service Center in Portland. Activities: workshops/seminars. Benefits: bookstore discounts.

Newsletter: *The Bloodletter.* Editors: Deb Hendrix, Stanley Johnson. Frequency: 4-5 times per year. Submissions: press releases; articles; book reviews.

INTERNATIONAL ASSOCIATION OF BUSINESS COMMUNICATORS.
One Hallidie Plaza, Ste. 600. San Francisco, CA 94102. (415) 433-3400. Fax (415) 362-8762. President, Norm Leaper, ABC; Membership Recruitment, Ann Fraley. Founded: 1970. Members: 11,500. International dues: $150, plus $30 applicaton fee.

Purpose: to further excellence in the area of business communication. Membership criteria: qualification and payment of fees. Activities: chapter meetings, workshops, international conference. Benefits: directory; resource/information library.

Magazine: *Communication World.*

IDAHO
Southern Idaho Chapter (Boise). Contact person: David A. Cuoio, Coordinator of Employee Communication. J.R. Simplot Co. PO Box 27. Boise, ID 83707. (208) 336-2110. Dues: $201.

OREGON
Oregon/Columbia Chapter (Portland area). Contact person: Christine Normandin, Communications Consultant. 19412 Wilderness Dr. West Linn, OR 97068. (503) 697-8738. Dues: $221.

WASHINGTON
Eastside Chapter (East Seattle/Bellevue/Redmond/Kirkland/Issaquah areas). Contact person: David Miller, President. Miller Communications, Inc. 4670 191st Ave. SE. Issaquah, WA 98027. (206) 874-7129. Meetings: third Tuesday of every other month, beginning with January, 7:00 am. Dues: $226. Newsletter: *IABC Eastside Reporter.*

Metro Spokane. Contact person: Dan Ruddell, General Manager. Broadway Group Advertising. PO Box 14646. Spokane, WA 99214. (509) 534-1502. Dues: $211.

Seattle Chapter. Contact person: Sally Gadd. Washington Software. 18804 N. Creek Parkway, Ste. 112. Bothell, WA 98011. (206) 483-3323. Dues: $226.

INTERNATIONAL ASSOCIATION OF CRIME WRITERS (NORTH AMERICA).
JAF Box 1500. New York, NY 10116. (212) 757-3915. Executive Director, Mary A. Frisque. Founded: 1987. Members: 225. Dues: $50.

Purpose: to encourage communication among crime writers worldwide. Membership criteria: published writer or professional in the field (agent, editor, bookseller). Activities: meetings. Benefits: information about crime literature conferences abroad; chance to meet with foreign writers and editors.

Newsletter: *Border Patrol.* Editors: William Slattery, Bruce Cassiday, Mary Frisque. Frequency: quarterly. Submissions: press releases and articles (sometimes); book reviews (crime literature in English translations).

INTERNATIONAL BLACK WRITERS.
PO Box 1030. Chicago, IL 60690. (312) 995-5195. President, Mable Terrell; Membership, Carolyn Griffin. Founded: 1970. Members: 650. Dues: $15.

Purpose: to encourage, develop, and display writing talent. Membership criteria: the desire to write. Meetings: monthly. Activities: meetings, workshops/seminars, conference, contests. Benefits: monthly newsletter, free admission to conference.

Newsletter: *In Touch.* Editor: Mable Terrell. Frequency: monthly. Submissions: press releases, articles. Additional publications: *Black Writer's Journal,* a quarterly magazine that includes poetry, articles, short fiction, and writing tips and techniques.

INTERNATIONAL FOOD, WINE, AND TRAVEL WRITERS ASSOCIATION. PO Box 1532. Palm Springs, CA 92263. (619) 322-4717. President, Arthur Von Wiesenberger; Executive Director and Membership Chairperson, Wil Hanson. Founded: 1956. Members: 350 (international). Dues: $60.

Purpose: to provide a gathering point and resource base for professionals engaged in the food, wine, travel, and hospitality industries. Membership criteria: open to individuals, companies, and organizations maintaining professional interests in the above industries; must be nominated by a member or an officer. Activities: local and regional meetings; annual conclave; awards based on nominations by regular members, including the *Golden Fork Award*. Benefits: access to current information on press trips and other professional travel benefits, official IFW&TWA working press card, confidential membership directory; special discounts on rental cars, travel, hotel accommodations; writer participation in *Annual Guide Book*; networking relationship with members worldwide and associate member organizations.

Newsletter: *Hospitality World*. Editor: Wil Hanson. Frequency: monthly. Submissions: press releases, articles from members. Additional publications: *Window to the World* (guidebook).

INTERNATIONAL WOMEN'S WRITING GUILD. PO Box 810, Gracie Station. New York, NY 10028. (212) 737-7536. Contact Person: Hannelore Hahn. Founded: 1976. Members: 2500. Dues: $35; $45 foreign.

Purpose: The IWWG is a network for the personal and professional empowerment of women through writing. Membership criteria: none. Activities: meetings; workshops/seminars; conferences; networking/support. Benefits: manuscript referrals to literary agents; subscription to *Network*; 8 regional and national events; medical insurance at group rates.

Newsletter: *Network*. Editor: Tatyana Stoumen. Frequency: 6 times per year. Submissions: press releases. Additional publications: *Writing as an Act of Faith, Ringing the Gong: Writing to Change the World/the Environment, On Addictions and . . .*

MONTANA ARTS COUNCIL. 48 N. Last Chance Gulch. Helena, MT 59620. (406) 444-6430. Contact Person: Julie Smith.

Purpose: promotion of the arts in Montana. Activities: meetings; workshops/seminars; conferences. Benefits: biennial fellowship of $2000 for writers; biennial First Book Award (includes publication of winning manuscript).

Newsletter: *ArtistSearch*. Editor: Sue O'Connell/Martha Sprague. Frequency: monthly. Submissions: press releases, articles, book reviews.

MYSTERY WRITERS OF AMERICA. 236 West 27th St., Room 600. New York, NY 10001. (212) 255-7005. President, John Lutz; Membership Chairperson, Priscilla Ridgway. Founded: 1945. Members: 2200 (international). Dues: $65; $25 for corresponding members.

Purpose: to promote interests of mystery writers; to maintain recognition of mystery writing in publishing industry and reading public; to disseminate information and share benefits of associating with others interested in mystery writing. Membership criteria: includes categories for people actively writing mysteries, those published in other fields, and those who are unpublished or fans. Activities: conferences; Edgar Allan Poe annual awards dinner held in New York City in late April.

Newsletter: *The Third Degree*. Frequency: 10 issues yearly.

NATIONAL LEAGUE OF AMERICAN PEN WOMEN, INC. Pen Arts
Building. 1300 17th Street, NW. Washington, D.C. 20036-1973. (202) 785-1997.
President, Frances H. Mulliken. Founded: 1897. Members: 6000 (national). Dues:
$35, paid at branch level (200 U.S. branches).

Purpose: to further professional contacts and excellence in the arts. Membership criteria:
rigorous qualification process. Activities: national meeting in spring (biennial). Benefits:
national membership directory.

Newsletter: *The Pen Woman* (magazine). Editor: varies. Frequency: 9 times annually.
Contents: includes titles of books by our member authors and professional/skill criteria
updates, standards.

OREGON
Portland Branch. Contact person: Myrna Perkins. 2039 SE 45th Ave. Portland, OR 97215.

WASHINGTON
Grays Harbor Branch. Contact person: Carole Bodey. PO Box 482. Hoquiam, WA 98550.

Seattle Branch. Contact Person: Kay Stewart. 7584 Meadowmeer Lane, NE. Bainbridge
Island, WA 98110.

Spokane Branch. Contact person: May W. Whitney. East 212 Weile #1. Spokane, WA
99208.

Tacoma Branch. Contact Person: Joann Schafer. PO Box 45436. Tacoma, WA 98444.

NATIONAL WRITERS CLUB, THE. 1450 S. Havana, Ste. 620. Aurora, CO
80012. (303) 751-7844. Contact Person: Executive Director, James L. Young.
Founded: 1937. Members: 4000. Dues: Membership, $50, plus $15 one-time setup
fee. Professional membership, $60, plus $15 one-time setup fee (requires credits
covering sales to at least three national or regional magazines, a book sold to a
royalty publisher, a play produced, or employment as writer, journalist, or editor).

Purpose: to meet the needs of freelance writers for honest, sympathetic, and authoritative help.
Membership criteria: person must be serious about writing. Benefits: savings plan, group
insurance, discount on books and supplies, agent referral, acts as literary agent to small
presses, manuscript criticism, agent referral, correspondence courses in fiction and nonfiction.
National membership directory: *Professional Writers Directory* (inclusion is by choice).

Newsletter: *Authorship.* Frequency: six times per year. Additional publications: *NWC
Newsletter, NWC Market Update, Flash Market News.*

Note: For those interested, NWC now operates the **Associated Business Writers of America.**
If your writing expertise lies in this area, you may become a dual member at no extra charge.

NATIONAL WRITERS UNION. 13 Astor Pl., Seventh Floor. New York, NY
10003. (212) 254-0279. National Director, Anne Wyville. Founded: 1983. Members:
3000 (national). Dues: $55-$135 (sliding scale).

Purpose: trade union for freelance writers; to gain equity, fair standards, and payment for
freelance writers through collective action. Membership criteria: publish a book or play, three
articles, five poems, one short story, or an equivalent amount of newsletter, publicity,
technical, commercial, governmental, or institutional copy; or have similar portfolio of
unpublished work and be actively seeking publication. Activities: delegates' assembly
annually in June, chapter meetings, workshops, conferences. Benefits: medical insurance,
collective bargaining, individual contract advice, press credentials, grievance handling.

Newsletter: *The American Writer.* Editor: Ed Hedemann. Frequency: quarterly. Additional
publications: Boston chapter has published *An Insider's Guide to Freelance Writing in New
England.*

NO FRILLS WRITER'S WORKSHOP. 1118 Hoyt Ave. Everett, WA 98201.
Contact Person: Ron Fleshman. (206) 259-0804. Founded: 1986. Members: 18. Dues: $40.

Purpose: to improve members' writing skills through interaction, information sharing, and study. Membership criteria: serious intention. Meetings: every Wednesday, 6:30-9:30 pm. Activities: workshops/seminars.

NORTHWEST ASSOCIATION OF BOOK PUBLISHERS. PO Box 633.
Marlyhurst, OR 97036. (503) 293-8583. President, George Van Patten. Members: 150+. Dues: $35.

Purpose: to promote professionalism in publishing and provide a support network for independent publishers. Membership criteria: open to all who support our purpose. Meetings: last Thursday of every month (except December), 10 am-12 pm at Marlyhurst College, West Linn. Annual meeting: Thursday before Thanksgiving.

Newsletter: *Publisher's Focus*. Editor: Doug Dubosque. (503) 829-6849. Frequency: monthly. Submissions: articles on independent publishing and related themes.

NORTHWEST OUTDOOR WRITERS' ASSOCIATION. 3421 E. Mercer
St. Seattle, WA 98112. (206) 323-3970. Contact Person: Stan Jones. Founded: 1978. Members: 275. Dues: $25 (active); $50 (supporting).

Purpose: improvement of craft and exchange of ideas. Membership criteria: published writers, broadcasters, photographers in the outdoor field. Meetings: winter, summer, and fall at various sites. Activities: workshops/seminars, conferences, contests. Benefits: monthly newsletter, participation in craft workshops, membership directory.

Newsletter: *NOWA Newsletter*. Editor: Stan Jones. Frequency: monthly. Submissions: press releases; articles; book reviews (member books primarily).

OREGON ASSOCIATION OF CHRISTIAN WRITERS. 17768 SW
Pointe, Forest Court. Aloha, OR 97006. President, Elsie Larson, (503) 643-6321; Editor, Sally Stuart, (503) 642-9844. Founded: 1963. Members: 280. Dues: $25.

Purpose: to promote higher craftsmanship in writing and a greater sense of responsibility in journalism. Membership criteria: a desire to write and portray a personal Christian faith. Meetings: February in Salem; May in Eugene; October in Portland. Activities: workshops/seminars, conferences, contests. Benefits: discount on annual conference; free attendance for quarterly seminars and workshops; quarterly newsletter with marketing update; membership directory.

Newsletter: *Writer*. Editor: Sally Stuart. Frequency: quarterly. Submissions: press releases, articles from members only, books reviews (not yet, but would be interested in some applying to writing, publishing, or other helps for writers).

OREGON COAST COUNCIL FOR THE ARTS. PO Box 1315. Newport,
OR 97365. (503) 265-9231. Executive Director, Sharon Morgan. Founded: 1977. Members: 3000+\-. Dues: $10-$1000.

Purpose: to change lives through the arts. Membership criteria: interest. Meetings: monthly on the fourth Wednesday at the Newport Performing Arts Center. Activites: workshops/seminars, conferences, contests. Benefits: discounts; advisory mailing of artists' opportunites (by discipline), monthly newsletter, referrals via artists' registry, insurance.

Newsletter: *OCCA Newsletter*. Editor: Helena Moore. Frequency: monthly. Submissions: press releases. Additional publications: *Applause* (magazine).

OREGON COUNCIL FOR THE HUMANITIES. 812 SW Washington, Ste. 225. Portland, OR 97205. (503) 241-0543. (800) 735-0543. Executive Director, Richard A. Lewis. Founded: 1971.

Purpose: to promote the humanities in public life in Oregon. Activites: meetings, workshops/seminars, conferences on an irregular basis; grants for public humanities programs (primary activity).

Magazine: *Oregon Humanities*. Editors: Richard A. Lewis, Carolyn Buan. Frequency: 2 times per year. Submissions: press releases on humanities-related events; articles (call or write for guidelines); book reviews.

OREGON COUNCIL OF TEACHERS OF ENGLISH. PO Box 2515. Portland, OR 97208. (503) 591-4690, ext. 256. Contact Person: Joseph Fitzgibbon. Founded: 1948. Members: 1100. Dues: $15.

Purpose: to promote teaching of the language arts. Membership criteria: an interest in the language arts. Meetings: quarterly around the state. Activities: workshops/seminars, conferences. Benefits: publications, information on latest teaching techniques, contact with state department of education, conferences with other teachers.

Newsletter: *Chalkboard*. Editor: Bill Mull. Frequency: 5 times per year. Submissions: press releases; article submissions; book reviews. Additional publications: *Oregon English*. Editor: Ulrich Hardt.

OREGON WRITERS ALLIANCE. 5060 SW 182nd Ave. Beaverton, OR 97007. Contact Person: Sheila Marler. Founded: 1987. Members: 20. Dues: $10.

Purpose: support/critique group for writers. Criteria: sincere interest in improving writing skills and a desire to publish. Meetings: second and fourth Wednesday in the Beaverton city meeting room, Hall and Fifth St. Activities: workshops/seminars. Benefits: monthly meetings, speakers, workshops, newsletter, updates on contests, access to OWA library.

Newsletter: *Oregon Writers Alliance*. Editor: Charlyn Salb. Frequency: quarterly. Submissions: press releases, book reviews (only books related to improved writing skills).

PEN INTERNATIONAL. 38 King St. London, WC2E 8JT. England. Executive Director, PEN USA Center West: Richard Bray. Founded: 1921 (London, England). Members: 2000 (USA). Dues: $45 (USA Center West).

Purpose: international, nonprofit organization to promote free expression in the arts and "to protect the principles of unhampered transmission of thought and to preserve the concept of a free press within each nation and among all nations." Activities: international congresses, programs, advocacy, contests, and awards.

PEN USA Center West. 1100 Glendon Ave., Ste. PH. Los Angeles, CA 90024. (213) 824-2041. Fax (213) 824-1679. Membership criteria: open to all qualified writers and members of the literary community who subscribe to PEN's ideals and aims. Activities: international congresses, programs, workshops/seminars (co-sponsored with other organizations), and contests. Benefits: newsletter, membership directory, announcements, events, awards, committee work, publicity kits for new authors, imprisoned writers' advocacy.

Newsletter: *PEN Center USA West* newsletter. Editor: Victoria Branch. Frequency: quarterly. Submissions: press releases, articles related to PEN's interests.

POETS & WRITERS, INC. 72 Spring St. New York, NY 10012. (212) 226-3586. Executive Director, Elliott Figman. Founded: 1970. Members: over 6800 listed writers. Dues: none; $5 listing fee.

Purpose: nonprofit corporation organized for literary and educational purposes. Membership criteria: we are not a membership organization but require publication in order to be listed. Activities: Writers Exchange Program; competitions; Readings/Workshops Grants Program, which offers matching grants to writers in New York and California (program is expanding to other states in the next couple of years); National Literary Information Center (NLIC) answers practical writing questions from 11:00-3:00 EST, Monday through Friday, and provides addresses for the writers listed with them.

Newsletter: *Poets & Writers Magazine*. Editor: Darylyn Brewer. Frequency: bimonthly. Submissions: articles. Additional publications: references, source books, how-to guides, several newsletters.

Poets & Writers West (West Coast Office): 1862 Euclid Ave., Box 292. Berkeley, CA 94709. (415) 548-6618. West Coast Coordinator, Stuart Robbins. Activities: readings/workshop programs.

PUBLISHERS MARKETING ASSOCIATION. 2401 Pacific Coast Highway, Ste. 102. Hermosa Beach, CA 90254. (213) 372-2732. Fax (213) 374-3342. Executive Director, Jan Nathan. Founded: 1983. Members: 1200. Dues: vary; start at $75 for companies having up to 9 employees. Affiliates: Pacific Northwest Book Publishers Asociation, Marin Small Publishers Association, Book Publishers Northwest.

Purpose: to cooperatively market our titles and to educate the independent publisher. Membership criteria: must be a publisher or about to become a publisher. Meetings: monthly. Activities: workshops, seminars, conferences, trade shows, contests. Benefits: cooperative marketing programs to libraries, bookstores, schools, and speciality markets; membership directory.

Newsletter: *PMA Newsletter*. Editor: Jan Nathan. Frequency: monthly. Submissions: press releases, articles.

ROMANCE WRITERS OF AMERICA, INC. 13700 Veterans Memorial Dr., Ste. 315. Houston, TX 77014-1023. (713) 440-6885. Members: 4800 (national). Dues: $45, plus $10 one-time processing fee.

Purpose: to provide support and education for romance writers. Membership criteria: must join national organization before joining local. Activities: annual national conference (1000+ attendees).

Newsletter: *Romance Writer Report*. Frequency: bimonthly.

ALASKA

Alaska Chapter #73. Contact person: Ramona Rolle-Berg. 4200 E. 145th Ave. Anchorage, AK 99516. (907) 345-7108.

IDAHO

North Idaho #21. Contact person: Beverly Goding. PO Box 797. Sagle, ID 83860. (208) 263-0869 (evenings), (208) 772-4094 (days).

Southern Idaho #64. Contact person: Pat Tracy. 4696 E. 113th N. Idaho Falls, ID 83401. (208) 524-5438.

OREGON

Greater Portland #59. Contact person: Isabel A. Ibarra. 4825 NE 17th. Portland, OR 97211. (503) 284-4200.

Heart of Oregon #3. Contact person: Ann Simas. 1140 Waverly St. Eugene, OR 97401-5235. (503) 485-0583.

Portland #50. Contact person: Iona Lockwood. 7000 SE Thiessen Rd. Milwaukie, OR 97267. (503) 659-2559.

Wilammette Valley #32. Contact person: Pat Kennedy. 5911 NW Pinewood Pl. Corvallis, OR 97330. (503) 753-0349.

WASHINGTON

Inland Empire #63. Contact person: Joy Tucker. N. 1703 Dakota St. Spokane, WA 99207. (509) 482-2063.

Peninsula #84. Contact person: Glenda Geister. PO Box 92. Lilliwap, WA 98555. (206) 877-5097.

Seattle #62. Contact persons: Angela M. Butterworth. 4603-163rd Ct., SE. Bellevue, WA 98006. (206) 643-7739. Pam Lee. 9908 NE 124th, #903. Kirkland, WA 98034. (206) 823-6148.

Tacoma #67. Contact person: Carol S. Duncan. 4142 N. 7th St. Tacoma, WA 98406. (206) 759-4623.

Yakima #20. Contact Person: Janie P. Hulett. 1053 Stone Rd. Yakima, WA 98908. (509) 965-4365.

SCIENCE FICTION WRITERS OF AMERICA (SFWA). Executive Secretary, Peter Dennis Paulz. 3505 Parris Bridge Rd. Spartanburg, SC 29305. West Coast Regional Director, Stephen Goldin. 6251 Havenside #4. Sacramento, CA 95831. Founded: 1965. Members: 1200 (national). Dues: $75.

Purpose: to inform science fiction writers of professional matters; to promote professional welfare; to help in dealing with publishers, agents, editors, and anthologists. Membership criteria: sale to professional publishers (reduced subscription rate available to unpublished writers). Activities: conferences, meetings, small meetings at many science fiction conventions, annual awards banquet to present the Nebula Award, the most important award in the science fiction genre. Benefits: model contracts, legal advice and representation under certain circumstances, meeting room at conventions, bookstore discounts, free review copies of books and magazines, three quarterly publications, membership directory.

Newsletter: *Bulletin of the Science Fiction Writers of America.* Editor: Pamela Sargent, Box 486, Johnson City, NY 13790. Frequency: quarterly. Submissions: press releases, articles. Additional publications: *SFWA* (letters), *Nebual Awards Report.*

SOCIETY FOR TECHNICAL COMMUNICATION. 901 N. Stuart St. Arlington, VA 22203. (703) 522-4114. Founded: 1953. Members: 13,000 (national). Dues: $75, $10 one-time initiation fee; $25 student rate; payable at national level.

Purpose: the advancement of the theory and practice of technical communication in all media. Membership criteria: be engaged in or have an interest in any phase of technical communication. Meetings: open to the public in all chapters. Activities: annual arts and publication contest; annual international conference in April.

Newsletter: *Technical Communication* (quarterly journal); *Intercom* (monthly newsletter).

SOCIETY OF AMERICAN TRAVEL WRITERS. 1155 Connecticut Ave., Ste. 500. Washington, D.C. 20036. (202) 429-6639.

SOCIETY OF CHILDREN'S BOOK WRITERS. PO Box 66296. Mar Vista Station. Los Angeles, CA 90066. (818) 347-2849. President, Stephen Mooser; Chairperson of Board of Directors, Sue Alexander. Founded: 1968. Members: 6600 (national). Dues: $35.

Purpose: to serve as a network of information and support for professional writers and illustrators of children's literature. Membership criteria: full members (published writers and illustrators of children's literature); associate members (anyone interested in children's literature). Activities: meetings, workshops, seminars, conferences (national conference every August), annual awards. Benefits: manuscript exchange, writing grants, medical insurance, membership directory, market guides.

Newsletter: *The Bulletin*. Editor: Stephen Mooser. Frequency: bimonthly. Submissions: from members only.

ALASKA
Alaska Chapter. Contact person: Nancy White Carlstrom. 2731 Alaska Range Lane. Fairbanks, AK 99708.

IDAHO/NEVADA
Idaho/Nevada Chapter. Contact person: Teddy Swecker. 155 McCoy St. Winnemucca, NV 89445.

OREGON
Northwest Chapter. Contact person: Elizabeth Vaughan. 2513 SE Taylor. Portland, OR 97214. (503) 235-6210. Dues: $10. Meetings: workshops and conferences 3-4 times annually. Activities: workshops/seminars; conferences; retreat. Benefits: local and national newsletter; national grants and awards; pamphlets, brochures, and market information; reduced rates on conferences and workshops. Membership directory available to members.

Newsletter: *SCBW NewsWorthy* (local). Editors: Robin Koontz, Darcie McNally. Frequency: bimonthy. Submissions: press releases; articles; book reviews. Additional publications: *NW Authors for Young People* (pamphlet); guides for citizens groups; other pamphlets.

WASHINGTON
Washington Chapter. Contact person: Eva Nixon. 18505 55th Ave., 3rd floor. Seattle, WA 98155-4318.

WYOMING
Rocky Mountain Chapter (includes Colorado, Utah, Nebraska, New Mexico). Contact person: Kathleen Phillips. 1054 Grant Place. Boulder, CO 80302.

WESTERN WRITERS OF AMERICA. PO Box 823. Sheridan, WY 82801. (307) 672-0889. Membership Chairperson, Barbara Ketcham. Founded: 1950. Members: 500 (international). Dues: $60.

Purpose: to advertise professional writers and help promote their books. Membership criteria: associate member must have published one book or five articles; full member must have published 3 books or 30 articles. Benefits: promotion and publicity; membership directory. Meetings: none. Activities: annual conference, fourth week in June, location varies.

Newsletter: *WWA Newsletter* (bimonthly) and *The Roundup* (quarterly magazine).

WOMEN IN COMMUNICATIONS, INC. 2101 Wilson Blvd., Ste. 417.
Arlington, VA 22201. (703) 528-4200. Executive Vice President, Susan Lowell Butler; Membership Director, Michele Grassley Franklin. Founded: 1909. Members: 11,500+ (national). National dues: $85, plus $25 one-time processing fee.

Purpose: a national organization of women and men who work to unite all communications professionals, support First Amendment rights, recognize outstanding communication achievements, and promote the advancement and equitable treatment of women communicators. Membership criteria: professional status requires at least two years of work as a professional in creative communications and 20 hours weekly in a professional capacity; associate status covers those with less than two years' experience; student memberships are also available. Activities: annual national convention, workshops, seminars, advancement fund for scholarship and awards programs. Benefits: networking, toll-free national job hotline, professional development, governmental representation, professional publications, membership directory, life, medical, and disability insurance.

Magazine: *The Professional Communicator.* Editor: Linda Russman. Frequency: bimonthly. Submissions: press releases, articles. Additional publications: *Washington Memo* (legislative newsletter); *Leading Change* (all-member newsletter).

MONTANA
Great Falls Chapter. Contact Person: Kathleen Cronin. College of Great Falls. 1301 20th St. S. Great Falls, MT 59405. (406) 761-8210.

OREGON
Portland Chapter. Contact Person: Janet Ross Klippstein. 11515 SE Lincoln Ct. Portland, OR 97216. (503) 255-5481.

WASHINGTON
Mid-Columbia Chapter. Contact Person: Kathryn S. Lang. 414 Scot. Richland, WA 99352. (509) 375-3474.

Seattle Chapter. Contact Person: Joan Carufel. World Cavalcade Travel Film. 5th and Union. Seattle, WA 98101. (206) 682-5255.

Spokane Chapter. Contact Person: Maxine M. Harris. Goodwill Industries. #130 3rd. Spokane, WA 99202. (509) 838-4246.

WOMEN IN FILM. 6464 Sunset Blvd., Ste. 900. Los Angeles, CA 90028. (213) 463-6040. President, Billie Beasley Jenkins. Founded: 1973. Members: 1500. Dues: $125. International organization with branches in United States.

Purpose: to increase equal opportunity of employment of women in film and television and create greater visibility of work by women. Membership criteria: three years professional experience with two member sponsors. Meetings: monthly. Activities: workshops, seminars, conferences, job referral service, screenings, retreat, festival. Benefits: medical insurance, contacts with professionals, other benefits outlined in membership information.

Newsletter: *Reel News.* Editor: Karen Lustgarten. Frequency: monthly.

WOMEN'S NATIONAL BOOK ASSOCIATION, INC. 160 5th Ave. New York, NY 10010. (212) 675-7805. President, Patti Breitman. Founded: 1917.

Purpose: a nonprofit, tax-exempt corporation providing educational and literary programs to those interested in the publishing industry; also serves as a channel of communication for topics of interest in the book world. Membership criteria: open to women and men in all occupations associated with the publishing industry. Benefits: membership directory.

Newsletter: *The Bookwoman.*

WORLD ACADEMY OF ARTS AND CULTURE. Secretary General, Rosemary Wilkinson. 3146 Buckeye Court. Placerville, CA 95667. (916) 626-4166. Dues: $30 first year, $10 annual renewal.

Purpose: international organization that gathers world poets in annual conference to promote world brotherhood and peace through poetry. Activities: liason for information for poets, international conferences.

Newsletter: *The Voice of Poets.* Frequency: before and after international conference.

WRITERS GUILD OF AMERICA, WEST. 8955 Beverly Blvd. West Hollywood, CA 90048. (213) 550-1000. Public Relations Director, Cheryl Rhoden. Founded: 1933. Members: 7000 (Western United States). Dues: $1500 initiation; then 1.5 percent of annual income plus $25 per quarter.

Purpose: collective bargaining agency representing writers in the film and broadcasting industries. Membership criteria: rigorous qualification process. Activities: annual meeting of membership, conferences. Benefits: pension plan, medical and dental insurance, membership directory. Some services available to nonmembers.

Newsletter: *The Journal.* Editor: Bill Meis. Frequency: monthly.

Conferences

Conferences are a great place to make professional contacts, discover new information, and get motivated. In this section we've listed conferences covering a diverse range of writing and publishing topics.

How to Use the Information in This Section

We've listed conferences by their official names and included other pertinent information such as sponsors' names, addresses, and telephone numbers. We've also included a contact person (often the conference director) whenever possible.

When no information on a particular topic or section was provided by conference personnel or the sponsoring organization, we have omitted that topic from the listing.

Location: Many conference locations change, and we have indicated those that vary, along with information on the locations for specific years when known. Where locations are constant, we have listed specific places.

Date: We have listed the time of the year the conference is usually held and added specific dates whenever information was available.

Frequency: Most conferences are held annually. Some, however, are offered every two years.

Length: This indicates the length of the conference, from one day to several weeks.

Fee: Conference fees are often two-tiered to offer discounts to the sponsoring organizations' members. The conference fee may cover tuition, accommodations, meals, and special activities, or it may cover only tuition. Some conferences also make registration available for individual days or events.

Attendees: This indicates the number of people expected to attend the conference.

Theme or title: If a conference lists a theme or specific title, its workshops and seminars will usually tie in to that theme.

Subjects: The subjects a particular conference covers may be broad, with many offerings in all categories, or the conference may be narrowly focused.

Format: This information indicates the method of presentation and how much time is allotted for topics or sessions. Formats vary from hourly workshops, formal and informal panel discussions, and guest speaker presentations to intensive, daylong sessions. Request the conference brochure and check to see if the subject areas and format appeal to you.

Special events: In addition to educational activities, conferences sometimes include activities such as sunset cruises, banquets, wine tastings, receptions, job fairs, silent auctions, book signings, awards presentations, and informal evening sessions.

Faculty: The total number of guest speakers, teachers, workshop facilitators, and the like is given here.

Additional information: Any other information that the conference director wants you, the prospective attendee, to know is included in this section.

AMERICAN MEDICAL WRITERS ASSOCIATION ANNUAL CONFERENCE.
Sponsored by American Medical Writers Association. 9650 Rockville Pike. Bethesda, MD 20814. (301) 493-0003. Contact Person: call the national office.

Location: varies, major cities. Date: fall. 1991 conference: October 23-26 in Toronto, Ontario, Canada. Frequency: annually. Length: 4 days. Fee: $175 members; $240 nonmembers. Day rate available.

Subjects: various aspects of medical communication, e.g., writing, editing, publishing, advertising, marketing, audio-visual, pharmaceutical, etc. Format: activities offered include plenary and other open sessions on medical communications topics; 50-60 in-depth workshops; formal networking events; opportunities to discuss professional concerns with peers. Special events: basic registration fee covers admission to the general session, plenary sessions, forums, paper presentations, fitness program, receptions, and hospitality room. Workshops, meals, and tours are priced separately.

See also **WESTERN REGIONAL CONFERENCE OF THE AMERICAN MEDICAL WRITERS ASSOCIATION.**

AMERICAN SOCIETY OF INDEXERS ANNUAL MEETING.
1700 18th St., NW. Washington, DC 20009. (202) 328-7110. Contact Person: David Billick.

Location: varies (San Antonio, Texas, 1992; Washington, D.C., 1993). Frequency: annually. Length: 1-2 days. Fee: call for information. Attendees: 100+/-.

Theme: Indexing in the '90s. Subjects: on indexing. Format: individual speakers, panel discussions. Special events: presentation of the Wilson Awards; indexing software publishers exhibition.

ARTS AT MENUCHA. Sponsored by Creative Arts Community. PO Box 4958. Portland, OR 97208. (503) 234-6827. Contact Person: Connie Cheifetz.

Location: Menucha Retreat Center, Corbett, Oregon. Date: August. Frequency: annually. Length: 2 one-week conferences run consecutively. Fee: $450 per week or $750 for both. Included: room and board. Reduced rate for members: $25 discount. Attendees: 80-100.

Subjects: writing children's books (August 4-10); songwriting (August 11-17); story illustration (August 11-17). Format: week-long residential workshop classes from 9-12 am and 1-4 pm. Special activities: evening programs from all instructors make for a rich disciplinery cross-over of ideas. Musical program one night each week. Faculty: 18.

ASIAN AMERICAN JOURNALISTS ASSOCIATION NATIONAL CONVENTION. Sponsored by Asian American Journalists Association. 1765 Sutter St., Room 1000. San Francisco, CA 94115. (415) 346-2051. Contact Person: Diane Yen-Mei Wong.

Location: varies. Date: August. 1991 conference: August 21-24 in Seattle, Washington. Frequency: annually. Length: 4 days. Fee: $150 members; $225 nonmembers. Included: meals. Attendees: 600.

Subjects: newspaper and magazine freelancing; TV and radio broadcasting; ethnic community news. Format: speakers, workshops, panels, critiquing sessions. Special events: banquet, job fair, reception.

BUMBERSHOOT, THE SEATTLE ARTS FESTIVAL. Sponsored by Bumbershoot, The Seattle Arts Festival. 414 Pontius Ave. N. Seattle, WA 98109. (206) 622-5123.

Location: Seattle Center Festival Grounds. Date: Labor Day weekend. 1991 festival: August 30-September 2. Frequency: annually. Fee: $6 admission at the gate.

Subjects: national guest writers, mixed media, writers-in-performance, book fair, panel discussions, word works, writers forums, special projects. Events are part of a wider festival programming.

CLARION WEST SCIENCE FICTION AND FANTASY WRITERS WORKSHOP. Sponsored by Clarion West. 340 15th Ave. E., Ste. 350. Seattle, WA 98112. (206) 322-9083. Contact Person: Linda Jordan.

Location: Seattle Central Community College. Date: June-July. 1991 conference: June 16-July 26. Frequency: annually. Length: 6 weeks. Fee: $1000. Attendees: 20.

Subjects: writing, editing, publishing in the areas of science fiction, fantasy, horror, poetry, and nonfiction. Format: established writers/editors each teach one week of writing and critique manuscripts that are written at the workshop. Special events: readings, lectures, conferences and individual counseling, and social events. Faculty: 6.

COSMEP PUBLISHERS CONFERENCE. Sponsored by COSMEP, The International Association of Independent Publishers. PO Box 703. San Francisco, CA 94101. (415) 922-9490. Contact Person: Richard Morris.

Location: Boston, Chicago, San Francisco, and Los Angeles in successive years. Date: fall. 1991 conference: October 2-4, in Boston. 1992 conference: September 14-17 in Chicago. Frequency: annually. Length: 4 days. Fee: $175, member rate. Attendees: 200-250.

Subjects: book promotion, distribution, and marketing. Format: 4 one-day seminars. Faculty: number varies.

EDMONDS ARTS COMMISSION *see* **WRITE ON THE SOUND.**

ENVIRONMENTAL WRITING INSTITUTE. Sponsored by The University of Montana and Teller Wildlife Refuge, Inc. Center for Continuing Education. The University of Montana. Missoula, MT 59812. (406) 243-6486.

Location: Teller Wildlife Refuge, Corvallis, Montana. Date: mid-May. Frequency: annually. Length: 7 days. Fee: $500. Included: lodging and meals. Commuter rate: $400. Attendees: 14.

Subjects: environmental and nature writing. Format: daily workshops with faculty, readings, special guests. Faculty: Peter Matthiessen (1991) plus special guests.

FLIGHT OF THE MIND SUMMER WORKSHOP FOR WOMEN. 622 SE 29th Ave. Portland, OR 97214. (503) 236-9862. Contact Person: Judith Barrington.

Location: McKenzie Bridge, Oregon. Date: July/August. 1991 conference: July 28-August 4. Frequency: annually. Length: 1 week. Fee: $475. Included: meals and accommodations. Attendees: 65.

Subject: writing for women. Format: choice of one of five classes. Students meet with chosen teacher three hours per day, six days, for workshop in chosen genre. Special events: evening readings by teachers and participants, bookstore, leisure activities (river rafting, hiking, swimming). Faculty: 5.

INTERNATIONAL ASSOCIATION OF BUSINESS COMMUNICATORS INTERNATIONAL CONFERENCE. One Hallidie Plaza, Ste. 600. San Francisco, CA 94102. (415) 433-3400. Contact Persons: Carole Sears, Heather Caldwell.

Location: varies. Date: May-June. 1992 conference: May 24-27 in San Francisco. Frequency: annually. Length: 4 days. Fee: $450-$520 members; $550-$620 nonmembers. Included: meals. Attendees: 1000-1200.

Title: Learning How to Influence: Gaining Authority, Status and Power (1991). Format: major presentations, seminars, workshops, InFocus Councils. Special events: luncheons, opening night reception, banquet.

INTERNATIONAL BLACK WRITERS CONFERENCE. Sponsored by International Black Writers. PO Box 1030. Chicago, IL 60690. (312) 995-5195. Contact Person: Mable Terrell.

Location: Chicago. Date: second weekend in June. Frequency: annually. Length: 3 days. Fee: $85; $20 for workshop and poetry celebration. Conference is free to members. Attendees: 200-350.

Theme: varies. Subjects: writing-related workshops on fiction, nonfiction, poetry, self-publishing, and desktop publishing. Format: workshops. Special events: awards, tribute to current writers, songwriters' luncheon, play. Faculty: 20.

INTERNATIONAL WOMEN'S WRITING GUILD CONFERENCE, THE. Sponsor: The International Women's Writing Guild. PO Box 810. Gracie Station. New York, NY 10028. (212) 737-7536. Contact Person: Hannelore Hahn, executive director and founder.

Fourteenth Annual IWWG Summer Conference. Location: Skidmore College, Saratoga Springs, New York. Date: August 9-16, 1991. Frequency: annually. Length: 1 week. Fee: $630 single, $580 double; $50 commuter registration. Included: room and board. Reduced rate for members: $20 discount. Attendees: 300.

Title: Writing and Higher Values II. Subjects: every aspect of writing, including mythology, values, and personal transformation. Format: 23 workshops on the nuts and bolts of writing, 10 workshops on mythology and values, 10 workshops on writing and personal transformation, 5 workshops on the arts. Special events: guest speakers in the evenings, readings of work in progress, critiquing. Faculty: 50.

Additional information: weekend retreat available August 16-18.

Second IWWG Washington State Conference. Location: The Annie Wright School, Tacoma, Washington. Date: September 14-15, 1991. Frequency: annually. Length: weekend. Fee: $65 per day. $10 per day reduced fee to members. Includes: lunch. Attendees: 100.

Subjects: writing and the creative process; the environment. Format: workshops and discussions. Special events: still in the planning stage. Faculty: 6.

MONTANA CULTURAL CONGRESS. Sponsored by the Montana Arts Council. 48 N. Last Chance Gulch. Helena, MT 59620. (406) 444-6430. Contact Person: Kathleen Burt.

Location: varies. Date: September of even-numbered years. Length: 3-4 days. Fees: $40-$75.

NATIONAL LEAGUE OF AMERICAN PEN WOMEN BIENNIAL CONFERENCE. Pen Arts Building. 1300 17th St., NW. Washington, DC 20036. (202) 785-1997. Contact Person: Edna A. Falbo (current, changes every two years).

Location: varies; in Washington, D.C., every four years; in other states by invitation of local chapter. Date: April of even-numbered years. 1992 conference: April 3-5 in Washington, D.C. Length: 3-5 days. Fees: registration is $35-$45 for each biennial segment; approximately $200 for all activities. Some hotels offer reduced rate to members. Attendees: 200-300.

Special events: contests for members in music composition; poetry, article, novel contests; art show competition with exhibit open to public.

NATIONAL PROFESSIONAL CONFERENCE. Sponsored by Women in Communications, Inc. 2101 Wilson Blvd., Ste. 417. Arlington, VA 22201. (703) 528-4200.

Location: varies. Date: October. 1991 conference: October 10-13 in Atlanta, Georgia. Chicago, Illinois, 1992; Pittsburgh, Pennsylvania, 1993. Frequency: annually. Length: 3 days. Fee: varies based on type of membership. Higher fees for nonmembers. Individual seminar tickets are available. Group discounts available. Includes: some meals. Attendees: 500.

Subjects: advanced track for senior communicators; integrated communications; war journalism; how Atlanta won the Olympics; "The Future of the News"; entrepreneurs' track for those operating and planning their own businesses. Format: featured speakers, seminars. Special events: night out.

NATIONAL WRITERS UNION ANNUAL CONFERENCE. Sponsored by the National Writers Union. Local #3. 236 West Portal Ave., #232. San Francisco, CA 94127. (415) 654-6369. Contact Person: Bruce Hartford.

Location: San Francisco or Berkeley. Date: spring. Frequency: annually. Length: 1 day. Fee: $55-$75. Attendees: 130-150.

Theme: writing. Subjects: technical writing, travel writing, freelance contracting, agent/author relationship, third-world authors, contracts, environmental writing, rights of writers, and others. Format: panels and workshops. Special events: keynote speaker, party.

OREGON ASSOCIATION OF CHRISTIAN WRITERS ALDERSGATE CONFERENCE. 17768 SW Pointe, Forest Court. Aloha, OR 97006. (503) 726-8320. Contact Person: Patricia Harbaugh. 437 Kirby St. Roseberg, OR 97474.

Location: Aldersgate Conference Center, Turner, Oregon (near Salem). Date: mid-August. 1991 conference: August 21-24 at Aldersgate. Frequency: annually. Length: 3 days. Fees $195-$275 (deluxe). Included: meals, accommodations, and tuition. Commuter rate: $120-$135. Reduced rate to members: $25 discount. Attendees: 125.

Subjects: fiction, nonfiction, poetry, photo-journalism, beginning to advanced writing for both books and periodicals. Format: hands-on morning workshops with a professional writer coaching the same small group all three days. Afternoons are a variety of 90-minute learning labs, different each day. Special events: tours to historic and scenic sights. Faculty: 16.

OREGON COAST COUNCIL FOR THE ARTS *see* **THE WORKSHOP AT NEWPORT.**

OREGON COUNCIL OF TEACHERS OF ENGLISH. PO Box 2515. Portland, OR 97208. Contact Person: Michelann Ortloff.

Location: Lake Oswego High School, Portland. Date: October. 1991 conference: October 11 at Lake Oswego High. Frequency: annually. Length: 1 day. Fee: $40. Included: meals. Reduced rate to members: $10 discount. Attendees: 500.

Title: The Art of Language Arts. Subjects: student writing; teachers as writers. Format: 45 workshops, keynote speakers, variety of programs geared for teachers of kindergarten through twelfth grade. Special events: contest, exhibits, autographing sessions.

OREGON WRITERS' WORKSHOP. 1219 SW Park. Portland, OR 97205. (503) 239-0504. Contact Person: Kathleen Culligan.

Location: Pacific Northwest College of Art, Portland. Date: school terms in fall, winter, and spring. Length: 10 weeks. Attendees: 40-50 per term.

Subjects: graduate level classes in fiction, nonfiction, and poetry. Format: classes meet for three hours one night a week for ten weeks. Methodology varies, but all classes involve extensive writing. It is assumed that students are serious and committed to the art. Special events: winter faculty reading. Other events planned by individual class. Faculty: 6-8 per term.

PORT TOWNSEND WRITERS CONFERENCE. Sponsored by Centrum.
PO Box 1158. Port Townsend, WA 98368. (206) 385-3102. Contact Person: Carol Jane Bangs.

Location: Fort Worden State Park, Washington. Date: July. 1991 conference: July 11-21 at Fort Worden. Frequency: annually. Length: 10 days. Fee: $225-$295. Commuter rate: $45 per day. Attendees: 160.

Subjects: poetry, fiction, nonfiction, writing for children. Format: daily munuscript workshops, lectures, readings. Special events: panels, receptions, open-mike readings.

PUBLISHERS MARKETING ASSOCIATION/ABA PUBLISHING UNIVERSITY. Sponsored by Publishers Marketing Association. 2401 Pacific Coast Hwy., Ste. 206. Hermosa Beach, CA 90254. (213) 372-2732. Contact Person: Jan Nathan, executive director.

Location: varies. Date: prior to ABA convention. Frequency: annually. Length: 2 days. Fee: varies. Reduced rate for members. Attendees: 300+.

Theme: A Book Publishing Course. Subjects: marketing, design, production. Format: two- and three-hour seminars, multiple tracks. Special events: exhibits. Faculty: 20+.

ROMANCE WRITERS OF AMERICA ANNUAL CONFERENCE.
Sponsored by Romance Writers of America. 13700 Veteran's Memorial Dr., Ste. 315. Houston, TX 77014. (713) 440-6885. Contact Person: Bobbi Stinson.

Location: varies; New Orleans, 1991; Midwest, 1992. Date: July. Frequency: annually. Length: 4 days. Fee: $275. Included: workshops, agent/editor appointments, meals. Reduced rate for members. Attendees: 1200.

Subjects: romance and mainstream women's fiction. Format: keynote address, 62 workshops, writing award for contest that precedes the conference, agent/editor appointments (10 minutes each). Special events: cocktail party, banquet, Sunday brunch. Faculty: 100.

SEATTLE ARTS FESTIVAL *see* BUMBERSHOOT.

SEATTLE PACIFIC CHRISTIAN WRITERS CONFERENCE.
Sponsored by Seattle Pacific University. Humanities Department. Seattle Pacific University. Seattle, WA 98119. (206) 281-2109. Contact Person: Linda Wagner.

Location: Seattle Pacific University, Third W. and Bertona. Date: last week in June. 1992 Conference: June 29-July 1 at Seattle Pacific University. Frequency: annually. Length: 3 days: Fee: $150 tuition; meals and housing extra. Reduced rate for members: $10 discount if they bring a new attendee. Attendees: 150.

Theme: Christian writing. Subjects: fiction, nonfiction, selling, different genres (devotionals, children's, poetry, screenwriting, etc.). Format: whole-group motivational and inspirational sessions, choice of small workshops throughout day. Special events: banquet, writing contest, individual manuscript consultations, editor appointments. Faculty: 24.

SELLING TO HOLLYWOOD. Sponsored by Writers Connection. 1601 Saratoga-Sunnyvale Rd., Ste. 180. Cupertino, CA 95014. (408) 973-0227. Contact Person: Meera Lester.

Location: Santa Clara County, California. Date: August. 1991 conference: August 9-11, Doubletree Hotel, Santa Clara, California. Frequency: annually. Length: weekend. Fee: $55-$360. Reduced rate for members, individual events, and single days. Included: all sessions and individual consultation with faculty member for full registrations. Attendees: 200-300.

Theme: Selling to Hollywood. Subjects: Workshops and panel discussions provide specific information for writers interested in selling literary properties to the film industry. Format: panels of producers, story editors, and literary agents; individual presentations and workshops. Special events: individual consultations with film industry professionals (with full registration only), bookstore, autograph session. Faculty: 12-20.

SITKA SYMPOSIUM ON HUMAN VALUES AND THE WRITTEN WORD. Sponsored by The Island Institute. PO Box 2420. Sitka, AK 99835. (907) 747-3794. Contact Person: Carolyn Servid.

Location: Sitka, Alaska. Date: June. Frequency: annually. Length: 6 days. Fee: $150 tuition; $150-$275 housing and meals.

SOCIETY FOR TECHNICAL COMMUNICATION'S INTERNATIONAL CONFERENCE. Sponsored by Society for Technical Communication (STC). 701 N. Stuart St., Ste 304. Arlington, VA 22203. (703) 522-4114.

Location: varies. Date: spring. Frequency: annually. Length: 4 days. Fee: approximately $200/members; $285/nonmembers.

Subjects: the changing role of the technical communication specialist in relation to factors such as technology, literacy levels, corporate and national cultures, and international business.

Additional information: Submissions of papers, workshops, panels, and discussion topics for the conference are invited.

See also **WRITER IN THE WORKPLACE.**

SOCIETY OF CHILDREN'S BOOK WRITERS AND ILLUSTRATORS NORTHWEST CONFERENCE. Sponsored by SCBW (Northwest). Contact Person: Margaret Bechard. 12180 SW Ann Place. Tigard, OR 97223. (503) 639-5754.

Location: varies. Date: July. Frequency: alternate years. Length: 3 days. Fee: $200. Meals included. Reduced rate for members: $20 discount. Attendees: 60-100.

Subjects: writing for children; picture book illustration; generating ideas; marketing strategies; nonfiction and textbook markets, etc. Format: daily keynote speakers, several choices of afternoon sessions. Special events: critiquing groups, small group discussions. Faculty: 5-7 speakers, 6-8 critiquing facilitators.

Additional information: also sponsors five-day retreat in alternate years.

SQUAW VALLEY COMMUNITY OF WRITERS ANNUAL WORKSHOP. Sponsored by Squaw Valley Creative Arts Society. PO Box 2352. Olympic Valley, CA 95730. (916) 583-5200. Contact Persons: Carolyn Doty, fiction; Gil Dennis, scriptwriting.

Location: Squaw Valley, California. Date: second week in July (poetry); second week in August (fiction, screenwriting). Frequency: annually. Length: 1 week. Fee: $450 per program. Included: 1 dinner. Attendees: prose/screenwriting, limit 125; poetry, limit 56.

Theme: to help the writer attain his or her potential by providing the concentrated attention of established writers, editors, agents, and fellow participants to the writer's work. Subjects: prose, poetry, screenwriting. Format: small, intensive workshops. Special events: movies, poetry readings, fiction readings. Faculty: 25.

Additional information: separate 1-week, concurrent programs for prose, poetry, and screenwriting; afternoon meetings open to public.

STANFORD PUBLISHING COURSE. Sponsored by Stanford University.
Stanford Alumni Association. Bowman House. Stanford, CA 94305-4005. (415) 725-1083. Fax (415) 725-8676. Contact Person: Bill Merz, program manager, Stanford Alumni Association. (415) 725-1083.

Location: Stanford University. Date: July. Frequency: annually. Length: 12 days. Fee: $2500; $2400/Stanford Alumni Association members. Included: books, working materials, receptions, small breakfast, all luncheons, opening banquet, closing barbecue. Attendees: 165.

Subjects: new publishing technologies, editing, design, production, finance and marketing, functions of publishing. Format: lectures, hands-on workshops. Faculty: 65.

Additional information: Application deadline is beginning of May. Preview videotape available for loan. Admissions standards are a minimum of three years' experience in professional publishing, or a waiver at the discretion of the course director must be granted.

SUMMER IN FRANCE WRITING WORKSHOPS. Sponsored by Paris
American Academy. HC 01, Box 102. Plainview, TX 97092. (806) 889-3533. Contact Person: Bettye Givens.

Location: Paris, France. Date: July. Frequency: annually. Length: 1 month. Fee: 5500 French francs. Attendees: 15.

Subjects: poetry, short stories, overcoming resistances to writing, discovering ideas and stories. Format: meet twice weekly in a formal setting; remainder of conference informal. Includes a survey of American writers who lived or worked in or were influenced by Paris, and also art history slide lectures that precede visits to cultural locations. Special events: special evening readings are organized with established writers as guests. Faculty: 10.

UNIVERSITY OF MONTANA *see* YELLOW BAY WRITERS' WORKSHOP.

WESTERN REGIONAL CONFERENCE OF THE AMERICAN MEDICAL WRITERS ASSOCIATION. Sponsored by the American Medical
Writers Association. Contact Person: Michele Vivirito. c/o Herbert Laboratories. 2525 Dupont Dr. Irvine, CA 92715. (714) 752-4500.

Location: Asilomar Conference Center, Pacific Grove, California. Date: spring. Frequency: annually. Length: 5 days. Fee: $300 AMWA members; $325 nonmembers. Included: accommodations (double occupancy), meals. Attendees: limited to 50.

Theme: medical writing. Subjects: evolution of medical journals, writing in the pharmaceutical industry, on-line medical databases, what editors and writers should know about publishing, business aspects of a freelance writing career. Faculty: 20+.

WESTERN WRITERS OF AMERICA ANNUAL CONVENTION. PO
Box 823. Sheridan, WY 82801. (307) 672-0889. Contact Person: Barb Ketcham.

Location: varies. Date: last full week of June. 1992 conference: June 23-27 at Snow King Resort, Jackson, Wyoming. Frequency: annually. Length: 4 days. Fee: $130-$150. Included: meals. Attendees: 300.

Subjects: Western writing. Format: panels made up of members covering various aspects of writing; a panel of editors, publishers, and agents; individual interviews. Special events: Spur Finalist Luncheon, Spur Banquet.

WOMEN IN COMMUNICATION *see* **NATIONAL PROFESSIONAL CONFERENCE.**

WORKSHOP AT NEWPORT, THE. Sponsored by the Oregon Council for the Arts and Oregon Writers Workshop. The Workshop at Newport. 10130 Slab Creek Rd. Newskowin, OR 97149. (503) 392-3968. Contact Person: Gerard Killeen.

Location: Newport, Oregon. Date: late July. 1991 conference: July 28-August 3 at The Naterlin Center, SW Highway 101, Newport. Frequency: annually. Length: 1 week. Fee: $150. Attendees: 50 registered students.

Subjects: fiction writing, poetry, creativity enhancement. Format: manuscript workshops daily from 9 am to noon; afternoon craft lectures; readings at night by well-known writers; constant writing. Special events: nighttime readings are open to the public for a nominal fee; end of workshop reading and party by and for the students. Faculty: 5 nationally known teachers.

WORLD CONGRESS OF POETS. Sponsored by the World Academy of Arts and Culture. 3146 Buckeye Court. Placerville, CA 95667. (916) 626-4166. Contact Person: Rosemary C. Wilkinson. For conference in Turkey, contact: Dr. Osman Turkay. 22, Avenue Mansions. Finchley Rd. London NW3 7AX, England.

Location: varies. Length: 5-day symposium. Frequency: annually, by invitation of Cultural Minister/Minister of Education of host nation. Fee: not yet set. Reduced rate for members. Attendees: 300-500.

Theme: World Brotherhood and Peace through Poetry. Subjects: poetry, literature, culture, education, art, music. Format: plenary sessions with afternoon workshops and evening cultural events. Special events: side trips to museums, ancient sites, libraries, etc. Faculty: 10+.

WRITE ON THE SOUND. Sponsored by the Edmonds Arts Commission. 700 Main St. Edmonds, WA 98020. (206) 775-2525, ext. 269. Contact Person: Linda McCrystal.

Location: Anderson Cultural Center, 700 Main St., Edmonds. Date: October. 1991 conference: October 11-12 at Anderson Cultural Center. Frequency: annually. Length: Friday night keynote session and all-day Saturday conference. Fee: $25. Attendees: 150.

Subjects: fiction, poetry, how-to, characterization development, children's literature, self-publishing, working with an agent, religious writing, how to get published (varies from year to year). Format: concurrent seminars and workshops. Special events: concluding social hour on Saturday with the speakers. Faculty: 8-9.

WRITER IN THE WORKPLACE. Sponsored by Society for Technical Communication and American River College. PO Box 1292. Roseville, CA 95661. (916) 484-8425. Contact Person: Connie Warloe.

Location: American River College, Sacramento, California. Date: February. Frequency: annually. Length: 1 day. Fee: $65. Included: meals. Attendees: 200.

Theme: changes every year. Subjects: technical, business writing, and communications. Format: keynote address and workshops. Special events: reception at end of day. Faculty: 30.

YELLOW BAY WRITERS' WORKSHOP. Sponsored by The University of Montana. Center for Continuing Education. The University of Montana. Missoula, MT 59812. (406) 243-6486. Contact Person: Judy Jones.

Location: Flathead Lake Biological Station, Montana. Date: August. 1991 conference: August 25-31 at Flathead Lake. Frequency: annually. Length: 7 days. Fee: $350 tuition; $225 lodging and meals. Commuter rate: $350. Attendees: 60.

Subjects: fiction, poetry, creative nonfiction, or personal essay. Format: daily workshops with faculty with ratio of 15:1, craft lectures, readings. Special events: lectures and readings; some recreational activities available. Faculty: 4 or more special guests for readings and discussions.

Protection, Trademarks, and ISBNs

How Do You Protect Your Work?

Copyright law in the United States changed significantly when the Copyright Act of 1976 took effect on January 1, 1978. For works copyrighted prior to 1978, the previous law still applies, except that the renewal term is now 47 rather than 28 years. For more information on early copyrights, write to the Copyright Office and request circulars R15a and R15t.

Works created in 1978 or after are automatically protected by copyright from the moment of creation (as soon as they are "fixed in tangible form"). Copyright ordinarily lasts for the author's life plus 50 years (or in the case of multiple authors of the same work, 50 years after the death of the last surviving author).

You need take no action to copyright your work other than to put it in written form, whether that form is printed or stored on electronic media. However, including a notice of copyright on the first or title page of documents is common practice. Notice serves as a clear statement that the work is not in the public domain (available for any use, reproduction, etc.) and is protected under the Copyright Act of 1976, not under the previous law that required either publication or registration. Notice also has relevance for international copyright law.

Copyright gives you, the author or creator, the exclusive right to do, or to authorize others to do, the following:

- Reproduce the work
- Prepare derivative works based on the content or characters of the original work
- Distribute the work for public sale, rent or lease copyright for the term of publication, or transfer specific rights (as to magazine publishers)
- Perform the work, as with music, drama, motion pictures, etc.
- Display the work in the case of visual art

No one else has the right to do any of these things without your express written permission or your agreed-upon transfer of specific rights.

In order to claim copyright, you need only be the original creator. Your notice of copyright should contain all of the following elements:

- The symbol © or the word "Copyright" or the abbreviation "Copr."
- The year of first publication or creation in tangible form
- The name of the owner of the copyright, for example: "Copyright 1991 by Jane Buck" or "© 1991 John Doe"

Material you cannot copyright includes works that have not been fixed in tangible form, such as improvised speeches; titles, names, short phrases, slogans, familiar symbols or designs, ornamentation or lettering, or listings of ingredients or contents; ideas, procedures, methods, systems, processes, concepts, principles, discoveries, or devices as distinguished from a description, explanation, or illustration; and works consisting entirely of information that is common property, such as calendars, height and weight charts, etc.

You can register your copyright by requesting the proper form from the Copyright Office (TX for manuscripts), completing the form, and returning it with the required payment ($20 in 1991). Registration offers these advantages:

- Establishes a public record of the copyright claim
- Is usually necessary before infringement suits can be filed in court
- Gives the copyright owner certain legal advantages in court regarding presentation of evidence and the extent of damages the court will award

Copyright forms are available from the Copyright Office at no charge; write to Copyright Office, Library of Congress, Washington, DC 20559, or call (202) 707-9100. You may duplicate forms, but the photocopy must be identical to the original.

For a copy of the actual copyright law, send $3.75 to the Superintendent of Documents, U.S. Government Printing Office, Washington, DC 20401-9371, or contact your nearest government printing office and request Copyright Office Circular 92, stock number 030-002-00168-3.

What Are Trademarks and How Are They Used?

Trademarks are not copyrights. Rather, they are a separate means of protecting business or product names, titles, logos, symbols, or designs. Most companies are diligent about protecting their trademarks because once allowed to enter common usage, trademarks become generic and are no longer protected as the sole property of a company. Thus the term escalator, once a brand name for a moving staircase, is now part of our everyday language.

To exercise your responsibility as a writer, you should be aware of trademarks and the rules that govern their use. They should be used only as adjectives, be capitalized, and be followed by the appropriate generic noun, as in Kleenex tissues.

In nonfiction articles that discuss specific products, this requirement generally poses no problem. But in fiction, when characters stop off for a couple of Cokes, writing that "Bill and Ted bought Coca-Cola soft drinks at the corner store" calls too much attention to a minor action. For fiction, the terminology is too self-conscious.

In nonfiction written for national publications, you would be wise to follow the letter of the law. For fiction, where trademark references are much less common, strict adherence may not be as important, though technically you can still be asked by a company to either use the proper form or not mention their product. At the very least, however, trademark names must always be capitalized.

For more information or a list of common trademarks, write the U. S. Trademark Association, 6 East 45th Street, New York, NY 10017, or call (212) 986-5880.

What Is an ISBN?

The ISBN number is a worldwide identification code that distinguishes different works of like titles and facilitates book ordering. The system is administered by R. R. Bowker for the International Standard Book Numbering Agency. Published books are assigned numbers by the agency or, in most instances, by the publisher from a series of numbers assigned to that publisher by the ISBN Agency.

If you are a self-publisher, you will need to apply for your own ISBN number. If you intend to publish more than one book, you should apply for more than one number, as receipt of your designated numbers is often a drawn-out process, and the part of the number that designates the publisher will change with each new issue.

For information or to apply, write to the ISBN Agency (U. S.), 121 Chanlon Road, New Providence, NJ 07974, or call (908) 665-6770.

Books for Writers

Most of the following writing- and publishing-related books are available from the Writers Connection bookstore. Those not sold through Writers Connection are marked with an asterisk (*). Inquire at your local bookstore or check your library for copies or information. Writers Connection members are entitled to a 15% discount off the retail prices of books ordered from our bookstore. Availability and prices are subject to change; call (408) 973-0227 for current information. To order by mail, use the order form on page 183.

Fiction

CREATING UNFORGETTABLE CHARACTERS
Linda Seger
Invaluable character techniques for all fiction writers, from scripts to novels. 1990.
F46—$12.95

FICTION WRITER'S RESEARCH HANDBOOK, THE
Mona McCormick
How to locate historical data using various sources. 1988.
F44—$9.95

HOW TO CREATE LIVING CHARACTERS (booklet)
Phyllis Taylor Pianka
A handbook of methods for drawing believable characters. 1983.
F31—$2.35

HOW TO WRITE A DAMN GOOD NOVEL
James N. Frey
A step-by-step no-nonsense guide to dramatic storytelling. 1987.
F32—$14.95

HOW TO WRITE A SYNOPSIS (booklet)
Phyllis Taylor Pianka
A guide to writing the all-important novel synopsis. 1990.
F11—$2.35

HOW TO WRITE DYNAMIC DIALOGUE (booklet)
Phyllis Taylor Pianka
Ways to use believable dialogue to improve your writing. 1990.
F15—$2.35

HOW TO WRITE ROMANCES
Phyllis Taylor Pianka
Everything you need to know about writing and selling the romance novel, including a sample query and synopsis. 1988.
F33—$13.95

HOW TO WRITE TALES OF HORROR, FANTASY & SCIENCE FICTION
J. N. Williamson
How-to essays from 26 top speculative fiction writers. 1987.
F16—$15.95

MYSTERY WRITER'S HANDBOOK
Mystery Writers of America, revised edition
Top mystery writers share tricks of the trade. 1982.
F17—$11.95

PLOTTING THE NOVEL (booklet)
Phyllis Taylor Pianka
Plot patterns; the seven elements of plot and how to use them. 1990.
F20—$2.35

WRITING THE MODERN MYSTERY
Barbara Norville
How to research, plot, write, and sell a modern mystery. 1986.
F29—$15.95

WRITING THE NOVEL FROM PLOT TO PRINT
Lawrence Block
Every step is fully described. 1985.
F30—$10.95

Nonfiction

FREELANCE INTERVIEW TIPS AND TRICKS (booklet)
Pat Kite
Techniques for landing the interview and methods for putting the interviewee at ease for best results. 1991.
NF6—$3.25

HOW TO SELL 75% OF YOUR FREELANCE WRITING
Gordon Burgett
The best book on marketing. 1990.
NF10—$9.95

HOW TO WRITE A BOOK PROPOSAL
Michael Larsen
A step-by-step guide by a leading literary agent. 1990.
NF11—$10.95

HOW TO WRITE A QUERY (booklet)
Phyllis Taylor Pianka
A guide to writing queries and proposals for articles and books. 1990.
NF12—$2.35

HOW TO WRITE THE STORY OF YOUR LIFE
Frank Thomas
A step-by-step guide to recording your life; 500 "memory sparkers" and 100 topic ideas. 1989.
NF39—$11.95

QUERY LETTERS/COVER LETTERS
Gordon Burgett
How to write the most compelling queries, cover letters. 1986.
NF24—$9.95

SYNDICATING YOUR COLUMN (booklet)
Pat Kite
Tips and directions for getting columns syndicated into weekly or daily newspapers. 1987.
NF33—$5.00

TRAVEL WRITING FOR FUN AND PROFIT
Ruth Wucherer
A veteran travel writer shares her trade secrets. 1984.
NF28—$9.95

WRITING FAST, FUN MONEY FILLERS (booklet)
Pat Kite
How to make money on short paragraphs. 1988.
NF30—$3.25

Desktop/Publishing

DESKTOP PUBLISHER'S LEGAL HANDBOOK, THE
Daniel Sitarz
How to make best use of your rights as a publisher and avoid infringing rights of others. 1989.
DP 15—$19.95.

HOW TO GET AN AGENT (booklet)
Phyllis Taylor Pianka
How to select and work with an agent. 1990.
DP11—$2.35

HOW TO SELF-PROMOTE YOUR BOOK (booklet)
Kite/Nelson
Tips on self-publicizing for new authors. 1989.
DP7—$3.55

LITERARY AGENTS
Debby Mayer
A writer's guide; includes interviews with well-known agents. 1983.
DP9—$6.95

SELF-PUBLISHING MANUAL, THE
Dan Poynter
New, revised edition of a complete guide to the self-publishing process. 1991.
DP13—$19.95

Specialized Markets

CHILDREN'S PICTURE BOOK, THE
Ellen Roberts
How to write it; how to sell it. 1986.
SM12—$16.95

CHILDREN'S WRITER'S & ILLUSTRATOR'S MARKET
Lisa Carpenter
Constructing a story, handling illustration, and getting published. Updated annually.
SM9—$16.95

HOW TO WRITE AND ILLUSTRATE CHILDREN'S BOOKS
Bicknell/Trotman
Covers constructing a story, illustrating, and getting published. 1991.
SM10—$22.50

HUMOR AND CARTOON MARKETS
Edited by Bob Staake
Over 500 listings of magazines, newsletters, greeting card companies, comic book publishers, advertising agencies, and syndicates for humor writers and illustrators. Updated annually.
SM1—$16.95

INTRODUCTION TO CHRISTIAN WRITING, AN
Ethel Herr
Effective techniques and marketing strategies for Christian writers. 1988.
SM6—$8.95

NONFICTION FOR CHILDREN
Ellen Roberts
How to create and sell "real-world" subjects to children from preschoolers to teenagers. 1986.
SM13—$16.95

WRITING FOR THE EDUCATIONAL MARKET
Barbara Gregorich
A complete resource manual for writing/publishing in the various educational applications. 1990.
SM18—$13.95

WRITING FOR THE ETHNIC MARKETS
Meera Lester
Provides writing tips, marketing strategies, and listings of book and magazine publishers and film and TV companies that buy ethnic material. Due out fall 1991.
SM19—$14.95

WRITING TO INSPIRE
Gentz/Roddy
A guide to writing and publishing for the expanding religious market. 1987.
SM5—$14.95

WRITING YOUNG ADULT NOVELS
Irwin/Eyerly
How to write the stories today's teens want to read. 1988.
SM11—$14.95

Scriptwriting

HOW TO SELL YOUR SCREENPLAY
Carl Sautter
Comprehensive explanation from a seasoned professional of how to sell your screenplay. 1988.
SC18—$22.95

HOW TO WRITE FOR TELEVISION
Madeline DiMaggio
Tips and techniques from a successful scriptwriter. 1990.
SC23—$10.95

MAKING A GOOD SCRIPT GREAT
Linda Seger
How to get a script back on track and preserve the original creativity; a guide for writing and rewriting. 1987.
SC8—$10.95

PRACTICAL SCREENWRITING HANDBOOK
Michael McCarthy
Light but thorough "how-to" guide for motion pictures and feature films, from title page to "the end." 1980.
SC2—$12.95

SCREENPLAY
Syd Field
The foundations of screenwriting; a step-by-step guide from concept to finished script. 1982.
SC9—$8.95

SCREENWRITER'S WORKBOOK, THE
Syd Field
Exercises and step-by-step instruction for creating a successful screenplay; a workshop approach. 1984.
SC10—$8.95

Resource/Reference

AMERICAN SLANG *
Robert L. Chappman, Ph.D., ed.
Dictionary of slang words and phrases with meanings, examples, dates, and origins. 1987.
Check local bookstores. Published by Harper and Row, New York.

ASSOCIATED PRESS STYLEBOOK AND LIBEL MANUAL
Addison-Wesley
Authoritative word on rules of grammar, punctuation, and the general meaning and usage of over 3,000 terms; insight into journalistic techniques. 1987.
RR1—$10.95

CALIFORNIA AND HAWAII PUBLISHING MARKETPLACE
Writers Connection
Comprehensive directory of publishers, magazines, agents, newspapers, organizations, and conferences. 1990.
RR48—$16.95

CHICAGO MANUAL OF STYLE
University of Chicago Press
A comprehensive, authoritative guide to journalistic and reference techniques. 1982.
RR41—$37.50

COPYEDITING, A PRACTICAL GUIDE
Karen Judd
A comprehensive field guide to copyediting, publishing. 1990.
RR23—$19.95

DIRECTORY OF POETRY PUBLISHERS *
Len Fulton, ed.
Over 2000 poetry markets with indexes. Updated annually.
Available from Dustbooks, PO Box 100, Paradise, CA 95967.

EDITING YOUR NEWSLETTER
Mark Beach
A complete guide to writing and producing a successful newsletter—on schedule and within budget. 1988.
RR2—$18.50

FINDING FACTS FAST
Alden Todd
Comprehensive research techniques to save you hours; a gold mine of information sources and research techniques. 1979.
RR40—$5.95

GET IT ALL DONE AND STILL BE HUMAN
Tony and Robbie Fanning
New revised edition of time management strategies for writers and others. 1990.
RR24—$9.95

GRANTS AND AWARDS *
PEN American Center
A directory listing of grants and prizes available to American writers. 1990/91.
Available from PEN American Center, 568 Broadway, New York, NY 10012.

HOW TO BULLET-PROOF YOUR MANUSCRIPT
Bruce Henderson
How to check manuscripts for potential libel and other legal problems. 1986.
RR20—$9.95

HOW TO WRITE WITH A COLLABORATOR
Hal Z. Bennett
How to team up with another writer, an expert, or a celebrity to co-author books, articles, and short stories. 1988.
RR3—$11.95

INTERNATIONAL DIRECTORY OF LITTLE MAGAZINES & SMALL PRESSES *
Len Fulton, ed.
A standard worldwide publishing and market reference for writers. Updated biannually.
Available from Dustbooks, PO Box 100, Paradise, CA 95967.

JUST OPEN A VEIN
William Brohaugh
A collection of essays by writers, for writers. 1987.
RR6—$15.95

LITERARY AGENTS OF NORTH AMERICA *
Author Aid/Research Associates International
Comprehensive five-index listing of agencies, contacts, and commission rates, plus profiles of agency heads, number of clients, and fee schedules. Updated annually.
Contact AA/RAI, 340 East 52nd Street, New York, NY 10022; or call 1-212-758-4213.

LITERARY MARKET PLACE (LMP) *
R.R.Bowker
The most widely used national directory of book publishers, editorial services, and agents, with complete reference book listing. Updated annually.
Available at most public libraries, or contact R.R. Bowker, 1-800-521-8110.

MENTOR GUIDE TO PUNCTUATION, THE
William C. Paxson
Quick and easy answers to punctuation problems. Organized for easy access. 1986.
RR9—$4.95

NORTHWEST PUBLISHING MARKETPLACE
Writers Connection
Comprehensive directory of writers' markets and more for Alaska, Idaho, Montana, Oregon, Washington, and Wyoming. 1991.
RR50—$14.95

NOVEL & SHORT STORY WRITER'S MARKET
Robin Gee
Marketing information on fiction publishers with interviews of fiction writers, publishers, and editors. Updated annually.
RR15—$18.95

PROFESSIONAL WRITERS GUIDE, THE
Bower/Young
An indispensable, comprehensive guide on all aspects of the writing business. 1990.
RR47—$16.95

REWRITE RIGHT!
Jan Venolia
Most writing can be improved by the simple process of reviewing and rewriting. 1987.
RR5—$6.95

SOUTHWEST PUBLISHING MARKETPLACE
Writers Connection
Comprehensive directory of writers' markets and more for Arizona, Colorado, Nevada, New Mexico, Texas, and Utah. 1991.
RR49—$14.95

12 KEYS TO WRITING BOOKS THAT SELL
Kathleen Krull
Develop a more professional attitude toward writing and marketing your book. 1989.
RR25—$12.95

WRITE RIGHT!
Jan Venolia
The best summary of grammar available for writers. 1988.
RR32—$5.95

WRITER'S DIGEST GUIDE TO MANUSCRIPT FORMATS, THE
Writer's Digest
Illustrated, easy-to-follow guide to all types of manuscript formats, including books, articles, poems, and plays. 1987.
RR44—$17.95

WRITER'S GUIDE TO COPYRIGHT, A
Poets & Writers
A summary of the current copyright law for writers, editors, and teachers. 1990.
RR29—$6.95

WRITER'S HANDBOOK, THE *
Sylvia K. Burack, ed.
Essentials and techniques from many successful writers, plus listings of markets for manuscripts. Updated annually.
Check local bookstores or contact The Writer, Inc., 120 Boylston Street, Boston, MA 02116.

WRITER'S LEGAL COMPANION, THE
Brad Bunnin
How to deal successfully with copyrights, contracts, libel, taxes, agents, publishers, legal relationships, and marketing strategies. 1988.
RR8—$14.95

WRITER'S MARKET
Writer's Digest
Where and how to sell what you write; thousands of markets for fiction and nonfiction articles, books, plays, scripts, short stories, and more. Updated annually. 1991.
RR25—$24.95

WRITERS NORTHWEST HANDBOOK *
Media Weavers, ed.
Listings of markets and resources in the Northwest, plus articles, tips, etc. Fourth edition.
Available from Media Weavers, Route 3, Box 376, Hillsboro, OR 97124.

WRITING AFTER FIFTY
Leonard L. Knott
How to start a writing career after you retire. 1985.
RR37—$12.95

WRITING DOWN THE BONES
Natalie Goldberg
Guidelines for freeing the writer within. 1986.
RR38—$9.95

YEARBOOK OF EXPERTS, AUTHORITIES, & SPOKESPERSONS, THE *
Mitchell P. Davis, ed.
An encyclopedia of ads and listings of sources for interviews, programs, etc., with index by subject or topic. Updated annually.
Available from Broadcast Interview Source, 2233 Wisconsin Avenue, NW, Washington, DC 20007, (202) 333-4904.

A Writer's Glossary

Advance. Your payment from the publisher prior to the publication of your book. The amount is then deducted from your royalties.

All rights. Magazines that purchase all rights to your material own the right to publish it wherever and whenever they choose without additional payment to you. Also, you lose the right to sell reprint rights to another publication. Book publishers that negiotiate all rights do so as a function of your contract, which spells out how or what you will be paid for each separate right. (*See also* **subsidiary rights.**)

Anthology. A collection of writings, usually short stories or essays, published in a single book. Anthology rights are different from first time or one-time rights and should be negotiated separately.

ASCII. A way of storing a computer file without formatting so that it can be read by most word-processing programs.

Assignment. When an editor asks you to write an article for which you will be paid upon completion. Acceptance of the finished piece is implied in the request.

Avant-garde. An article or story with nontraditional ideas and often written in an unusual format.

Backlist. A list of the publisher's books that were not published during the current season, but which are still in print.

Belles lettres. Writing to be enjoyed for its aesthetic qualities, rather than read for information.

Bio. A short biography of those details of your life and experience directly related to your credibility as an author in your specific field.

Byline. The credit that lists you by name as the author with your published work.

Chapbook. A short collection of poetry or stories published in a very small edition.

Children's. Writing for children ages 2 through 12. Often called juvenile literature.

Clips. Copies from newspapers or magazines of your previously published works. Clips are often requested by editors as examples of your writing.

Compatible. Refers to different computers that can read the same computer disk.

Co-publishing. An agreement between publisher and author to split the costs of publication, often resulting in a higher author's royalty. Also known as cooperative publishing and sometimes employed by universities and well-established presses that obtain funds from sources other than the author. Do not confuse co-publishing with vanity or subsidy publishing. Read your contract carefully.

Copyright. A legal protection of your work. (For more information, see the section on "Protection, Trademarks, and ISBNs.")

Cover letter. Rarely sent with a proposal and not to be confused with a query, this letter can accompany a submission and be a response to an editor's questions or a brief communication of material you want the editor to know.

Cover price. The retail price of your published book. Cover price may be used as the basis for determining your royalty.

Disk. A flat, magnetic recording surface used to store computer data.

Experimental fiction. Fiction that uses an unusual approach or uncommon subject.

Feature. The lead article in a magazine, a special department at the magazine, or an article dealing with people rather than facts.

Filler. Short and often amusing or intriguing items used in newspapers and magazines to finish out a column or page.

First North American serial rights. The right to first publish material in a periodical before it appears in book form in the United States and Canada.

First run. The number of copies printed by the publisher the first time your book is printed.

Freelance submissions. Manuscripts submitted by writers who are not on the staff of a publication and who, as independents, manage their own work and submit to a variety of markets.

Genre. In commercial fiction, the specific categories of writing, such as mysteries, romances, or Westerns. In scholarly terms, genre can mean types of writing, such as poetry or essays.

Hard copy. Printed copy as opposed to a computer file.

Honorarium. A small amount of money offered as payment.

Illustrations. Drawings, lithographs, or visual art forms, but not photographs.

Imprint. A division within a publishing house which publishes a special category of books and is named differently than the parent company.

Juvenile *see* **children's.**

Kill fee. A portion of the total payment for an assigned article that is paid to you in lieu of full payment when the editor decides not to run your article.

Literary fiction. Relies more on stylistic elements, details of character and atmosphere, and character's thoughts than on physical action. Often experimental in style and subject.

Literary agent. A person who represents you, the author, in finding a publisher or arranging contract terms on a literary project.

Mainstream fiction. A more in-depth treatment of characters, situations, and plots than the genre novel, or a book promoted as a potential best-seller by a publisher's marketing campaign.

Manuscript. Your unpublished, written work.

Mass market paperback. A paperback book on a popular subject, published with a cover designed to attract the "impulse" buyer at the drugstore, market, or bookstore.

Midlist. Books that the publisher decides to bring out but does not heavily promote. These books are not expected to be best sellers but are often thought to have some literary or educational value. Not a good situation for an author.

Model release. Written permission given to a photographer to use a picture of you for a specific stated purpose or purposes. A guardian must sign for a minor child.

Multiple submissions. Copies of the same manuscript that you send for consideration to more than one publisher at the same time.

Net receipts. Money the publisher receives from sales of your book. An important part of negotiating your contract is the basis upon which royalties are paid. Payment used to be based on a percentage of the cover price. More common now is a royalty based on the amount of money a book publisher receives from the wholesale price of the book, often after all promotional and incidental expenses are deducted.

Novella or novelette. A short novel or long story of about 7000 to 15,000 words.

On spec *see* **speculation or spec.**

One-time rights. Gives the publisher permission to publish your story or book one time only. After publication, all rights revert back to you.

Outline. A one- or two-sentence summary for each chapter or topic, often included with your book proposal or sent with your query to magazines or newspapers.

Page rate. Rather than pay by the inch or by the word, many magazine publishers pay by the published page; the term does not refer to manuscript pages.

Payment on acceptance. The editor reads your article, decides to publish it, and sends you a check by return mail: the preferred method for writers.

Payment on publication. The editor reads your article, accepts it for publication, publishes it, and then sends your check, often weeks or months later. If a publisher pays on publication, try to negotiate for a kill fee should the publisher later decide not to publish your article.

Photo feature. A piece that focuses on beautiful, interesting, or compelling photos. Written text supports the photos.

Periodical. A publication, not including newspapers, produced in serial issues at regular or stated intervals with the intent of continued publication.

Proposal. The sales tool you send to book publishers to convince them to accept your nonfiction manuscript. Often includes a query, outline, information on the intended audience, and bio. Several good books discuss how to assemble a proposal.

Query. A letter to an editor meant to raise interest in a work you propose to write.

Reading fee. A fee charged by some agents to read your manuscript. The fee may be returned if your manuscript is accepted and/or sold by the agent.

Reprint rights. Permission to publish material that has already been published in another periodical or book. You retain this right only if you have not sold all rights or produced a work-for-hire. When offering reprint rights to publishers, always inform them where and when the material was originally published.

Royalties. A negotiated amount of money paid to you, the author, by the publisher. The royalty can be figured on the cover price or the publisher's net receipts. (*See also* **cover price** and **net receipts.**)

SASE. Self-addressed stamped envelope. Include one with your query or proposal.

Second serial rights. Permission for a periodical to reprint your work after it has been previously published in another magazine or a book. *See also* **reprint rights.**

Sidebar. A short piece that complements or expands a feature article.

Simultaneous submissions. Sending the same manuscript or article to several publishers at the same time. Inform publishers in your query letter to avoid problems should more than one accept your material. *See also* **multiple submissions.**

Slant. The approach, angle, tone, or point of view you use in writing an article.

Speculation or spec. The condition when you agree to write an article with no promise from the editor that it will be accepted when it is finished.

Subsidiary rights. Rights granted to the publisher by your contract, allowing the publisher to sell your manuscript anywhere and in any form, including for serial (periodical) publication, book clubs, anthologies, and radio, television, and video reproduction. Negotiate these rights carefully.

Subsidy publishing. You pay a company to publish your book, and then you receive all copies and market them yourself, with little or no help from the publisher. Also known as vanity publishing.

Syndication rights. A story, article, or column series sold to a business service that makes a wide variety of features available to many publications.

Synopsis. A limited-length summary of your story (from one to eight pages) included with sample chapters (usually the first three).

Trade. A book, often in paperback, on a general-interest subject directed toward a general rather than a professional audience and sold primarily in bookstores.

Transparencies. Positive color slides; not color prints.

Unsolicited manuscript. A manuscript you send to a publisher without its being requested. In many cases, unsolicited submissions are returned unopened or thrown out. Send a query or proposal first.

Work-for-hire. Work you do for a company or publisher as part of your employment, whether in a permanent or contract (temporary) position. You are paid for your writing, and the company owns the copyright and other rights. Specific legal conditions govern determination of a work-for-hire.

Writer's guidelines. The publisher's instructions on what subjects, forms, lengths, etc., are appropriate for the material you submit. Send for guidelines whenever they are available.

Young adult (YA). Books written for readers ages 12 through 18.

Book Subject Index

This index is alphabetized using the letter-by-letter system and is divided into three sections: fiction, nonfiction, and co-publishing or subsidy publishers.

When indicating fiction and nonfiction index topics, some publishers selected more subjects than were named in their initial list of interests. Additional topics may indicate future interests or identify subcategories within the publisher's basic focus, such as folklore in Native American books or children's books for a publisher of science materials.

Fiction

Adventure
Council for Indian Education 14
Glacier House Publications 18

Afro-American
Story Line Press 34

Avant-Garde/Experimental
Box Dog Press 11

Children's/Young Adult
Alaska Native Language Center 8
Graphic Arts Center Publishing Co. 20
Hapi Press, The 21
HarperCollins Children's Books 21
Harvest House Publishers 21
Multnomah Press (Christian theme) 28
Northwest Parent Publishing 29
Questar Publishers, Inc. 32
Romar Books, Ltd. 33

Contemporary/Modern
Arrowood Books, Inc. 9
Council for Indian Education 14
Intertext 23

Ethnic
Alaska Native Language Center 8
Council for Indian Education 14

Erotica
Box Dog Press 11

First Novels
Arrowood Books, Inc. 9
Box Dog Press 11
Council for Indian Education 14
Glacier House Publications 18
Mother of Ashes Press 26

Mountain Meadow Press 27
Questar Publishers, Inc. 32
Story Line Press 34

Folklore
Alaska Native Language Center 8
Council for Indian Education 14
Edmonds Arts Commission Books 16

General
Story Line Press 34

Historical
Council for Indian Education 14
Edmonds Arts Commission Books 16
Harvest House Publishers 21
Maverick Publications, Inc. 25
Mountain Meadow Press 27
Questar Publishers, Inc. 32

Horror
Box Dog Press 11

Humor
Box Dog Press 11
Council for Indian Education 14

Literary
Edmonds Arts Commission Books 16
Intertext 23
Mother of Ashes Press 26
Story Line Press 34

Mystery
Romar Books, Ltd. 33
Story Line Press 34

Native American
Alaska Native Language Center 8
Council for Indian Education 14
Maverick Publications, Inc. 25
Mountain Meadow Press 27
Sandpiper Press 33

Nonfiction

Subsidy or Co-Publishing Basis

Magazine and Newsletter Subject Index

This index is alphabetized using the letter-by-letter system and is divided into two sections: fiction and nonfiction.

When indicating fiction and nonfiction index topics, some editors selected more subjects than were named in their initial list of interests. Additional topics may indicate future interests or identify subcategories within the publication's basic focus, such as celebrity profiles for a regional publication or ethnic issues for a family magazine.

State Index

This index is organized by state with book, magazine, and newsletter entries alphabetized using the letter-by-letter system. Magazine and newsletter listings are in italics.

Washington

Wyoming

Comprehensive Index

This index is alphabetized using the letter-by-letter system. Magazine, newsletter, and newspaper listings are in italics.

N

O

P

Timely and useful information for writers delivered to you each month in the *Writers Connection* newsletter

Features and how-to tips for writers, self-publishers, freelancers, technical and business writers, editors, and scriptwriters

Plus

Publishing and film industry news and market listings
Contests for writers and poets
Events on the West Coast and nationwide
Issues of concern to writers
Writers' software and computer news

Here are just a few article titles from past issues:

How to Define a Blockbuster Novel—And Write One
Writing for the Screen: How to Make Your Own First Break
Mid-List Crisis: Promoting Your Novel after Publication
Audio-Visual Writer's Primer: Guide to a Growing Market for Writers
Strategies for Creativity: Learning to Write from Your Creative Center
Publicize or Perish: Suggestions for Small Presses and Self-Publishers

All this and services, opportunities, consultant referrals for writers, and **updates to the Publishing Marketplace directories**

Special Discount Offer:

One full year (12 issues) for just $12 (regular price $18)
Only with the order form on page 183 (no photocopies, please)
Offer good through August 31, 1992

Writers, expand your opportunities and ideas with *Writing for the Ethnic Markets*

Endorsed by Alex Haley and other well-known writers, this exciting, new book combines chapters of how-to information with three directories—book publishers, periodical publishers, and film and TV producers of ethnic-oriented material.

Price: $14.95
ISBN: 0-9622592-4-1

Aimed specifically at writers, this book provides guidance in learning

- how to develop an "ethnic lens"

- how to write from passion, obsession, and other points of power

- how to use dreams as a creative tool

- how to market ethnic articles, short stories, novels, and books

- how to sell ethnic projects to film and TV producers

Information on multicultural resources, an annotated list of suggested writing books, and several indexes make this book a valuable resource for all writers regardless of their ethnic origins, but especially for those interested in writing about their own ethnicity or the cultures of others.

Available Fall 1991 from Writers Connection Press. To order your copy, use the form on page 183 or call (408) 973-0227.

Find hundreds of freelance writing opportunities in the Publishing Marketplace Series

Compiled and edited by a writer and experienced research librarian, the Marketplace books provide writers with a wealth of information on markets and resources in the western United States. Each book includes:

Book Publishers—Select from small, mid-size, and large presses. Find submission editors, subjects of interest, acceptance policies, contact information, and marketing channels.

Magazines—Locate hundreds of new markets. Discover submission editors, editorial needs, acceptance policies, contact information, and tips.

Newspapers—Find submission and book review editors. Learn submission, book review, and travel editors and circulation.

Literary Agents—Choose the right agent for your book or script. Evaluate subjects of interest, agency policies, contact information, represented titles, and tips.

Professional Organizations—Maximize your contacts. Locate national and state branches, contacts, purpose, dues, membership criteria, activities, and newsletters.

Writers Conferences—Gain insights, information, and contacts. Discover locations, frequency, fees, themes, subjects, and format.

Reference Books—Expand your sources of information. An annotated bibliography of writing and publishing books.

Indexes—Find what you need quickly. Separate subject index for books and magazines and also comprehensive and state indexes.

Use these comprehensive directories of submission information, editorial guidelines, and reference sources to get your material to the right person, in the right format, for the right market.

The *California and Hawaii Publishing Marketplace* provides access to information on the largest publishing market outside of New York.

292 pages, $16.95
ISBN: 0-9622592-1-7

"My copy already bears the marks of an essential tool: dog-eared pages replete with margin remarks and rays of bright yellow highlighting."

Trish Kaspar, writer and technical editor

"There's a place for this one! Right between your dictionary and your thesaurus."

Antoinette May, biographer and weekly columnist for the *San Francisco Chronicle*.

The *Southwest Publishing Marketplace* provides a comprehensive listing of new and untapped markets in Arizona, Colorado, Nevada, New Mexico, Texas, and Utah.

176 pages, $14.95
ISBN: 0-9622592-2-5

"With its comprehensive listings and cross-references, the *Southwest Publishing Marketplace* fills a gap as big as the Grand Canyon! Finally writers will be able to zero in on the right markets right away with this easy-to-use directory."

Mary Westheimer, writer, editor, and founding member of the Arizona Authors' Association Advisory Board

"Whether your written work has a regional slant or you would just like to connect with authors and publishers in your area, this book should prove a helpful resource."

Steve Davis, author and publisher of *The Writer's Yellow Pages*

Be among the first to increase your sales to markets in these rapidly growing writing/publishing regions. To order your copy, use the form on page 183 or call (408) 973-0227.

182

How does a writer break into Hollywood?
Find an agent? Write the stories Hollywood wants?

Nineteen top Hollywood pros answer these questions and more in the hottest new resource for scriptwriters—the *Writing for Hollywood* and *Selling to Hollywood* videotapes. In the broadcast quality style of network television, these tapes provide an insiders' look at the complex and intriguing process of writing and selling screenplays for motion pictures and television.

Selling to Hollywood

86 minutes

- **Breaking In**
  written and unwritten rules of the game
  using the "spec" script to open doors
- **Protecting Your Material**
  registering scripts with WGA
  sending follow-up letters to pitches
- **Agents**
  selling without an agent
  how to find and work with an agent
- **Selling to the Studios and Independents**
  rejection/acceptance factors
  the development process
- **"Hot" Scripts**
  elements of the equation
  writing with original voice & style
- **Pitching**
  elements of a good pitch
  log lines, set pieces, plot points
- **Opportunities and Alternatives**
  production deals with studios
  getting character-driven pieces to the stars

Writing for Hollywood

83 minutes

- **The Prewriting Process**
  stepping out the scenes
  determining the major turning points
- **Structure**
  the three-act structure
  the character's journey from A to Z
- **Dialog & Characterization**
  creating interesting characters
  advancing the story
- **Rewriting**
  time sequence in scriptwriting
  questions to ask during the rewrite
- **Story Analysis and Script Evaluation**
  how professional analysts evaluate scripts
  researching for accurate period pieces
- **Collaboration**
  how to become your own worst enemy
  collaborators as allies
- **TV Sitcoms**
  the sitcom structure
  creating cliffhangers

You don't have to live in Hollywood to be a successful screenwriter. Learn how to write the stories Hollywood wants and discover how to sell them to an increasingly competitive industry where million-dollar deals are made over lunch.

Produced by Paul Edwards Production Group and Writers Connection. Individual VHS tapes are priced at $79.95 each; the set is $129.95. Writers Connection member price is $71.95 per tape; $116.95 for the set. To order, use the order form on page 183 or call (408) 973-0227.

Order Form

Information/Membership/Subscription

❏ Send me a Writers Connection newsletter/seminar catalog

❏ Enroll me as a Writers Connection member
includes subscription—$40 per year $_____

❏ Send me 12 issues of the *Writers Connection* newsletter
without membership—$12 (includes shipping) $_____

Books/Tapes

Check the items you wish. Price code: **member**/nonmember price.

❏ Send me _____ copies of the **Northwest Publishing**
Marketplace—$12.71/$14.95 each $_____

❏ Send me _____ copies of the **California and Hawaii**
Publishing Marketplace—$14.41/$16.95 each $_____

❏ Send me _____ copies of the **Southwest Publishing**
Marketplace—$12.71/$14.95 each $_____

❏ Send me _____ copies of **Writing for the**
Ethnic Markets—$12.71/$14.95 each $_____

❏ Send me _____ copies of the **Writing for Hollywood** VHS
videotape—**$71.95/$79.95** each $_____

❏ Send me _____ copies of the **Selling to Hollywood** VHS
videotape—**$71.95/$79.95** each $_____

❏ Send me _____ sets of both videotapes at the special
package price—**$116.95/$129.95** each $_____

❏ Send me the following titles from the books for writers
listing. Writers Connection members can deduct 15 percent.
Please enter code, title, and price for each book below.

                                                                                                    $_____
_____ $_____
_____ $_____
                                                          Book/tape subtotal $_____
                                           Calif. residents add 7% sales tax $_____
      Add $3.00 per book/tape ($6 max.), $.75 per newsletter for shipping $_____
                                                                        Total $_____

Name_____

Address_____

City_____ State_____ Zip_____

Daytime phone _____ Membership number_____

❏ Check or money order enclosed

Please charge my: ❏ Visa ❏ MasterCard Account #_____

Expiration date _____ Signature_____

Please return to: **Writers Connection**
1601 Saratoga-Sunnyvale Rd., Suite 180, Cupertino, CA 95014
Phone orders using a Visa or MasterCard are accepted: **(408) 973-0227**

Notes